Teach...
Inspire...
Lead...

With REA's TExES 101 test prep, you'll be in a class all your own.

Free!
Diagnostic Exam
www.rea.com/texes

M000106073

Research & Education Association

The Best Teachers' Test Preparation for the

TExES
Texas Examinations of Educator Standards

101 Generalist EC-4

Luis A. Rosado, Ed.D.
Associate Professor
Director of Center for Bilingual and ESL Education
The University of Texas at Arlington

And the Staff of
Research & Education Association

Visit our Educator Support Center at:
www.REA.com/teacher

The competencies presented in this book were created and implemented by the Texas State Board for Educator Certification (SBEC). For further information visit the SBEC website at *www.sbec.state.tx.us*.

Research & Education Association
61 Ethel Road West
Piscataway, New Jersey 08854
E-mail: info@rea.com

The Best Teachers' Test Preparation for the Texas Examinations of Educator Standards (TExES) *101 Generalist EC–4 Test*

Published 2009

Printed in the United States of America

Library of Congress Control Number 2006938059

ISBN-13: 978-0-7386-0166-3
ISBN-10: 0-7386-0166-7

REA® is a registered trademark of Research & Education Association, Inc.

CONTENTS

Author's Dedication vii

About the Author. vii

About Research & Education Association vii

Author's Acknowledgments viii

REA Acknowledgments viii

INTRODUCTION   ix

DOMAIN I: ENGLISH LANGUAGE ARTS AND READING   3

Competency 001 (Oral Language) 3

Competency 002 (Phonological and Phonemic Awareness) 10

Competency 003 (Alphabetic Principle) 13

Competency 004 (Literacy Development) 15

Competency 005 (Word Analysis and Decoding) 22

Competency 006 (Reading Fluency) 25

Competency 007 (Reading Comprehension) 26

Competency 008 (Research and Comprehension Skills in the Content Areas) 31

Competency 009 (Writing Conventions) 35

Competency 010 (Development of Written Communication) 40

Competency 011 (Assessment of Developing Literacy) 44

DOMAIN II: MATHEMATICS   51

Competency 012 (Mathematics Instruction) 51

Competency 013 (Number Concepts, Patterns, and Algebra) 56

Competency 014 (Geometry, Measurement, Probability, and Statistics) 63

Competency 015 (Mathematical Process) 70

DOMAIN III: SOCIAL STUDIES   77

Competency 016 (Social Science Instruction) 77

Competency 017 (History) 87

Competency 018 (Geography and Culture) 104

Competency 019 (Government, Citizenship, and Economics) 109

DOMAIN IV: SCIENCE — 115

Competency 020 (Science Instruction) 115
Competency 021 (Physical Science) 117
Competency 022 (Life Science) 122
Competency 023 (Earth and Space Science) 127

DOMAIN V: FINE ARTS, HEALTH, AND PHYSICAL EDUCATION — 133

Competency 024 (Visual Arts) 133
Competency 025 (Music) 139
Competency 026 (Health) 145
Competency 027 (Physical Education) 153

PRACTICE TEST — 159

Answer Sheet 161
Test 163
Answers, Sorted by Competency 178
Answer Key 180
Detailed Explanations of Answers 181

INDEX — 197

Author's Dedication

This book is dedicated to Kelly, Koko, and Alex, because through their natural behavior and development, they guided me to see the connection between theory and practice.

About the Author

Dr. Luis A. Rosado is the Director of the Center for Bilingual and ESL Education at the University of Texas at Arlington. He holds degrees from the University of Puerto Rico, Boston State College, and Texas A & M University–Kingsville. He has published in the areas of parental involvement, cross-cultural communication, and Spanish linguistics. Dr. Rosado has more than 19 years of teaching experience at the elementary, high school, and college levels. He has taught in Puerto Rico, Massachusetts, and Texas.

About Research & Education Association

Founded in 1959, Research & Education Association is dedicated to publishing the finest and most effective educational materials—including software, study guides, and test preps—for students in middle school, high school, college, graduate school, and beyond.

REA's Test Preparation series includes books and software for all academic levels in almost all disciplines. Research & Education Association publishes test preps for students who have not yet entered high school, as well as for high school students preparing to enter college. Students from countries around the world seeking to attend college in the United States will find the assistance they need in REA's publications. For college students seeking advanced degrees, REA publishes test preps for many major graduate school admission examinations in a wide variety of disciplines, including engineering, law, and medicine. Students at every level, in every field, with every ambition can find what they are looking for among REA's publications.

REA's practice tests are always based upon the most recently administered exams and include every type of question that you can expect on the actual exams.

Today REA's wide-ranging catalog is a leading resource for teachers, students, and professionals.

We invite you to visit us at *www.rea.com* to find out how "REA is making the world smarter."

Author's Acknowledgments

I wish to thank teacher candidates throughout Texas and especially my students who motivated me to write this book. I would like to thank Christina Jones-Barnes for her input and feedback throughout the duration of this project. I would also like to acknowledge the support and guidance of Anne Winthrop Esposito, REA Senior Editor, who kept me focused.

REA Acknowledgments

We would like to thank REA's Larry B. Kling, Vice President, Editorial, for supervising development; Pam Weston, Vice President, Publishing, for setting the quality standards for production integrity and managing the publication to completion; Anne Winthrop Esposito, Senior Editor, for project management and preflight editorial review; Diane Goldschmidt, Senior Editor, and Molly Solanki, Associate Editor, for post-production quality assurance; Terry Casey for indexing; Marcy S. Kramer for proofreading; Christine Saul, Senior Graphic Artist, for cover design; and Caragraphics for typesetting.

Teach...
Lead...
Inspire...

INTRODUCTION

About This Book

REA's *The Best Teachers' Preparation for the TExES 101 Generalist EC–4* is a comprehensive guide designed to assist you in preparing to take the TExES (Texas Examinations of Educator Standards) battery required for teaching in Texas. To enhance your chances of success in this important step toward your career as a teacher in Texas schools, this test guide:

- presents an accurate and complete overview of the TExES 101 Generalist EC–4

- identifies all of the important information and its representation on the exam

- provides a comprehensive review of every domain

- presents sample questions in the actual test format

- provides diagnostic tools to identify areas of strength and weakness

- provides a full-length practice test based on the most recently administered TExES

- replicates the format of the official exam, including level of difficulty

- supplies the correct answer and detailed explanations for each question on the practice test, which enables you to identify correct answers and understand why they are correct and, just as important, why the other answers are incorrect

This guide is the result of studying many resources. The editors considered the most recent test administrations and professional standards. They also researched information from the Texas Education Agency, professional journals, textbooks, and educators. This guide includes the best test preparation materials based on the latest information available.

About the Test

Below are the domains used as the basis for the TExES 101 Generalist EC–4 examination, as well as the approximate percentage of the total test that each competency occupies. These competencies represent the knowledge that teams of teachers, subject area specialists, and district-level educators have determined to be important for beginning teachers. This book contains a thorough review of these competencies, as well as the specific skills that characterize each area.

Domain	Percentage
1. English Language Arts and Reading	40%
2. Mathematics	15%
3. Social Studies	15%
4. Science	15%
5. Fine Arts, Health, and Physical Education	15%

When Should the TExES Be Taken?

The test should be taken just before or after graduation for those seeking certification right out of school. The TExES is a requirement to teach in Texas, so if you are planning on being an educator, you must take and pass this test.

Paper-based TExES tests are usually administered six times a year at several locations throughout Texas. The usual testing day is Saturday, but the test may be taken on an alternate day if a conflict, such as a religious obligation, exists. Computer-based tests are available more frequently.

The TExES Registration Bulletin offers information about test dates and locations, as well as registration information and how to make testing accommodations for those with special needs. To receive a registration bulletin, visit *www.texes.ets.org*.

Registration bulletins are also available at education departments of Texas colleges and universities.

The Texas State Board for Educator Certification (SBEC) can be reached at (888) 863-5880 or (512) 936-8400 or via e-mail through the SBEC website. You can also find information about the test and registration on the SBEC website at *www.sbec.state.tx.us*.

Call Center/Customer Service activities are handled by ETS (Educational Testing Service). The phone number is (800) 205-2626. Hours of operation are Monday to Friday, 8:00 am to 5:00 pm, Central Time.

Is There a Registration Fee?

To take the TExES, you must pay a registration fee. If you are using the registration form, all fees must be paid in full by personal check, cashier's check, or money order payable to ETS. All payments must be made in U.S. dollars. Cash will not be accepted. If you are registering via the Internet or phone during the emergency registration period, payment must be made by VISA or MasterCard.

How to Use This Book

How Do I Begin Studying?

Review the organization of this test preparation guide.

1. To best utilize your study time, follow our TExES Independent Study Schedule. The schedule is based on a seven-week program, but can be condensed to four weeks if necessary.

2. Take the diagnostic test online at *www.rea.com/texes*.

3. Review the format of the TExES.

4. Review the test-taking advice and suggestions presented later in this chapter.

5. Pay attention to the information about domains, content, and topics on the test.

6. Spend time reviewing topics that stand out as needing more study.

7. Take the practice test, review the explanations to your answers carefully, study the competencies that your scores indicate need further review.

8. Follow the suggestions at the end of this chapter for the day before and the day of the test.

When Should I Start Studying?

It is never too early to start studying for the TExES. The earlier you begin, the more time you will have to sharpen your skills. Do not procrastinate! Cramming is not an effective way to study, since it does not allow you the time needed to learn the test material.

Studying for the TExES 101 Generalist, EC–4

It is very important for you to choose the time and place for studying that works best for you. Some individuals may set aside a certain number of hours every morning to study, while others may choose to study at night before going to sleep. Other people may study during the day, while waiting in line, or even while eating lunch. Only you can determine when and where your study time will be most effective. Be consistent and use your time wisely. Work out a study routine and stick to it.

When you take the practice tests, simulate the conditions of the actual test as closely as possible. Turn your television and radio off, and sit down at a quiet table free from distraction. As you complete each practice test, score your test and thoroughly review the explanations to the questions you answered incorrectly; however, do not review too much at any one time. Concentrate on one problem area at a time by reviewing the question and explanation, and by studying our review until you are confident that you have mastered the material.

Keep track of your scores. By doing so, you will be able to gauge your progress and discover general weaknesses in particular sections. Give extra attention to the reviews that cover your areas of difficulty, as this will build your skills in those areas.

TExES 101 Generalist, EC–4 Study Schedule

The following study schedule allows for thorough preparation for the TExES. The course of study here is seven weeks, but you can condense or expand the timeline to suit your personal schedule. It is vital that you adhere to a structured plan and set aside ample time each day to study. The more time you devote to studying, the more prepared and confident you will be on the day of the test.

Week 1.   Take the online diagnostic exam. The score will indicate your strengths and weaknesses. Make sure you simulate real exam conditions when you take the test. Afterward, score it and review the explanations, especially for questions you answered incorrectly.

Week 2.   Review the explanations for the questions you missed, and review the appropriate chapter sections. Useful study techniques include highlighting key terms and information; taking notes as you review the book's sections; putting new terms and information on note cards to help retain the information.

Weeks 3 and 4.   Reread all your note cards, refresh your understanding of the exam's competencies and skills, review your college textbooks, and read over class notes you've previously taken. This is also the time to consider any other supplementary materials that your counselor or the Texas Education Agency suggests. Review the agency's website at *www.sbec.state.tx.us*.

Week 5.   Begin to condense your notes and findings. A structured list of important facts and concepts, based on your note cards and the book's competencies, will help you thoroughly review for the test. Review the answers and explanations for all missed questions.

Week 6.   Have someone quiz you using the index cards you created. Take the practice test, adhering to the time limits and simulated test-day conditions.

Week 7.   Review your areas of weakness using all study materials. This is a good time to retake the practice test.

Format of the TExES

The TExES (101) Generalist, EC–4, includes 100 scorable multiple-choice items and approximately 10 nonscorable items. Your final scaled score will be based only on scorable items.

All multiple-choice questions are designed to assess your knowledge of the domains and related skills mentioned above and reviewed in this book. In general, the multiple-choice questions are intended to make you think. You are expected in most cases to demonstrate more than an ability to recall factual information; you may be asked to think critically about the information, analyze it, consider it carefully, compare it with knowledge you have, or make a judgment about it.

Answering the multiple-choice questions is straightforward. You will have four choices labeled A, B, C, and D. You must mark your choice on a separate answer sheet. You should have plenty of time in which to complete the test, but be aware of the amount of time you are spending on each question so that you allow yourself time to complete the whole test. Although speed is not very important, a steady pace should be maintained when answering questions. Using the practice tests will help you prepare for this task.

The TExES (101) Generalist, EC-4 is also offered as a computer-based test. Please see the SBEC website for further information.

About the Review Sections

The reviews in this book are designed to help you sharpen the basic skills needed to approach the TExES, as well as provide strategies for attacking the questions.

Each teaching competency is examined in a separate chapter. The skills required for all five domains are extensively discussed to optimize your understanding of what the 101 Generalist EC–4 test covers.

Your schooling has taught you most of what you need to answer the questions on the test. The education classes you took should have provided you with the know-how to make important decisions about situations you will face as a teacher. Our review is designed to help you fit the information you have acquired into specific competency components. Reviewing your class notes and textbooks together with our competency reviews will give you an excellent springboard for passing the exam.

Scoring the TExES (101) Generalist EC-4

How Do I Score My Practice Test?

There are 100 multiple-choice questions on the TExES 101 Generalist, EC–4 practice test. You must get 70 or more of the questions correct to pass.

If you do not achieve a passing score on the practice test, review the detailed explanations for the questions you answered incorrectly. Note which types of questions you answered wrong, and re-examine the corresponding review. After further review, you may want to re-take the practice tests.

When Will I Receive My Score Report and What Will It Look Like?

Approximately four weeks after the paper-based exam, or one week after the computer-based exam, your score report will be available. The report will indicate whether you have passed the test. It will also include:

- a total test scaled score that is reported on a scale of 100–300. The minimum passing score is a scaled score of 240. This score represents the minimum level of competency required to be an entry-level educator in this field in Texas public schools

- your performance in the major content domains of the test and in the specific competencies of the test. This information may be useful in identifying strengths and weaknesses and can be used in preparing for the test should you need to retake it

- information to help you interpret your results

You will not receive a score report if you are absent or choose to cancel your score.

Test-Taking Tips

Although you may not be familiar with tests like the TExES, this book will help acquaint you with this type of exam and help alleviate your test-taking anxieties. Listed below are ways to help you become accustomed to the TExES, some of which may be applied to other tests as well.

Tip 1. Become comfortable with the format of the TExES. When you are practicing, stay calm and pace yourself. After simulating the test only once, you will boost your chances of doing well, and you will be able to sit down for the actual TExES with much more confidence.

Tip 2. Read all of the possible answers. Just because you think you have found the correct response, do not automatically assume that it is the best answer. Read through each choice to be sure that you are not making a mistake by jumping to conclusions.

Tip 3. Use the process of elimination. Go through each answer to a question and eliminate as many of the answer choices as possible. By eliminating two answer choices, you have given yourself a better chance of getting the item correct since there will only be two choices left from which to make your guess. Do not leave an answer blank; it is better to guess than to not answer a question on the TExES test.

Tip 4. Make note of the questions on which you guessed, then recheck them later if you have time.

Tip 5. Work quickly and steadily to avoid focusing on any one problem too long. Taking the practice test in this book will help you learn to budget your precious time.

Tip 6. Learn the directions and format of the test. Familiarizing yourself with the directions and format of the test will not only save time, but will also help you avoid anxiety (and the mistakes caused by getting anxious).

Tip 7. On the paper-based exam, be sure that the answer circle you are marking corresponds to the number of the question in the test booklet. Since the test is multiple-choice, it is graded by machine, and marking one wrong answer can throw off your answer key and your score. Be extremely careful.

The Day of the Test

Before the Test

On the day of the test, make sure to dress comfortably, so that you are not distracted by being too hot or too cold while taking the test. Plan to arrive at the test center early. This will allow you to collect your thoughts and relax before the test, and will also spare you the anguish that comes with being late.

You should check your TExES registration information to find out what time to arrive at the testing center.

Before you leave for the test center, make sure that you have your admission ticket and two forms of identification, one of which must contain a recent photograph, your name, and signature (e.g., driver's license). Your name must appear on your identification exactly as it appears on your registration documents. You will not be admitted to the test center if you do not have proper identification.

You must bring several sharpened No. 2 pencils with erasers, as none will be provided at the test center.

If you would like, you may wear a watch to the test center. However, you may not wear one that makes noise, because it may disturb the other test takers. Cell phones, electronic equipment, dictionaries, textbooks, notebooks, calculators, briefcases, or packages will not be permitted. Drinking, smoking, and eating are prohibited.

During the Test

Procedures will be followed to maintain test security. Once you enter the test center, follow all of the rules and instructions given by the test supervisor. If you do not, you risk being dismissed from the test and having your scores cancelled.

On the paper-based test, when all of the materials have been distributed, the test instructor will give you directions for filling out your answer sheet. Fill out this sheet carefully since this information will be printed on your score report.

Once the test begins, mark only one answer per question, completely erase unwanted answers and marks, and fill in answers darkly and neatly.

On the computer-based test, you will be given 15 minutes, before the test begins, to review the directions. No oral instruction will be provided. At any time during the test, you may use the "Help" button to review the general directions. To answer a question, click on a response. To move on to the next question, click on "Next." To return to a previous question, click on "Back." You will be provided with scratch paper.

Can I Retake the Test?

If you don't do well on the TExES, don't panic! You can take it again, and in fact many candidates do. A score on the TExES that does not match your expectations should not change your plans about teaching. You can register to retake it at any subsequent test administration. To retake a test, submit a new registration along with the correct payment. It is recommended that you wait for your scores before reregistering. If you choose to register again for the same test before receiving your scores from a previous administration, you assume responsibility for test fees and any applicable late or emergency registration fees for both test dates.

After the Test

When you finish your test, hand in your materials and you will be dismissed. Then, go home and relax—you deserve it!

TExES

Texas Examinations of Educator Standards

101 Generalist EC-4

Review

Domain I: English Language Arts and Reading

Competency 001 (Oral Language)

The teacher understands the importance of oral language, knows the developmental processes of oral language, and provides children with varied opportunities to develop listening and speaking skills.

All teacher candidates need a clear understanding of the basic components of language, which are phonology, morphology, syntax, lexicon, semantics, and pragmatics. **Phonology** is the study of the sound system of a language. The basic units of sound are called **pho-** **nemes**. Phonemes are represented by **graphemes**, or letters. For example, the word *through* has seven graphemes (letters) that represents only three sounds /th,r,u/. Teachers should stress the difference between letters in a word and the sounds that the letters represent.

Morphology is the study of the structure of words and word formation. **Morphemes** are the smallest representation of meaning. For example, the word *cars* is made of two morphemes, the basic word or root word *car*, and the plural morpheme *s*. Knowledge of morphology will help students in the word analysis that is required to decode printed information.

Syntax describes the organization and word sequence in a complete sentence. The English language has specific basic sentence structures, called kernel sentences. The four most common sentence structures in English are:

1.	**Noun**	**Intransitive Verb**	**Predicate Nominative**
Example:	Katrina	was	a hurricane.
2.	**Noun**	**Intransitive Verb**	**Predicate Adjective**
Example:	Katrina	was	destructive.
3.	**Noun**	**Transitive Verb**	**Direct Object**
Example:	*Bear Mountain*	won	an Oscar.
4.	**Noun**	**Transitive Verb**	**Indirect Object Direct Object**
Example:	Mark Cuban	gave	the Mavericks an incentive.

Lexicon refers to the vocabulary of a language. Vocabulary is the most changeable component of language. The meanings of words change based on context and historical framework. For example, today the word *hot* can have several different meanings based on the speech act, e.g., high temperature, fashionable, or lucky. In a few more years, any of these more recent meanings might change or become obsolete.

Semantics describes the way that meaning is conveyed in a language. Language represents the meaning system, which is based on the culture and context of the conversation. Language uses connotation and denotation to convey meaning.

Connotation refers to the implied meaning of words and ideas. Idiomatic expressions use implied meaning as a communication tool; and therefore, speakers must have knowledge of the culture to understand an expression's implied meaning. This requirement often presents a challenge to English language learners (ELLs) because they generally lack the familiarity with American culture that native speakers have. Teachers need to teach idioms in a contextualized situation and also need to describe their intended meanings.

Denotation refers to the literal meaning of words and ideas. A sign that reads "Dog Bites" might seem obvious because all dogs have the capability (literal meaning) to bite. However, the pragmatics of communication will guide people to go beyond the literal meaning and understand the intended meaning of the statement—this specific dog is aggressive and might attack. The *Amelia Bedelia* series written by Peggy Parish presents many situations where the main character understands everything only literally. This limited understanding creates many communication problems and comedic situations.

Pragmatics describes how context can affect the interpretation of communication. Pragmatics describes the hidden rules of communications understood by native speakers of the same language. Native speakers often call these rules "commonsense rules." However, these rules might be only common to native English speakers. These rules are not immediately evident to ELLs; thus, teachers introduce these rules within a context. In English, a person greets another person with a routine statement such as "How are you?" The rules of pragmatics require the receiver to answer with a generic statement such as "Not bad," "I am OK," or "Fine." English language learners and people who are new to the culture might misinterpret the routine question as a literal inquiry and try to answer it directly, which often creates confusion.

Principles of First Language Acquisition

Language learning results from the combination of innate ability, imitation of speech, and environmental influences. Children are born with innate mechanisms

to develop language, but language only emerges if the mechanism is triggered by stimuli from people in the child's environment. Noam Chomsky, from the Massachusetts Institute of Technology (MIT), called this mechanism a Language Acquisition Device (LAD).

Imitation is a learning strategy that young children frequently use until age two, but imitation decreases in effectiveness as language learning becomes more complex. Children who are at the one-word stage of language acquisition use the strategy of imitation for language development. Due to memory limitations, infants appear to pay more attention to the ends of sentences or words. For example, a question such as, "Do you want to go out?" might receive a reply of "out." This reply probably means, "Yes, I want to go out."

After age two, imitation alone cannot meet the communication needs of children and so they become rule makers. Toddlers begin testing language rules on their own as a way of trying to figure out how the language operates. For example, imitation alone cannot explain idiosyncratic statements such as "I goed out yesterday." This non-standard utterance shows that the child is field-testing language rules. In this case, the child is testing the rule for the formation of the regular past tense, and has applied it to an irregular verb. This type of overgeneralization characterizes the process of first language acquisition during most of the early childhood years. Direct correction will not generally help in this situation. Often, parents present the standard version of the word and the child will ignore it until he or she is ready to internalize it. However, parents and teachers are always encouraged to address the communication needs of the child while modeling the standard version of the language.

Language Is Learned in Social Settings

In mainstream American culture, parents often allow the participation of children in the conversation of adults. Participation in conversation provides children with the vocabulary and the format of conversations (Stewig and Jett-Simpson 1995). Parents do not always engage in direct language teaching but they help language acquisition by communicating with the child and using the adult version of the language. As a result of this linguistic support, most children come to school with a strong vocabulary and language background. Conversely, some ethnic and linguistic groups might not follow the same pattern of linguistic interaction with children. The expression "Children are to be seen, not heard" represents an example of how some groups view the appropriate interaction of children with adults. Children who are brought up in a society where participation in adults' conversations is restricted might not have the same language development and will begin school behind their classmates.

Children Are Concerned with Meaning

Children quickly understand that the main purpose of language is communication. They are not concerned with grammar, and they just want to communicate to get their needs met. Because of this, direct error correction has little impact in the language development of preschool children. They expect language to make sense and rely on sympathetic listeners to understand them. Therefore, modeling is always the best way to support language development in preschool children.

Stages of Language Development

The process of first language acquisition is characterized by certain stages, which are regulated by the maturation process and by the level and quality of exposure to the native language. It is difficult to assign a definite age for each of these stages, but we will provide an average age in order to develop a working framework for readers. A description of these stages follows.

Babbling or Pre-Language Stage (0–6 months)

Children at this state send and receive messages and use reflexive crying to communicate with caregivers. They play vocally by producing multiple linguistic and non-linguistic sounds, (e.g., mmm, gugu, dada). Infants can identify the voices of parents and family members, and they are able to follow certain commands. They also begin understanding the intonation patterns used to convey anger or excitement and the patterns used to ask questions.

Holophrastic One-Word Stage (11–19 months)

Children at the one-word stage begin imitating inflections and facial expressions of adults. They recognize their name, and follow simple instructions presented in contextualized situations. Children begin using adults as tools by pointing to objects and requesting assistance. They understand **word concepts** and use these to conceptualize complete ideas.

Two-Word Stage (13–24 months)

At the two-word stage, children begin producing rudimentary types of sentences. These constructions are characterized by a combination of two types of words— Pivot and Open words. **Pivot** refers to words that can be used to accomplish multiple functions, i.e., *no, up, all, see, more,* and *gone*. The **open** class contains words that are generally used to refer to one concept. Words like *home, milk, doggy, juice, pants,* and *shoe* are words that are used mostly to refer to one particular situation. Based on the vocabulary limitations of this stage, children use combinations of these two classes to create the subject and the predicate of the sentence. Some possible examples of utterances produced at this stage are: "See baby," "see mommy," "no more," and "all gone."

Telegraphic Stage (18–27 months)

The telegraphic stage represents a higher degree of linguistic development in which the child goes beyond the two-word stage. Most of the words used at this stage are **content words** with high semantic value that can be used in multiple situations. Some examples of function words are nouns, adjectives and verbs. The use of **function words**, such as prepositions and articles, is very limited at this stage because they do not convey as much information as content words. The typical sentence at this stage consists of subject, verb, object or adjective format. Some possible examples of utterances produced at this stage are: "no more TV," "milk all gone," and "that's not nice."

Two to Three Years

At age two children have about 200 to 300 words in their speaking repertoire, and generally can produce short rudimentary sentences. They also begin using prepositions and pronouns with some level of inconsistency. The vocabulary of three-year-olds grows to about 900 to 1000 words. Three-year-olds begin creating three- to four-word sentences. They are able to follow two-step commands and engage in short dialogues about familiar topics. In schools with programs for three-year-olds, children get exposed to informal and formal registers—variants of a language used for a particular purpose depending on the social setting. Children begin to request instead of demand, use courteous vocabulary, and begin following conversation formats.

Age Four

Four-year-olds generally have about 1,500 words in their speaking repertoire. They use more complex sentence structures, but their speech still contains pronunciation problems and overgeneralizations. Four year-olds are able to understand more than what they are able to verbalize. They can answer factual questions in contextualized situations, but have difficulties explaining the rationale for their answers.

Age Five

Five-year-olds have a vocabulary of about 2,100 words and a working knowledge of the grammar of the language. They may have problems dealing with compound sentences and sentences with embedded meaning. They are beginning to understand time concepts and use verbs accordingly. Most children at this stage have mastered the use of the progressive (-ing), regular past tense (-ed), and plurals (-s). Irregular verbs still constitute a challenge for five-year-olds. They are able to identify and produce specific sounds and blends (combinations of phonemes like in the word <u>bl</u>ock). The vocabulary continues to increase as children have more contact with peers and teachers in school.

Age Six and Seven

Six- to seven-year-olds have a speaking vocabulary of about 2,100 words and a comprehension vocabulary of more than 20,000 words. They use well-constructed sentences using all parts of speech. They still might have problems with certain words and structures, but their speech is fluent and clear. However, speakers at this age might still have problems with words containing sounds like /v/, /th/, /ch/ and /sh/. Some children will use the sound of the /w/ in place of the required /r/ and /l/ sounds. They are able to separate words into syllables and begin decoding written language. They are beginning to understand and address questions that call for reasons for an action. For example, they can explain their actions and answer questions such as "Why did you pick number five as the answer?" After age six,

children continue to polish their language skills, and add new and more sophisticated vocabulary.

Age Eight to Ten

The speaking repertoire of eight-year-olds continues growing and improving. They begin using relative pronouns clauses (i.e., The boy *that* you met yesterday is my friend.) They also begin to use subordinated clauses that begin with *when, if, and because* (i.e., *If* you bother me, I am going to tell the teacher). The gerund is also becoming common for speakers of this age (i.e., *Cheating* is bad). Children begin using more complex sentences, vocabulary, and verb construction. Their speech is more coherent though the use of connectors like *first, during, after,* and *finally*.

Assessing the Speaking Ability

Intelligibility

A child's speaking ability is generally assessed informally in class as part of daily activities. First, teachers have to determine if the speech of the child is **intelligible** and can be understood by native speakers with minimum effort. Communication or intelligibility problems in native speakers can be caused by developmental issues, the use of dialectical variations, or speech disorders. To assess the speech of the child, teachers need an understanding of the developmental patterns in the process of language mastery, and use these patterns as a foundation for assessing a child's performance. Teachers should also develop an understanding of features from dialects spoken in the community to avoid confusion with features that contrast with Standard English. For example, speakers of **Ebonics**, a language variant used by some African American children, and speakers of the **Boston dialect** drop the /r/ after a vowel. One of example of this is in the statement "...park the car in Harvard yard" [Pahk the kah in Hahvud yahd]. In this case, the omission of post-vocalic *Rs* cannot be identified as a pronunciation problem. Because of this, teachers need a working knowledge of the dialects used in the community in order to make accurate assessments of the children's speech.

Language Interference

Teachers have to take into account how the first language of an ELL interferes in the pronunciation of English. Phonologically, language interference can happen at the word or sentence level. The most noticeable form of language interference happens when students use the phonology of their first language to pronounce words in English. For example, most Spanish dialects do not use the /v/ sound; instead, they replaced it with the /b/ sound. This feature creates semantic problems when native Spanish speakers pronounce the English word, *vowel* as *bowel*, which can create an embarrassing situation for the speaker.

Korean and Japanese speakers might also experience language interference when using the English /r/ sound because this sound is not present in their language. Chinese has both the /r/ and /l/ sounds; however, native Chinese speakers may experience problems with these two sounds when learning English. This is because they have the tendency to substitute the /r/ with the /l/ sound. This feature can create semantic problems when native Chinese, Korean, and Japanese speakers pronounce the English word *rice as lice*. A second type of interference can be caused by the application of incorrect **word stress** in English. For example, in Standard English most speakers will place the primary stress of the word *com.po.si.tion* on the second to last syllable, but never on the last syllable. However, Spanish speakers and speakers of Caribbean English might place the primary stress on the last syllable, resulting in nonstandard English pronunciation. Language interference can create communication problems and potentially embarrassing situations for ELLs. Thus, teachers have to become aware of conflicting language sounds and provide appropriate language support to ELLs.

Communication Style and Culture

Culture plays an important role in the way that people communicate orally and in written form. In oral communication, English uses a linear rhetorical pattern that allows little flexibility to deviate from the topic. Other languages like Spanish, Russian, and Arabic allow for a more flexible progression to convey information. This flexibility is identified as a **curvilinear** approach, because it allows speakers the option of deviating from the main topic without being penalized. This cultural and linguistic difference can create problems in assessing the speaking capabilities of children who are native speakers of languages other than English. Teachers have to be vigilant to determine how the first language (L1) and culture affect the performance of children in the second language (L2).

Speaking Checklist

The speaking ability can also be assessed in the classroom with a structured checklist identifying specific features that teachers want to observe. Lapp et al. (2001) developed an instrument to assess the speaking ability called The Speaking Checklist. A summary of key elements is presented below.

Speaking Checklist

1. Sticks to the topic
2. Builds support for the subject
3. Speaks clearly
4. Takes turns and waits to talk
5. Talks so others in the group can hear
6. Speaks smoothly
7. Uses courteous language
8. Presents in an organized and interesting way
9. Supports the topical thesis
10. Answers questions effectively
11. Is comfortable speaking publicly
12. Maintains listeners interest
13. Volunteers to answer in class

The Texas Education Agency (TEA) also developed a new instrument to comply with the No Child Left Behind (NCLB) state accountability system called the Texas Observation Protocol (TOP). This instrument was designed to assess the language proficiency of ELLs in Texas. This instrument contains a speaking component that assesses the speaking ability based on four language proficiencies: Beginning, Intermediate, Advanced, and Advanced High (TEA, 2006). This instrument is also an observation tool that uses holistic scoring, administered by teachers in the bilingual or ESL classroom. A performance that is scored at the Advanced High proficiency is generally required to be reclassified as a fluent

English speaker. A description of the Advanced High proficiency follows:

1. Students are able to participate in extended discussion in a variety of social and grade-appropriate academic topics.

2. Students are able to communicate effectively using abstract and concrete content-based vocabulary during classroom instruction.

3. Students are able to use complex English grammar structures and complex sentences at a level comparative to native speakers.

4. Students rarely make linguistic errors that interfere with overall communication.

5. Students rarely use pronunciation that interferes with overall communication.

Listening and Speaking

Language uses a complex system for creating meaning through socially shared conventions. During the first months of life, babies are active listeners. Long before they can respond orally, they communicate non-verbally by waving their arms, smiling, or wiggling. They are also capable of communicating their needs and wants through non-verbal communication, including body language and crying. Through listening, they develop the receptive language needed to begin communicating orally. Although listening is used extensively in communication, it does not receive much attention at school.

While there is no well-defined model of teaching listening skills, some theorists link listening skills to reading skills. They feel that reading and listening both make use of similar language comprehension processes. Listening and reading both require the use of skills in phonology, syntax, semantics, and knowledge of the structure of text, and both language skills seem to be controlled by the same set of cognitive processes. A number of studies suggest that the teaching of listening can be done by engaging in the kinds of activities that have been successful in developing reading, writing, and speaking proficiencies. For example, teachers can guide students' listening activities by setting a purpose for listening, providing questions before and after the listening activity, and encouraging children to

forge links between the new information that was just heard and the knowledge already in place. In addition, children need to be coached in the use of appropriate volume and speed when they speak, and in the rules to participate in discussions. Students also need to follow the rules for maintaining a polite conversation, which include staying on a topic and taking turns without interrupting speakers.

Communication Disorders

A communication disorder occurs when a person's speech interferes with the ability to convey messages during interactions with community members. The four classifications of language disorders are disorders in voice, fluency, articulation, and language processing (Piper, 2003).

Voice Disorders

Voice disorders describe any type of distortion of the pitch, timber, or volume of spoken communication. There are two types of voice disorders: phonation and resonance. **Phonation** disorder describes any kind of abnormality in the vibration of the vocal fold. For example, *hoarseness* or extreme breathiness can interfere with comprehension. **Resonance** disorder describes abnormalities created when sound passes through the vocal tract. The most typical example of resonance disorder occurs when the sound passing through the nasal cavity changes oral sounds to nasal, which is called *hyper-nasal sounds*. This type of disorder should not be confused with the nasal quality of Southern dialects like the Texas twang.

Fluency Disorders

Fluency disorders refer to any kind of conditions that affect the child's ability to produce coherent and fluent communication. The most common types of fluency disorder are caused by *stuttering* and *cluttering*. **Stuttering** is characterized by multiple false starts or the inability to produce the intended sounds. **Cluttering** occurs when children try to communicate in an excessively fast mode that makes comprehension difficult.

Teachers have to be cautious when assessing ELLs who might experience temporary fluency dysfunction, such as hesitations, false starts, and repetition, that are created by anxiety or confusion with the two languages. Often ELLs stutter because they cannot find or might not know the appropriate word in English. Allowing students to code-switch from English to their first language can be used as a temporary remedy to stuttering. Additionally, children new to the language often use the intonation pattern and the speed of delivery of their native language. For example, when Spanish-speaking ELLs impose the Spanish intonation pattern and speed of delivery to English, the delivery might become incomprehensible and be mistaken as the speech disorder of cluttering.

Articulation Problems

Children may have problems with specific sounds that can cause unintelligibility and the production of esthetically displeasing sounds. The most common articulation disorder is *lisping*. **Lisping** is a term used when children (or adults) produce the sound /s/, /sh/, /z/, and /ch/ with their tongue between the upper and lower teeth. Some other sounds that can present challenges to children are the /w/, /l/, and /r/ sounds. Some of these problems might be developmental and will eventually be eliminated, while others might require speech therapy. Elmer Fudd and Sylvester the Cat, two popular cartoon characters, are well known for exhibiting these speech features (i.e., Sylvester lisping, and Elmer having difficulties with the /r/ sound like in "wabbit").

Language Processing

Language processing disorders are generally caused by a brain-based disturbance called aphasia. Three types of aphasia are known: receptive, expressive, and global.

Receptive aphasia, or "sensory aphasia" results from a lesion to a region in the upper back part of the temporal lobe of the brain. Receptive aphasia creates problems with listening comprehension and retrieval of words from memory. People affected with this condition have the tendency of repeating formulaic phrases and producing unintelligible sequences of words or sounds.

Expressive aphasia results from damage to the lower back part of the frontal lobe. This damage affects the speaking ability and causes specific problems with articulation and fluency. The speech produced is often very slow including multiple hesitations and problems with the supra-segmental features of language including intonation, rhythm, and stress. The sentences produced are generally very short and contain only the necessary features to convey the message. Their speech resembles the speech of children at the telegraphic stage of first language development.

Global aphasia is also a brain-based disorder that affects both the receptive and expressive features of language. Children with this kind of severe impairment of articulation and fluency produce minimal speech and their comprehension is very limited. This type of language disorder is also known as "irreversible aphasia," which suggests that little can be done to help children suffering from this condition.

Activities to Promote Oral Communication

The best way to promote oral communication is to guide students into using language in meaningful situations. In classroom situations, teachers can organize activities to resemble real-life situations in order to promote communication among students. Some of these activities are described below.

Dramatic Play

Dramatic play using prompts is an ideal activity to develop communication that resembles real-life situations. Students are given a situation and a specific role to play, and they improvise probable communications. For example, one child can play the role of a parent, another role of a student in trouble, and a third student can play the role of a teacher.

Language Play

Language play involves the use of language in rhyme, alliteration, songs, and repeating patterns to amuse children. Tongue twisters are commonly used to practice pronunciation and language patterns. Through these activities, children acquire language knowledge in a relaxed and fun environment. Teachers can also use nursery rhymes, poems, and stories that contain rhyme to introduce these language features.

Show and Tell

In show and tell, children bring artifacts and personal items to class. They show the object and describe its features to the class. In addition to the obvious benefit of oral communication, this kind of activity can be used to promote home and cultural pride.

Hand-Puppet Show

Hand puppets, finger-puppets, and string-puppets can be used to promote communication confidence among children. Students speak using the puppet as a cover for any errors made in communication. The use of puppets is an enjoyable and motivating activity for young learners.

Pair Interview

Another interesting strategy to promote oral communication is pair interview. In this strategy, children are paired to learn information from each other and then report their findings to the larger group. This strategy is ideal for the first day of class when students want to get to know each other.

Presentations to Address Different Audiences

Children can also be asked to develop short presentations for a given audience, and then modify the ideas to present the same information to address a different kind of audience. For example, children can be led to prepare an oral presentation to convince parents to donate money to purchase more computers for the school. Once the presentation is delivered, the students can be asked to modify the presentation to address members of the school board or a business executive.

Key Principles of the Competency

- Teach vocabulary words like preposition of places (under, over, between) to Pre-K children to allow them to verbalize their position relative to objects, i.e., under the desk…

- Promote the development of listening skills by implementing listening activities as a routine in the daily schedule.

- Do role playing using specific historical to help students understand different points of view. For example, ask students to role-play soldiers from the South and the North during the Civil War.

- Present listening skills for various purposes, and provides children with opportunities to engage.

- Provide instruction and opportunities for children to evaluate the content and effectiveness of their own spoken messages.

- Select and use appropriate technologies to develop children's oral communication skills.

Competency 002 (Phonological and Phonemic Awareness)

The teacher understands phonological and phonemic awareness and employs a variety of approaches to help children develop phonological and phonemic awareness.

Importance of Phonological and Phonemic Awareness for Reading

Phonological and phonemic awareness constitute the foundation for the development of the metalinguistic awareness that children need to become successful language learners and effective readers.

Phonemic awareness refers to the ability of a child to understand that words have smaller components called sounds, and these sounds together create syllables and words. Phonemic awareness is the basic linguistic principle required to develop an understanding of oral and written communication. Once children understand this principle, they begin discovering more sophisticated linguistic principles like phonological awareness. Children who have developed phonemic awareness are able to dissect a word into each phoneme, and put it back to re-create the word. The ability to manipulate spoken words has been linked to successful reading development.

Rhymes

Phonemic stress can be taught through the use of nursery rhymes, short poems, or stories like the traditional Humpty Dumpty character of Mother Goose nursery rhymes:

Humpty Dumpty sat on the wall, Humpty Dumpty had a great fall, All the king's horses and all the king's men, Couldn't put Humpty Dumpty together again.

The use of these rhythmic patterns in an enjoyable and relaxed environment introduces children to the sounds and music of language. Eventually, children will notice the ending of the words and how specific sounds relate to each other.

Alliteration is a literacy technique used to emphasize phonemes by using successive words that begin with the same consonant sound or letter. Tongue twisters are the best known form of alliteration. Children can repeat tongue twisters for fun and at the same time, develop an awareness of the sound-symbol correspondence. In the following example, the /p/ sound is emphasized:

Peter **P**iper **p**icked a **p**eck of **p**ickled **p**eppers.

Phonological awareness

Phonological awareness is the ability to recognize and manipulate components of the sound system of a language. It includes the ability to segment words into smaller units like syllables and phonemes (sounds). Phonological awareness also encompasses the ability to identify and separate words within a sentence, identify stress in individual words, and identify the intonation pattern used in sentences.

✳ Syllabication

Syllabication is an important component of phonological awareness. It refers to the ability to conceptualize and separate words into their basic pronunciation components, which are syllables. Syllables can be as a simple as one vowel, or can be a combination of vowels

and consonants. For example, the word *elegant* contains three syllables (el/**e**/gant), one of which is a vowel alone. Phonemes are the basic unit of a syllable, and syllables constitute the basic units for the pronunciation of the English language. Consequently, syllables influence the rhythm of the language, poetic meter, and word stress. Syllabication can be taught using the appropriate voice intonation in order to indicate the beginning and ending of a syllable. Teachers often use clapping to indicate syllable boundaries.

Word Stress

English has at least four levels of word stress but, for practical purposes, we only need to be concerned with the first two: main stress and secondary stress. Word stress can affect the ability to understand words, and can also alter meaning. For example, the word *pervert* can have two meanings depending on how it is pronounced. With the stress on the next to last syllable (*pérvert*) it becomes a noun, but if the stress is placed on the last syllable (*pervért*) it becomes a verb.

Intonation Patterns

The intonation pattern describes the pitch contour of a phrase or a sentence that is used to change the meaning of the sentence. In English, there are utterances that might appear to be identical but convey a different meaning. In the question below, the rising point at the verb *are* makes the utterance a question, while a slight change of intonation to the pronoun, *you*, changes the utterance to a reply to the question.

Question   How **are** you?

Reply   How are **you**?

Special Considerations when Teaching Phonemic and Phonological Awareness

1. It is easier to break sentences into words, and break words into syllables than to break syllables into phonemes.

2. Use a whole-to-the-parts approach to teach phonological awareness. Guide children to segment short sentences into words, and segment words into syllables first. Then, guide children to segment syllables into individual phonemes. Finally, reverse the process to recreate the word and eventually the whole sentence.

3. Begin teaching phonemic awareness using short monosyllabic words. Introduce words with a consistent word structure like consonant-vowel-consonant i.e., *bat* and *cat*, before introducing more difficult ones.

4. Begin segmenting short words into phonemes. Once children understand this component of phonemic awareness, introduce syllabication.

5. Teachers should introduce sounds in initial position, then sounds in final position, and finally (the most difficult ones) the phonemes in medial position.

6. Teachers should introduce phoneme awareness first with simpler concepts like rhyming and initial phoneme identification, and then introduce blending and segmenting words into syllables.

7. When teaching sound-symbol correspondence, introduce sounds that present the least chance for distortion. Sounds like the **nasal** /m/ and **sibilant** /s/ represent easier sounds for the child than the brief sounds created with **stop** sounds like /p/, /t/, and /k/.

Teaching Phonemic and Phonological Awareness

Teachers can promote the phonemic and phonological knowledge through a variety of strategies. A list of these strategies follows:

1. Teach the child to isolate phonemes. To follow a pattern from the simplest to the most difficult, begin with initial and final sounds first, and then add phonemes in the middle. Ask questions such as "What is the first sound of the word *boy*?"

2. Guide children to blend onset and rimes. Ask the child, "What word can you create when you blend the sounds *L* and *ake*, or *T* and *ake*."

3. Introduce blending by guiding children to identify the word created when the following sounds are blended: /b/, /a/, and /t/.

4. Guide children to identify a word like *tape* and then remove the onset and ask the child: "What word

is left when we remove the first sound?" (answer: *ape*.) Then ask students, "Is this a word?"

5. Teach word segmentation by saying a word, and then guiding children to identify the sounds that they hear. Teachers can begin with simple monosyllabic words like *car* and then expand to more sophisticated words.

6. Use onsets and rimes to teach the sound-symbol relationship. Guide children to create new words by substituting the first letter of monosyllabic words. For example, using the word *ring*, the child can replace the initial sounds to create additional words *sing*, *king*, and *spring*. This activity has two purposes: it emphasizes phonemic awareness and, at the same time, teaches how word families can support vocabulary development.

7. Teachers should lead children to segment or separate the sounds in words. Begin with words with consistent sound-symbol correspondence, like *bag* and *lag*, and later expand to words that contain clusters/blends like in the word **splash** and diagraphs like in the word **church**.

8. Introduce minimal pairs, which are sets of words that differ in only one phoneme like *pail* and *bail*, to guide students to notice the difference. Teachers should pronounce both words and ask students if the words are the same or different. Initially, contrast words with initial consonant sounds like in *pat* and *bat*, and later expand to include more sophisticated contrasting pairs like in **bit** and **beet**.

9. Say words and guide children to identify the number of sounds that they hear. Initially, avoid stop sounds because children might have difficulties perceiving the brief sound represented by these sounds.

10. Guide children to recite nursery rhymes or children's songs and then guide them to repeat the rhyme or song, changing the initial word. For example, a simple Mother Goose rhyme like *Go to bed Tom!* can be used to replace the parts of the rhyme. For example, students can repeat "*Go to bed, Tom!, Tired or not, Tom, Go to bed, Tom.*" Students can then replace Tom with other names. Students can also replace the initial sound of each line to create standard and non-standard words. For example, guide children to substitute the initial sound of each major word to see how it sounds

and to determine if the change created a word that they can recognize, i.e, *So* to *Sed*, *Som*, *So* to *Sed*, *Som*. In addition to teaching the phoneme system, children are guided to understand how phonemes can alter meaning.

Balanced Reading Program

The development of phonemic and phonological awareness is important for preparing students for formal reading instruction. However, a strong reading program must go beyond these components to incorporate a balanced reading program. The concept of a balanced reading program emerged as a result of the work of Catherine Snow, Susan Burns, and Peg Griffin (1998). The balanced reading program encompasses best teaching practices from two traditionally opposing reading instruction programs: the **skills-based** approach, which emphasizes phonics instruction, and the **meaning-based** approach, which promotes reading comprehension and enrichment. The researchers concluded that a balanced reading program, one that incorporates the best principles of phonics (skills-based) and whole language (meaning-based) instruction, can best address the reading needs of all children.

Competency 003 (Alphabetic Principle)

The teacher understands the importance of the alphabetic principle for reading English and provides instruction that helps children understand the relationship between printed words and spoken language.

The Alphabetic Principle

The **alphabetic principle** has been described as the ability to connect the letters of the alphabet with the sounds that they produce. In addition to knowing the letters of the alphabet, children need to understand that letters and letter patterns represents the sounds of spoken English. They also need to conceptualize that language contains predictable connections between phonemes and graphemes, and that these relationships can be applicable to other situations. Understanding the connection between the letters of the alphabet and the sounds that they represent, constitute one of the main hurdles children need to conquer to become literate.

Types of Writing Systems

Modern writing systems can be categorized into several classifications. Three of the most commonly used classifications are pictographic, syllabic, and alphabetic. *Pictographic* writing systems are designed to represent words or ideas with a visual image representing the concept. Pictographic writing was the first type of written language developed in the history of civilizations. Pictograms are used today in road signs and public buildings. For example, the figure of a spoon and a fork are pictographs that represent a restaurant, and a figure of a woman or man represents restroom facilities by gender.

Syllabic writing represents syllables with signs, and syllabic writing is more efficient than a pictographic writing system. Japanese is a syllabic language composed of about 100 syllables. The Japanese syllabic system is ideal because the entire language can be phonologically represented by a relatively small number of syllables and the language does not have consonant clusters.

Alphabetic writing system uses the sounds of the language as a basic unit for writing. English uses an alphabetic writing system that is based upon phonetic signs. Theoretically in this system, each symbol represents one unit of sound. However, this principle works better with languages with more consistent sound-symbol relationship. Many alphabetic languages like Spanish are more phonetically consistent than English. An analysis of the grapheme-phoneme correspondence of English follows.

The Grapheme-Phoneme Correspondence of English

The connection between graphemes and phonemes in English is not always consistent. English has 26 graphemes to represent 44 phonemes. The consonant system is more consistent than the vowel system. English has five letters to represent 12 vowel sounds, which makes decoding and pronunciation more challenging. This inconsistency is partially caused by the evolution of the English language and the influence of multiple languages in the development of modern English. Teachers need to be proactive by identifying these troublesome areas and organizing instruction to address these issues. Some of the potential areas of concern are:

1. Graphemes can represent multiple phonemes. For example the grapheme *s* can represent multiple phonemes: car**s**-/**z**/, call**s**-/**z**/, **s**ugar-/**sh**/, mis**s**ion-/**sh**/, and walk**s**-/**s**/. This grapheme-phoneme inconsistency represents a challenge when attempting to use a phonic approach to teach reading.

2. English has graphemes that represent a sound in some words and remains silent in other words. For example, the graphemes *s* and *l* become silent in the following examples without giving readers a reliable clue for this change: *island*, *calm*, and *palm*. (Some speakers will make an attempt to pronounce the /s/ and /l/ in these words.)

3. English has multiple consonant diagraphs, which are two or more letters representing one sound.

    *   Gh – Ghost
    *   Gn – Gnat
    *   Kn – Know
    *   Ght – thought
    *   Pn– Pneumonia
    *   Ps– Psychology
    *   Rh– Rhythm
    *   Wr– Write
    *   Sc– Scene

    This inconsistency presents a challenge to native English speakers as well as ELLs.

4. English uses multiple contractions in daily communication. These can create listening comprehension problems for students and especially for ELLs. Teachers should introduce contractions together with the long version of the words to avoid confusion. Table 1-1 presents a few examples of the type of confusion that contractions can cause.

Table 1-1. Contractions in English

Contractions	Regular form	Possible Confusion
They're	They are	there and their
He's	He is/He has	his
He'll	He will	Hill, hell or heel or heal
You're	You are	your

5. English has multiple initial consonant clusters, which require students to be able to blend the sounds and at the same time recognize the sounds of individual phonemes. These sounds also represent a challenge for native Spanish speakers because Spanish does not have words that begin with particular letter sequences that exist in English. These types of clusters occur in medial positions and they are always preceded by the vowel **e**, such as in the words e**sp**ero, e**sc**apar, and e**st**ar. Based on this feature, Latino children will place an **e** in front of English words containing the following clusters:

    SP (as in *speak*), SC (*school*), ST (*street*), SPR (*spring*), SCR (*scream*), STR (*stream*), SM (*small*), SN (*snow*), and SL (*slate*).

6. A lot of English words end in consonants and consonant clusters (e.g., ra**t**, co**rd**, fi**rst**, and ca**rd**.) Young native English-speaking children and ELLs may have difficulties blending clusters at the end of the words. For native Spanish speakers, these clusters represent a unique challenge because Spanish does not have words that end in consonant clusters. Based on this feature, Spanish-speaking children, and possibly most children in early childhood, may tend to simplify final consonant cluster in English. For example, the word *board* might become *boar*.

How Is the Alphabetic Principle Learned?

Traditionally, children go through specific stages in the process of learning new words and mastering the alphabetic principle (Ehri, 1998). Preschoolers are exposed to components of the alphabetic principle through their environment. They can identify the logo of stores like Wal-Mart or Burger King by their design instead of by the specific letters contained in the logo. But because they are not connecting the letters and the sounds of the logo, this stage is generally considered a pre-alphabetic phase (USDA, 2006). At home, children might also get exposed to the alphabet song, which most of them learn in a subconscious manner. Eventually children engage in a **partial alphabetic phase** as they get exposed to alphabet block playing and concrete letter objects that are typical in early childhood programs. They begin connecting the shape of the letters with the sound that they represent. Children are also often exposed to children's literature and books in which the sound-symbol correspondence is carefully controlled. Children also begin connecting initial letter with the sound of the names of peers, like the **N** of Nancy and **A** of Alex.

A third phase of learning new words is identified as the **full Alphabetic Stage**. At this stage, children begin making connections between the letters, the sounds that they represent, and the actual meaning of the word. Children get very excited during this stage because they are beginning to "crack" the written code of the language.

In the fourth and last state of development, called the **Consolidated Alphabetic Stage**, children begin conceptualizing that they can use components of words that they know to decode new words. They begin discovering how they can create new words with the use of onsets, rhymes, and other letter sequences. One of the main purposes of phonics instruction at this stage is to guide children into understanding the connection between the grapheme and phoneme and the sequence that they create to form words and sentences. This knowledge allows students the opportunity to expand the number of words that they recognize instantly (sight words), which prepares them for literacy.

Teaching the Grapheme-Phoneme Correspondence

The introduction of the grapheme-phoneme correspondence can be presented through games, songs, and other engaging activities; but eventually, the correspondence should be presented explicitly. Teachers have to bring the skills to the surface level and make students aware of the concepts and skills that they need to learn in order to become effective readers. Teachers should take into account the complexity of the language and the maturity level of the children when introducing children to the alphabetic principle. A list of considerations

and strategies for teaching the grapheme-phoneme connection follows.

1. The introduction of the letter-sound correspondence should be guided by the potential support of the children's efforts to become readers. That is, introduce the spelling of the letters that the child is most likely to encounter in text. For example the letters *m, a, t, s, p* and *h* are used more frequently in writing than letters like *x, q,* or consonant diagraphs like *ght or gn*.

2. It is also important to begin instruction in the grapho-phonemic relationship using sounds that present the least possible distortion or confusion with other sounds. Some of the sounds that are easier to perceive are the nasals /m/, /n/, the fricatives /f/, the sibilant /s/, and the English retroflex, /r/.

3. Teachers should postpone the introduction of less clear phonemes like the nasal /ng/, the distinction between the sibilants /s/ and /z/, the troublesome sounds in English like the voiced *th* in the word **th**em, and the voiceless counter part in words like **th**ink.

4. Introduce words with one or two consonants and one short vowel sound such as in the words *on* and *car*. Later, long vowel sounds can be introduced.

5. Next, add consonant blends like *try*, followed by digraphs like *th, sh,* and *ch* in words like *thanks, show, chop*. Digraphs can lead students to recognize common words such as *this, she,* and *chair*. Introduce single consonants and consonant blends or clusters in separate lessons to avoid confusion.

6. Avoid voiceless-stop sounds (/t/, /p/, /k/) at the beginning or middle of words because the short duration of these phonemes makes them difficult to perceive. Teachers should postpone the introduction of conflicting letter-sound correspondence of phonemes like the /b/ and /v/ or /i/ and /e/, or visually confusing graphemes like the *b* and *d* or *p* and *g*.

Competency 004 (Literacy Development)

The teacher understands that literacy develops over time, progressing from emergent to proficient stages, and uses a variety of approaches to support the development of children's literacy.

Literacy Development

Literacy development generally begins at home when parents begin reading stories to their children. Through such activities, they are helping their child to hear the similarities and differences in the sounds of words. As a result of linguistic stimulation, children begin to manipulate and understand sounds in spoken language, and eventually they will practice this understanding by making up rhymes and new words on their own. When children are able to follow the written text together with the oral production, they begin to learn the names of the letters and the different sounds that each letter represents. Finally, children link the letters of the alphabet with the sounds of the words they speak. At this point children begin developing the phonemic and phonological awareness needed to become emergent readers.

Stages of Reading Development

Children go through three main stages of reading development: emergent readers, early readers, and fluent readers.

Emergent Readers

Emergent readers understand that print contains meaningful information. They imitate the reading process and display basic reading readiness skills like directionality movement, i.e., eye movement from top to bottom and from left to right. Emergent readers can participate in shared reading activities and are able to follow and match words with their pronunciation when teachers point to the words as they are read. Additionally, children at this stage:

- Use illustration to support comprehension.

- Listen and follow a story attentively and develop an awareness of the story structure.

- Represent the main idea of a story through drawings, and can retell major events in the story.

- Use illustrations and prior experiences to make predictions and to support comprehension.

- Possess some degree of phonemic awareness and are able to connect the initial letter of words with its representing phoneme.

Early Readers

Early readers have mastered reading readiness skills and are beginning to read simple text with some degree of success. They are also developing an internal list of high frequency words in print. Their reliance on picture clues has decreased now that they can get more information from print. Children at this stage also:

- Begin using the cuing system to confirm information in the text.

- Rely on grapho-phonemic information to sound out words as a decoding strategy.

- Show preference for certain stories.

- Begin noticing features from language and text like punctuation and capitalization, as well as the use of bold print and variation in format.

- Retell stories read to them with detail and accuracy.

- Engage in discussion of stories read, and identify the main idea and story characters.

- Engage in self correction when text does not make sense to them.

Newly Fluent Readers

Newly fluent readers can read with relative fluency and comprehension. They are able to use several cuing systems to obtain meaning from print, i.e., semantic, structural, visual, and grapho-phonemic cuing systems. They self-monitor their reading, and can identify and correct simple errors with minimum external support. They ask clarification questions to develop an understanding of the content. Newly fluent readers can also:

- Summarize the part of the story that they have read, and make inferences about the content.

- Handle more challenging vocabulary through the use of context clues.

- Begin using literary terms and grammar concepts.

- Enjoy reading from a variety of genres for information and for pleasure.

Children at this stage are not totally independent readers but with practice and support from teachers, they soon become fluent and independent readers.

Literacy Development in School

As the child enters school, formal reading instruction begins. How children should be taught to read is a subject that stirs up intense debate. Basically, it comes down to a discussion about starting points, and how to proceed with instruction. The two most common approaches used to teach reading in public schools are the skills-based approach, and the meaning-based approach. The skills-based approach is also called the bottom-up approach and the meaning-based is also known as the top-down approach.

Bottom-Up Approach (Skills-Based)

The **bottom-up approach** proceeds from the specific to the general, or from the parts to the whole. This approach begins with phonemes and graphemes, and continues by expanding to the syllable, words, sentences, paragraphs, and then whole reading selections. The best representation of this approach is phonics instruction.

Phonics is a method of teaching beginners to read and pronounce words by teaching them the phonetic value of letters, letter groups, and syllables. Because English has an alphabetic writing system, an understanding of the letter-sound relationship may prove helpful to the beginning reader. However, this view of reading instruction is that these relationships should be taught in isolation, in a highly sequenced manner, followed by reading words that represent the regularities of English in print. The children are asked to read decodable texts by sounding out words. Typically, this approach uses reading programs that offer stories with controlled vocabulary that are made up of letter-sound relationships and words with which children are already familiar. Thus, children might be asked to read a passage such as:

The cat sat on a mat.

The cat saw the rat in the pan.

The rat saw the cat.

The rat and the cat ran and ran.

Writing instruction follows in the same way. Children are asked to write decodable words, and fill in the blanks with decodable words in sentences in workbooks. This is based on the assumption that, once the children progress past this initial reading instruction time frame, meaning will follow.

Phonics instruction was widely used in the late 1960s and 1970s. Phonics is still being promoted today. The flaw in this kind of instruction is that many English words, including the highest frequency words, are not phonetically regular. Also, comprehension of text can be limited in phonics, because there is not a great deal to comprehend in texts such as "pig did a gig." Modern approaches to phonics instruction have made the stories more enjoyable and interesting. For example, the *Progressive Phonics Book* series, which is available through the Genki English website, uses computer sound technology, visuals, and more involving stories to engage the reader. The following is an example of this approach.

Don't Scowl at My Vowel

I don't mind it if my dog

Tries to **pat** me with his **paw**

But I don't like it if my **cat**

Tries to scratch me with her **claw**.

The assumption is that textual meaning will become apparent in time. Furthermore, it must be stressed that teaching phonics is not the same as teaching reading. Also, reading and spelling require much more than just phonics; spelling strategies and word-analysis skills are equally important. Nor does asking children to memorize phonics rules ensure application of those rules, and, even if that were true, the word the child is attempting to decode is frequently an exception to the stated rule. Teaching children to use phonics is different from teaching them about phonics. In summary, the skills-based approach begins reading instruction with a study of single letters, letter sounds, blends and digraphs, blends and digraph sounds, and vowels and vowel sounds in isolation, and in a highly sequenced manner. The children read and write decodable words, with a great emphasis on reading each word accurately, as opposed to reading to comprehend the text as a whole.

The Genki English website provides examples of strategies to use for phonics instruction. This site also provides free use of games, songs and stories. The Genki English websites can be accessed at *http://www.genkienglish.net/phonics.htm*.

Top-Down Approach (Meaning-Based)

Another approach to promoting literacy is the **top-down approach**. This approach begins with the whole and then proceeds to its individual parts. That is, the top-down approach begins with whole stories, paragraphs, sentences, words and then proceeds to the smallest units of syllables, graphemes, and phonemes. The approach that best represents this view is the **Whole Language Approach**. The Whole Language Approach grew out of the work of Dr. Kenneth Goodman, who was a leader in the development of the psycholinguistic perspective. This approach suggests that to derive meaning from text, readers rely more on the structure and meaning of language than on the graphic information from the text. Dr. Goodman and other researchers demonstrated that literacy development parallels language development. One of Dr. Goodman's contributions to the field was a process called **miscue analysis**, which is a process that begins with a child reading a selection orally, and an examiner noting variations of the oral reading from the printed text. Each variation from the text is called a miscue and is analyzed for type of variation. Previously, teacher candidates were urged to read and reread texts with young children until the child could read every word in the text perfectly. Goodman suggested, however, that only miscues that altered meaning needed to be corrected, while other, unimportant miscues could be ignored.

The Whole Language Approach stands in sharp contrast to the emphasis on phonics that is promoted in the skills-based approach to reading. The meaning-based approach to reading emphasizes comprehension and meaning in texts. Children focus on the wholeness of words, sentences, paragraphs, and entire books, and seek meaning through context. Whole-language advocates stress the importance of reading high-quality children's literature and extending the meaning of the literature through conversation, projects, and writing. Instead of fill-in-the-blank workbooks, children are encouraged to write journals, letters, and lists, and to participate in writing workshops. Word recognition skills, including phonics, are taught in the context of reading and writing, and are taught as those things relate to the text in hand. Children are taught the four cueing systems, and are taught to ask themselves, "Does it look right? Does it sound right? Does it make sense?" The children are taught that the reason people read books is to make meaning. Thus, the focus of this approach is on both comprehension and making connections. The main flaw of the Whole Language Approach is that it makes heavy instructional demands on the teacher.

Balanced Reading Program

Today, many classrooms are places where young children enjoy learning to read and write in a balanced reading instructional program. Research into best practice strongly suggests that the teaching of reading requires solid skill instruction, including several techniques for decoding unknown words. These techniques include but are not limited to, phonics instruction embedded in interesting and engaging reading and writing experiences with whole and **authentic literature-based** texts to facilitate the construction of meaning. In other words, this approach to instruction combines the best skill instruction and the whole language approach in order to teach both skills and meaning as well as to meet the reading needs of individual children.

Some of the reading strategies used in a balanced literacy program are:

- Teacher directed/reading to students (read aloud)

- Shared reading, guided reading and reading workshops

- Student directed reading and independent reading

- Teacher directed writing, writing to/for students as part of classroom routines, and process writing

- Shared writing as in language experience/interactive writing, writing workshops

- Student directed writing and independent writing activities

Children's Literature

Genre is a particular type of literature that can be classified in multiple categories. Some of the most common genres used in elementary schools are science fiction, biography, and traditional literature, which encompasses folk tales, fables, myths, epics, and legends. Classifications of genre are largely arbitrary and are based on conventions that apply a basic category to an author's writing. Classifications give the reader a general expectation of what sort of book is being chosen. Teachers today are expected to share a wide range of texts with children. The most common type of books for children is picture books. **Picture books** are books in which the illustrations and the text work together to communicate the story. It is a very good idea to share picture books with children in several different formats. Sometimes, able teachers simply read the book to the child without showing any of the pictures. The story is then discussed, and the children are asked if they would like the book to be reread, this time with the pictures being shared. Typically, this technique sparks a lively conversation about why the book with its illustrations is better than hearing the words alone.

Traditional Literature

Traditional literature comprises the stories that have their roots in the oral tradition of storytelling and have been handed down from generation to generation. This genre also includes the modern versions of these old stories. Teachers can read and share multiple versions of old stories, and then compare and contrast each version. It is also interesting to read a number of folktales and keep track of the elements that these old stories have in common, and also to guide children towards noticing where these old stories show up in their day-to-day lives. Children enjoy sharing what they notice. Some examples of folk literature are:

- Animal tales where the characters are animals exhibiting human characteristics, e.g., *Anansi the Spider*.

- Fables where the main characters are also animals and these present a moral, e.g., *The Tortoise and the Hare*.

- The *Pourquois Tales* comprise stories from around the world that explain how things were created. Every culture may have a different version of the way things were created, e.g., *How the Sea was Created*, and *The Legend of the Bluebonnet*.

- Wonder tales describe stories of enchantment in far away lands. Traditionally, it presents the themes of Good vs. Evil, e.g., *Snow White*.

- Noodle head tales are stories of lovable fools. These stories include individuals that are not very bright, but manage to survive and often succeed, e.g., *Puss in Boots*.

- Cumulative tales represent stories where the information is presented in a sequence and all the events in the sequence are repeated, e.g., *The Gingerbread Man* and *The Three Little Pigs*.

- Tall tales describe the story of legendary people or fictitious characters that manage to accomplish great things in life, e.g., *Paul Bunyan*, *John Henry*, and *Pecos Bill*.

- Ghost stories have traditionally been used to regulate the behavior of children. For example, the Boogie Man has been used in multiple cultures to scare children and encourage them to behave properly. In the Mexican culture, the Boogie Man is called "El Cucuy"; in the Puerto Rican culture, "El Cuco."

Multicultural Literature

Multicultural literature is a term used to describe literature other than traditional European stories. Traditionally, these are stories from countries throughout the world that are written by people from those countries. Original works of people from other countries are regularly used in American public schools. The term **authentic multicultural** has been used to describe literature written by members of particular cultural groups that represent their own reality. Some examples of literature that reflect the Latino experience are *The Gold Coin* by Alma Florada, *Chato's Kitchen* by Gary Soto, *Hairs-Pelitos* by Sandra Cisneros, *Friends from the Other Side* by Gloria Anzaldua, *When I was Puerto Rican* by Esmeralda Santiago, and *Tomas and the Library Lady* by Pat Mora.

Modern Fantasy

Modern fantasy is a genre that presents make-believe stories that are the product of the author's imagination. Often, they are so beyond the realm of everyday life that the stories can't possibly be true. Extraordinary events take place within the covers of these books. Fantasy allows a child to move beyond the normal life in the classroom, and speculate about a life that never was, and may never be. Fantasy is a genre that typically sparks intense discussions, and provides ample opportunities to illuminate the author's craft for the child. The popular *Harry Potter* series by J. K. Rowling is a perfect example of both the genre and the debate generated by this type of fiction.

Historical Fiction

Historical fiction is fiction that is set in the past. This type of fiction allows children to live vicariously in times and places they can not experience in any other way. This type of fiction often has real people and real events depicted, with fiction laced around them. Historical fiction informs the study of social studies. Examples include *Don't You Know There's a War On?* by James Stevenson (WWII), *Klara's New World* by Jeanette Winter (Swedish immigrant family), *A Horse Called Starfire* by Betty Boegehold (Native Americans' first encounter with the horse), and *Wagon Wheels* by Barbara Brenner (an African American boy and family in 1870 Kansas).

Nonfiction

Nonfiction books have the real world as their point of origin. These books help to expand the knowledge of children when they are studying a topic; however, these books need to be evaluated for accuracy, authenticity, and inclusion of the salient facts. Nonfiction books can be used to support the teaching of content and to promote higher-level comprehension skills.

Biography

Biography is a genre that deals with the lives of real people. Autobiography is a genre that deals with the life of the author. These books invigorate the study of social studies because, through careful research, they often include information that transforms a name in a textbook into a person that one may like to get to know better.

Poetry

Poetry is a genre that is difficult to define for children, except as "not-prose." Poetry is the use of words to capture something: a sight, a feeling, or perhaps a sound. Poetry needs to be chosen carefully for a child, as poetry ought to elicit a response from the child—one that connects with the experience of the poem. All children need poetry in their lives. Poetry should be celebrated and enjoyed as part of the classroom experience, and a literacy-rich classroom will always include a collection of poetry to read, reread, savor, and enjoy. *The Owl and the Pussycat* by Edward Lear, Mother Goose rhymes, limericks, and haiku are all poems or type of poems that appeal to young children.

In summary, today there is an overwhelming variety of children's literature from which to choose. When selecting books for use in a classroom, a teacher has a number of issues to consider: Is the book accurate? Aesthetically pleasing? Engaging? Bear in mind that all children deserve to see positive images of children like themselves in the books they read, as illustrations can have a powerful influence on their perceptions of the world. Children also need to see positive images of children who are not like themselves, as who is or is not depicted in books can have a powerful influence on children's perception of the world. Teachers ought to provide children with literature that depicts an affirming, multicultural view, and the selection of books available should show many different kinds of protagonists. Both boys and girls, for example, should be depicted as able and strong.

To teach all components of all of the genres, teacher candidates should become aware of the terminology to analyze stories. They should also guide children to use the appropriate terms to describe different types of literature. This author taught elementary school after teaching for several years in high school and college, and quickly found that the term *fiction* was a foreign word for third graders. This author soon found out the magic word to refer to fiction for third graders was *make-believe*. Thus, teachers can introduce most of the terminology to study literature by using words to which students can relate. Once students understand the concept, teachers can introduce standard terminology to describe literature. Some of the concepts and terminology to describe literature follow:

1. Information about the story including the author and illustrators, the publishing company, and even the International Standard Book Number (ISBN)

2. Terminology to describe the characters of the story (the protagonist, the antagonist or villain, animals, humans)

3. For older students introduce the point of view of the author. A story's point of view can be first person (the author is one of the characters of the story, and the narrator), the omniscient point of view (the narrator is an outsider who knows what the characters are thinking or feeling), or the limited point of view, or subjective consciousness (the narrator is not a character in the story). In the limited point of view, the narrator guides readers to see the story from a point of view of one of the characters. The narrator also conveys information that might seem unnatural coming from a character in the story.

4. The setting refers to the geographical location and the general environment and historical circumstances of the story.

5. The theme of the story. The plot tell us what happens and the theme tells us why it happens. Some examples of themes are: problems of growing up, maturing, linguistic and cultural adjustment, love and friendship, family issues, and achieving one's identity.

6. Literary Style, which includes description of the following:

   • Exposition: It is usually used to introduce the background information and to understand or introduce characters

   • Dialogue: Communication among the characters

   • Vocabulary: Word choice, use of concrete vs. abstract terminology, i.e., Is the language vocabulary appropriate for intended audience?

   • Imagery: The use of words to create sensory impressions. It conveys sights, sounds, textures, smells, and tastes. Imagery includes the collection of images used to create an emotional response in the reader.

   • Tone: The author's mood and manner of expression. It might be humorous, serious, satirical, passionate, sensitive, childlike, zealous, indifferent, poignant, or warm.

   • Analysis of the story. It might be multicultural or traditional, or include possible stereotypes, sexism, religious issues, controversial elements, or words or ideas that might create controversy.

Key Principles of the Competency

• When students draw pictures and use invented spelling to write about them, we say that the child has developed the idea that print carries meaning.

• Discuss folk tales from around the world and guide students to discuss common features and unique features (oral activities).

• When assessing the literal comprehension of students in the emergent stage of reading development, provide students with visual aids and ask them to explain what happened in the story.

• The invented spelling of emergent readers can be used to determine their ability to apply phonic skills.

• To teach the connection between spoken and written words to emergent readers, the teacher should use a big book and point to each word as she/he reads the story aloud.

• Use a "story tree" or "story map" containing parts of the story to teach critical analysis of literature. A story map contains the following parts:

   a. Setting—It is a real place or imaginary? Is the place important to the story line? Does the story take place in the past, present or future?

   b. Characters—Who is the principal character? Who are the good and bad characters? Are the characters real or fictitious?

   c. Plot—What is the main problem? What caused the problem?

   d. Resolution—How did the story end? How did the problems get solved?

• To apply meta-cognitive skills and to enhance their comprehension, students should ask additional questions about the content and the story as a whole.

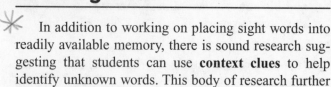

Competency 005 (Word Analysis and Decoding)

The teacher understands the importance of word analysis and decoding for reading and provides many opportunities for children to improve their word-analysis and decoding abilities.

Word Analysis Skills

Word analysis refers to the way that children approach a written word in order to decode and obtain meaning from it.

Vocabulary Sight Words

Vocabulary building is a skill that needs to be practiced daily in the classroom. One of the goals of this is to assist children in becoming skillful in rapid word recognition. Research suggests that fluent word identification needs to be accomplished before a child can readily comprehend text. If a child needs to painstakingly analyze many words in a text, the memory and attention needed for comprehension are absorbed by word analysis, and the pleasure in a good story is lost. Typically, children who are beginning readers decode each word as they read it. Through repeated exposure to the same words, instant-recognition vocabulary grows. It is particularly important that developing readers learn to recognize those words that occur very frequently in print. These words are called sight words.

Dolch Words

In 1948, Edward W. Dolch identified 220 of the most frequently used words in the English language. He believed that if children were exposed to these words and learned to recognize them as sight words, they would become fluent readers. Some examples of Dolch words are: *a, an, am, at, can, had, has, ran, the, after, but, got* and *away*. The introduction of these sight words can expedite the decoding process and develop fluency among early readers.

Decoding Clues

In addition to working on placing sight words into readily available memory, there is sound research suggesting that students can use **context clues** to help identify unknown words. This body of research further suggests that instruction can help improve students' use of context clues. There are three main kinds of context clues: **semantic, syntactic, and structural**.

Semantic Clues

Semantic clues require a child to think about the meanings of words, and what is already known about the topic being read. For example, when reading a story about hawks, teachers can help children to activate prior knowledge about the bird, and to develop an expectation that the selection may contain words associated with hawks, such as *predator, carnivorous, food chain*, and *wingspan*. This discussion might help a child gain a sense of what might be reasonable in a sentence. For ELLs who might not be familiar with the hawk, teachers need to identify equivalent species from their geographical area.

Syntactic Clues

The word order in a sentence might also provide clues to readers. For example, in the sentence, "Hawks are _____," the order of the words in the sentence indicates that the missing word must be an adjective. This open-ended sentence can lead students to words such as *carnivorous, predators*, or other descriptors for the bird. Furthermore, the illustrations in the book can often help with the identification of a word. A picture of a hawk eating prey can lead students to the words *predator* or *carnivorous*. Still, context clues are often not specific enough to allow students to predict the exact word. However, when context clues are combined with other clues such as phonics and structural clues, accurate word identification is usually possible.

Structural Clues

Another strategy to provide clues to readers is to pay attention to letter groups because there are many groups of letters that frequently occur within words, which are called morphemes. These specific clusters of letters

Table 1-2. Common Prefixes of English and Spanish

Roots	Meaning	English Words	Spanish Words
bio	life	symbiosis	simbiosis
fobia (phobia)	fear of	xenophobia	xenofobia
fono (phono)	sound	phonetics	fonética
foto (photo)	light	photography	fotografía
geo	land, earth	geology	geología

can be taught. Common **derivational morphemes** in the form of prefixes, suffixes, and **inflectional endings** should be pointed out to students. An analysis of derivational and inflectional endings follows.

Derivational Morphemes Most of the derivational morphemes come from foreign languages like Greek and Latin, and they represent relatively consistent meanings. For example, the meaning of the prefixes *pre*, *anti*, and *sub* is very consistent in English and in other languages; namely pre=before, anti=against, and sub=under.

A large number of English prefixes are common to multiple western languages such as Spanish, French, and German. See Table 1-2 above for examples for English and Spanish.

Derivational morphemes can change the syntactic classification of the word. That is, by adding a morpheme to a word it can be changed from a verb to a noun or from an adjective to an adverb. Table 1-3 presents some examples of syntactic changes.

Table 1-3. Derivational Morphemes and Syntactic Changes

Type of Modification	Word 1	Word 2
Verb to a noun	To Drive	Driver
Adjective to an adverb	Cautious	Cautiously
Adjective to a noun	Aware	Awareness

Children who are guided to recognize derivational morphemes will have a definite advantage when decoding words.

Inflectional Morphemes Inflectional morphemes do not change the syntactic classification, and typically follow derivational morphemes in a word. These are native of English and always function as suffixes. English has eight inflectional endings.

1. Short Plural **s**, e.g., Two *car***s**, three *pen***s**

2. Long plural **es**. Use long plurals after ch, sh, s, z, and x, e.g., *churches*, *washes, cases,* and *boxes*

3. Third person singular s, e.g., Mary *walk***s** quickly

4. Possessive **'s**, e.g., Martha**'s** boy

5. Progressive **ing**, e.g., She is *walk***ing**. The gerund is not included in this group, i.e., **Walking** is good for your health.

6. Regular past tense **ed**, e.g., He work**ed** very hard

7. Past participle **en** or **ed, e.g.,** She has beat**en** the system, or It has been ruin**ed**

8. Comparative and superlative **er** (**better**), and **est** (**best**), e.g.,—Alex Rodríguez is **better** than Derek Jeter, or He is the rich**est** player in the major leagues.

Understanding the meaning of these morphemes can definitely enhance students' decoding and comprehension skills.

Being able to rapidly and accurately associate sounds with a cluster of letters leads to more rapid and efficient word identification. As young readers build an increasing store of words that they can recognize with little effort, they can use the words they know to help them recognize other, possibly related, words that are unfamiliar. The best practice for helping students gain skill in word-recognition is real reading and writing activities. As children read and reread texts of their own choice, they have many opportunities to successfully decode a word, and realize that each time a letter combination such as *c-a-t* is found in the selection, it's read as *cat*. With each exposure to that word, the child reads the word more easily. A child who writes a sentence with that word is developing a greater sensitivity to meaning or context clues. The child attempting to spell that word is reviewing and applying what he knows about letter-sound associations.

Words That Can Create Comprehension Problems for Children

There are words that children can decode but they might have problems identifying the intended meaning. Some of these difficult words include homonyms and homophones. **Homonyms** are words that have the same sound and the same spelling but differ in meaning. Homonyms are common in the content areas and can create comprehension problems. The context will determine the meaning of the words. Examples of homonyms are presented in Table 1-4.

Table 1-4. English Homonyms

Word	Meaning 1	Meaning 2
Club	A place to socialize	A wooden stick
Fine	A penalty	To imply good or okay
Bank	Margins of a river	A place that holds money
Rock	Type of music	A stone

Homophones are words that sound the same but they are spelled differently and have different meaning. Examples of homophones are: blew and blue, cents and sense, heir and air, wait and weight, hear and here, eight and ate, to, two, and too, there and their, deer and dear, hair and hare. **Homographs** are words that are spelled the same way but have more than one pronunciation and different meanings. For example, the word *bow* has two pronunciations, the first referring to the front part of a ship or the way that people bend to salute; the second referring to the decorative knot used in clothing. Consider the use of the word

in the following sentence: The Japanese ambassador wore a red *bow*, stood on the *bow* of the ship and graciously *bowed* to the audience.

Compound Words

Compound words are created when two independent words are joined to create a new word. Often, knowing the meaning of the two words will guide students to understand the meaning of the compound word. For example, the compound word *birdhouse* is composed of the words *bird* and *house*. With this information, children can understand that the new word refers to a refuge or a house for birds. However, there are some examples of compound words where the two words can create confusion among children. Examples of these deceptive compound words are *butterfly*, *nightmare*, and *brainstorm*.

Key Principles of the Competency

- Understands that many children develop word-analysis and decoding skills in a predictable sequence

- Understands the importance of word recognition skills

- Knows a variety of formal and informal procedures for assessing children's word-analysis

- Teaches the analysis of phonetically regular words in a simple-to-complex progression

- Teaches children to read passages using decodable texts as appropriate

- Teaches children to recognize high-frequency irregular words by selecting words that appear frequently in children's books

- Teaches children ways to identify vowel-sound combinations and multi-syllabic words

- Provides instruction in how to use structural cues to recognize compound words, as well as the base word, prefix, and suffix

- Teaches children to use knowledge of English word order

- Uses formal and informal assessments to plan and adjust instruction

Competency 006 (Reading Fluency)

The teacher understands the importance of fluency for reading comprehension and provides many opportunities for children to improve their reading fluency.

Reading Fluency

Reading fluency is the ability to decode words quickly and accurately in order to read text with the appropriate word stress, pitch and intonation pattern (or prosody). Reading fluency requires automaticity of word recognition and reading with prosody to facilitate comprehension. **Automaticity** is the quick and accurate recognition of letters, words, and language conventions. Automaticity is achieved through continuous practice using texts written at the reading level of the child.

Fluency and Comprehension

Fluency is a prerequisite for language comprehension. Children struggling with fluency devote their time to mastering their language skills, which is an effort that takes away from the effort that they should be placing on reading comprehension. When students read aloud in class, the main purpose of the activity is to develop fluency. If after reading aloud, teachers ask the child comprehension questions, the child will most likely have to read the same passage silently to be able to respond to the questions. Thus, teachers should separate these two activities—read silently for comprehension, and read aloud to promote fluency.

What Is the Expectation?

Chapter 110.3 TEKS for English language arts and reading suggests that the typical child in first grade should be able to read about 60 words per minute (wpm) and the rate should increase by 10 words in each grade, i.e., second grade (70 wpm), third grade (80 wpm), and fourth grade (90 wpm). To determine the number of words per minute read, a simple formula is used; namely, words read in a minute, minus errors, equals word per minute (UT system/TEA, 2002). The expectation is that children in the first to fourth grade will be able to read independently with minimum difficulty, i.e., finding no more than 1 in 20 words difficult.

How Do We Teach Fluency?

Teachers can use several strategies to promote reading fluency. Descriptions of these strategies follow.

Guided Oral Repeated Reading

Teachers can promote opportunities for **guided oral repeated reading** using text at the reading level of the child. Teachers, parents and peers can provide support and feedback for these students. Allow the child to read the same story repeatedly to develop fluency.

Choral Reading

Reading in group is another activity used to promote reading fluency. This activity is ideal for ELLs and struggling readers because pronunciation and fluency problems will not be publicly noticed and they can use the model provided by fluent readers.

Pairing Students

Pairing proficient readers with ELLs or struggling readers can benefit both groups—the proficient child receives additional practice reading, and the ELLs and struggling readers are able to listen to fluent readers. ELLs and struggling readers can also read to their partners and receive input.

Interactive Computer Programs

Using interactive reading programs can provide individualized reading support for children. These computer programs often contain colorful pictures and interesting stories. The child should have the option of clicking on the words or pictures in order to have the selected word read aloud or to get animation of the word's meaning. The program can also read a story at normal speed while the child follows the highlighted words in a printed text.

Silent Sustained Reading

Guiding the child to read continuously for about 20 minutes a day can definitely improve reading fluency. This activity is also used to teach the child to read silently without moving their lips.

Readers' Theater

This activity has been used successfully to emphasize reading fluency. In this activity, a story is modified so that various characters have to read portions of the text. Students rehearse their reading part, and then create a theater format to present the reading. Children enjoy this new approach and it improves reading fluency.

Developing Reading Fluency

Pointing to words while reading helps students see the letter-sound correspondence; however, this practice can also affect the development of reading fluency. Second graders should be guided to discontinue this practice. Continuous monitoring of reading fluency is required to insure children develop and maintain reading fluency when they are exposed to more challenging text. To be sure that students maintain reading fluency, teachers can conduct individual assessment using teacher-developed check-lists or more standardized processes like running records.

Assessing Reading Fluency

A running record is an assessment strategy designed by Mary Clay (2002) to assess students' word identification skills and fluency in oral reading. As the teacher listens to a student read a page, the teacher uses a copy of the page to mark each word the child mispronounces. The teacher writes the incorrect word over the printed word, draws a line through each word the child skips, and draws an arrow under repeated words. In this activity teachers can identify the type of error made and can then provide additional support to individual learners.

Key Principles of the Competency
* Understands that fluency involves rate, accuracy, and intonation

* Understands how children's reading rate and fluency affect their comprehension
* Understands how children develop reading fluency
* Applies norms to identify and monitor children's fluency levels
* Selects and uses instructional strategies, materials, and activities to develop fluency
* Understand how to foster collaboration with families to promote reading fluency

Competency 007 (Reading Comprehension)

The teacher understands the importance of reading for understanding, knows the components of comprehension, and teaches children strategies for improving their comprehension.

Reading Comprehension

Helping students read for understanding is the central goal of reading instruction. Comprehension is a complex process involving the text, the reader, the situation, and the purpose for reading. There are a number of factors that come into play as a child attempts to comprehend a passage. First, students cannot understand texts if they cannot read the words. Thus, a teacher who is interested in improving students' comprehension skills needs to teach them to decode well. In addition, children need time during the school day to read texts that are easy for them to read, and also have time to discuss what has been read. Children need to read and reread easy texts often enough that decoding becomes rapid, easy, and accurate. It has been noted frequently in the literature that children who comprehend well have bigger vocabularies than children who struggle with reading. In part, this is true because their knowledge of vocabulary develops through contact with new words as they read text that is rich in new words. However, it has also been suggested that simply teaching vocabulary in isolation does not automatically enhance comprehension.

Background Knowledge

*Reading comprehension can be affected by **prior knowledge**, and readers who possess rich prior knowledge about the topic of a reading often understand the reading better than classmates with less prior knowledge. A discrepancy between the schema intended by the author and the schema that the reader brings to the reading process can create confusion and comprehension problems. This is especially important for students from linguistically and culturally diverse backgrounds, who might not possess the cultural information to understand stories written for middle class American students.*

Pre-Reading Activities

Prior knowledge also affects interest. Generally, students like to read about somewhat familiar topics. This is an area in which the skill and interest of the teacher can play a significant role. Teachers should identify interests in children and find appropriate stories to match their interests. An able teacher can also make a previously unfamiliar topic seem familiar through **pre-reading activities** during which prior knowledge is activated, new prior knowledge is formed, and interest is stirred up. Teachers of ELLs often have to spend more time in pre-reading activities than the actual time devoted to reading the stories.

Setting the Purpose for Reading

A good teacher will set a clear purpose for reading, and ask the students to gain an overview of the text before reading, to make predictions about the upcoming text, and then to read selectively based on their predictions. Best practice suggests that children should be encouraged to generate questions about ideas in text while reading. Successful teachers encourage children to construct mental images representing ideas in text, or to construct actual images from texts that lend themselves to this kind of activity.

Linking Prior Knowledge to New Knowledge

A successful teacher will help readers to process text containing new factual information through reading strategies, and helping children to relate that new information to their prior knowledge. Questioning techniques is a simple but powerful mechanism to guide children to link current knowledge to new knowledge. Through questioning, teachers guide children to question the facts, intent of the author, and also to check the answers through text verification. It is through conversation that children are able to compare their predictions and expectations about the content. It is also through these conversations that children see the need to revise their prior knowledge when compelling new ideas are encountered that conflict with prior knowledge. As part of these ongoing conversations, teachers will become alert to students who are applying the incorrect schema as they read, and will be able to encourage use of more appropriate knowledge. These conversations help children figure out the meanings of unfamiliar vocabulary words based on context clues, the opinions of others, and sometimes through the use of appropriate source materials such as glossaries, dictionaries, or an appropriate selection in another text. After reading activities, able teachers encourage children to revisit the text—to reread and make notes and paraphrase—in order to remember important points, interpret the text, evaluate its quality, and review important points. Children should also be encouraged to think about how ideas encountered in the text might be used in the future. As children gain competence, they enjoy showing what they know.

Story Grammar

Children should be encouraged to analyze stories using the story-grammar components of setting, characters, problems encountered by characters, attempts at solution to the problem, successful solution, and ending. Teachers can use graphic organizers to present a visual clue of these components. Story frames like the one listed in Figure 1-1 can be modified to introduce various components of literature, as well as an assessment tool to check for comprehension.

As children's comprehension grows more sophisticated, they move from merely attempting to comprehend what is in the text, to reading more critically. This means that they grow in an understanding that comprehension can go beyond the denotative components of the facts portrayed in text. With skillful instruction, children come to read not only what a text says, but also how the text portrays the subject matter. Students recognize the various ways in which every text is the unique creation of a unique author, and they also learn to compare and contrast the treatment of the same subject matter in a number of texts. For example, teachers can introduce the multiple versions of stories like *Cinderella* in order to discuss how stories can represent similar themes using unique settings and situations. Examples of variations on Cinderella are *Mufaro's Beautiful Daughters: An African Tale*, by John Steptoe; *Yeh-Shen, a Cinderella Tale from China*, by Ai-Ling Louie; and *The Egyptian Cinderella*, by Shirley Climo.

Teachers can help students grow in comprehension through stages. In the beginning, teachers are usually happy if children are able to demonstrate their comprehension of what a text says in some authentic way. The next stage is to have the children ponder what a text does—to describe an author's purpose, to recognize the elements of the text, and how the text was assembled. Finally, some children can attain the skill set needed to successfully engage in text interpretation, to be able to detect and articulate tone and persuasive elements, to discuss point of view, and to recognize bias. Over time, and with good instruction, children learn to infer unstated meanings based on social conventions, shared knowledge, shared experience, or shared values. They make sense of text by recognizing implications and drawing conclusions, and they move past the point of believing the content of a selection simply because it was in print.

Reflecting Reading—Bias in Traditional Stories

Traditional children's stories are filled with episodes of violence, sexism, and stereotypes. Fairy tales like *Cinderella* and *Snow White* portray women as weak creatures in need of support and rescuing. They also present old people as ugly and often as evil, e.g., the evil witch. Killing is also rampant in stories such as *Hansel and Gretel* where the main characters are left to die in the woods, and then are imprisoned by an "ugly and old witch" who they kill eventually. Thievery and killing are also promoted in the story of *Jack and the Beanstalk*. In the original story the main character, Jack, steals from the "ugly" giant and kills him. Teachers should not ignore violence and bias in literature, and they should use these stories as a foundation to guide children to discuss and challenge bias and stereotypes.

Teachers can use traditional stories to examine controversial events in the stories. Teachers can lead children to discuss the actions of characters like Jack in *Jack and the Bean Stalk* who steals the golden goose from the giant. Teachers can also introduce new stories and modern versions of traditional stories where stereotypes and violence are challenged. For example, in the Disney's version of the Chinese story of *Mulan*, the main character challenges the stereotypical role of women when she joins the Army disguised as a man in order to save the honor of the family and become a national heroine. In the *Paper Bag Princess*, the protagonist presents the idea that women do not always need to be saved by men or to marry a man who will protect them. In this story, the princess saves the prince from the dragon and even-

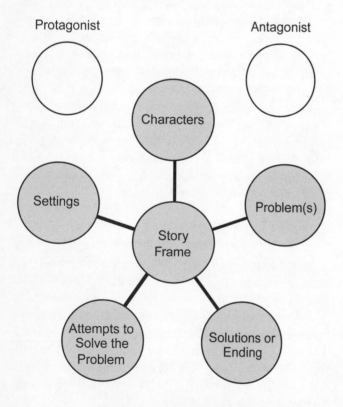

Figure 1-1. Story Frame

tually she decides not to marry him. Guiding children to examine themes and bias in literature can make them better readers and, more importantly, they can become reflective learners.

Monitoring Comprehension

Children need to be taught to monitor their own comprehension, and to decide when they need to exert more effort, or to apply a strategy to make sense of a text. The goal of comprehension instruction is for the child to reach a level at which the application of strategies becomes automatic. In summary, comprehension is maximized when readers are fluent in all the processes of skilled reading—from the decoding of words to the articulation and easy application of the comprehension strategies used by good readers. Therefore, teachers need to teach predicting, questioning, seeking clarification, relating to background knowledge, constructing mental images, and summarizing. The teaching of comprehension strategies has to be conceived as a long-term developmental process, and the teaching of all reading strategies is more successful if they are taught and used by all of the teachers on a staff. In addition, teachers need to allow time for in-school reading, and recognize that good texts are comprehended on a deep level only through rereading and meaningful discussions.

Monitoring Reading Comprehension in Pre-Literate Children

Story retelling is a strategy used with young children to assess listening and reading comprehension. This strategy can also assess sentence structure knowledge, vocabulary, speaking ability, and knowledge about the structure of stories.

An informal or more structured checklist can be used to assess a student's comprehension, sentence structure knowledge, and vocabulary development as they retell a story. Any checklist for listening comprehension should assess the ability of the child to (Lapp et al., 2001):

1. retell the story with details.

2. show evidence of comprehension of the story line and plot, including the characters, setting, author's intention, and literal and implied meaning

3. show evidence that the child understood major ideas and the ideas that support it

4. bring background information to the selection

5. analyze and make judgments based on facts

6. retell the selection in sentences that make grammatical sense

7. retell the story using sentences that include standard usage of verbs, adjectives, conjunctions, and compound sentences

8. use a rich and meaningful vocabulary with minimal use of slang and colloquial expressions

9. adapt spoken language for various audiences, purposes, and occasions

10. listen for various purposes including critical listening to evaluate a speaker's message, and listening to enjoy and appreciate spoken language

Reading Strategies

Looking at strategies used by proficient readers can help teachers make skillful choices of activities that will maximize student learning. Anne Goudvis and Stephanie Harvey (2000) offer the following suggestions for useful activities.

Activating Prior Knowledge

Readers pay more attention when they can relate to the text. Readers naturally bring their prior knowledge and experience to reading, but they comprehend better when they think about the connections they make between the text, their lives, and the larger world. This strategy is especially important when teaching children from diverse cultural and linguistic backgrounds. Teachers need to explore the schemata necessary for children to understand the story and the background knowledge that children bring to the reading process. One of the strategies used to explore a child's background is the KWL chart. This is a chart that asks students to describe what they **K**now, **W**ant to know, **L**earned and still want to learn, or areas that the students did not understand that well. Because this is a class activity, children can benefit from what others already know, what others want to learn, and what areas others had difficulties with.

Predicting or Asking Questions

Questioning is the strategy that keeps readers engaged. When readers ask questions, even before they read, they clarify understanding and forge ahead to make meaning. Asking questions is also at the heart of thoughtful reading. A variation of this strategy is to give students a true or false question about the content to be read. Once the students complete the questions, they then read to corroborate the answers.

Visualizing

Active readers create visual images based on the words they read in the text. These created pictures in turn enhance their understanding.

Drawing Inferences

Inferring is when the readers take what they know, garner clues from the text, and think ahead to make a judgment, discern a theme, or speculate about what is to come.

Determining Important Ideas

Thoughtful readers grasp essential ideas and important information when reading. Readers must differentiate between less important ideas and the key ideas that are central to the meaning of the text.

Synthesizing Information

Synthesizing information involves combining new information with existing knowledge to form an original idea or interpretation. Reviewing, sorting, and sifting important information can lead to new insights that change the way readers think.

Repairing Understanding

If confusion disrupts meaning, readers need to stop and clarify their understanding. Readers may use a variety of strategies to "fix up" comprehension when meaning goes awry.

Confirming Predictions

As students read and after they have finished reading, they should confirm the predictions they originally made. There is no wrong answer. One can confirm negatively or positively. Determining if a prediction is correct is a goal.

Using Parts of Book

Students should use book parts—such as charts, diagrams, indexes, and the table of contents, to improve their understanding of the reading content.

Reflecting

An important strategy is for students to think about, or reflect on, what they have just read. Reflection can be just thinking, or it can be more formal, such as a discussion or writing in a journal.

While providing instruction in a subject area, the teacher needs to determine if the reading material is at the students' level of reading mastery. If not, the teacher needs to make accommodations either in the material itself or in the manner of presentation.

Assessing Comprehension

A frequent device for assessing comprehension is the use of oral or written questions. A question may be **convergent**, which indicates that only one answer is correct, or **divergent**, which indicates that more than one answer is correct. Most tests, however, include a combination of question types.

Another device for checking on comprehension is a **cloze test**, or a passage with omitted words the test taker must supply. The test maker must decide whether to require the test taker to supply the exact word or to accept synonyms. Passing scores reflect which type of answer is acceptable. If assessing an understanding of meaning is the intent of the exercise, the teacher might accept synonyms and not demand the surface-level constructs, or the exact word.

The speed at which a student reads helps determine comprehension, up to a point. The faster that a student reads, the better that student comprehends, with some limitations. In general, the slow reader who must analyze each word does not comprehend as well as the fast reader. It is possible, however, to read too fast. Most students have had the experience of having to reread materials. For example, a student reading a chapter in preparation for a test might read more slowly than when reading a short story for pleasure or reading to get the main idea of a story.

Competency 008 (Research and Comprehension Skills in the Content Areas)

The teacher understands the importance of research and comprehension skills to children's academic success and provides children with instruction that promotes their acquisition and effective use of these skills in the content areas.

Transition From "Learning to Read" to "Reading to Learn"

Children from pre-K to second grade spend most of the language arts portion of their day trying to decode and make sense of written language. The main purpose of this stage is to read for pleasure. Traditionally, short stories with pictures that have a specific structure and predictable story line are used to guide the child in the process of "learning to read." However, in the upper elementary grades, the needs of the children go beyond decoding and reading for pleasure, and "reading to learn" becomes the main task. The "reading to learn" stages require students to decode written language, understand the content, and obtain vital information from the content. One important component of the process of "reading to learn" is to understand how text is organized in the content areas. Children need to identify key components of the organizational format and identify the type of information offered. Teachers have to guide children

to notice and study the structure of text, including the table of contents, titles, subtitles, and headings.

Structure of Text

Students need to look closely at the structure of text in order to comprehend it. To accomplish this task, skillful teachers guide the students through a picture, table, and graphic walk-through of the text while asking questions and pointing out useful text features to the students. Most texts have titles, subtitles, headings, glossaries, and bolded words. What techniques were used to make them stand out? Figuring out the structure of a text helps readers to read more efficiently. Children can anticipate what information will be revealed in a selection when they understand textual structure. Understanding the pattern of the text helps students organize ideas. Authors have a fairly short list of organizational patterns to choose from. The following are the most common patterns:

- Chronological order relates events in a temporal sequence from beginning to end

- Cause-and-effect relationships between described events, with the causal factors identified or implied

- Problem description, followed by solutions

- Comparisons and/or contrasts to describe ideas to readers

- Sequential materials, presented as a series of directions to be followed in a prescribed order

Once children understand how information in the content areas is organized, they can become more efficient readers.

Becoming More Efficient Readers

Students with strong comprehension skills and decoding ability are now ready to become more efficient readers by practicing the techniques of scanning and skimming to get content information. In **scanning**, children are guided to look for specific information in text. Children are taught to use headings, indices, bolding and italics to guide them to specific words or content. In **skimming**, students read major headings, table of contents, bold letters, graphic materials, and summary paragraphs to get the main idea of the content.

Study Skills

Students need to know how to study the information that has been presented to them in texts and other media. Graphic organizers help students to review material, and help them to see the relationships between one bit of information and another. For example, a Venn diagram helps students identify how things are alike and different. A Venn diagram can also be used to help students recognize how a single topic is treated in two readings, or how two books, animals, or ecosystems are alike and different. The student labels the two overlapping circles, and lists items that are unique to each one in each respective circle. In the area in the center where there is overlap, the student records the elements that the two items have in common.

Another skill students need to master is **note taking**. Unless a teacher wants to read passages directly out of an encyclopedia or other source material, he or she should take the time to actively teach note-taking techniques. Teachers should also think up an authentic task that requires students to accomplish higher-level manipulation of the given information. First, help the children to formulate a researchable question. Second, have them highlight the words that might be used as keywords in searching for information. Third, have students brainstorm in groups of other words to be used as keywords. Next, ask then to list appropriate sources. Finally, as they skim articles, they can fill in the chart with little chunks of information.

Graphic Organizers

Graphic organizers help students improve organizational skills, and provide a visual representation of facts and concepts and their relationships within an organized framework. The ability to organize information and ideas is fundamental to effective thinking.

To increase reading comprehension among ELLs, allow students to share information about the story or passage. Through this activity, students can help each other using peer scaffolding and oral language interaction. Semantic mapping can be used before and after readings to organize materials in new ways highlighting connections among ideas.

Think-Aloud

This strategy allows the teacher and students to problem solve together. The teacher poses a question to students and then, the teacher, group of students, or entire class responds at the same time. This strategy can be easily used to increase reading comprehension in the content areas.

Summarizing and Organization of Content

When children are guided to summarize and organize content, they are using basic reading comprehension and taking this content to higher level of thinking including evaluation, analysis, and synthesis. By guiding children to go beyond the literal meaning and guiding them to reorganize content requires students to develop a deeper understanding of content. Guide students to reorganize content (study skills) by creating their own tables, charts, and graphs. For example, students can develop a chart containing the longest rivers of the world organized by regions and countries. When children are required to process and present information using a new structure, comprehension and knowledge of the content area increases and memory retention is enhanced.

Study Plans

To increase content comprehension, teachers might acquaint students with several study plans to help them read content materials. Many of these plans are well known and easily accessed, and the teacher and the students can simply select the plan(s) that works best for them within various subjects. Students may use **mnemonic devices**, or memory-related devices, to help them remember the steps in reading a chapter effectively. Several other strategies follow.

SQ4R

Students often use plans like the **SQ4R** plan when reading text in content areas. The acronym stands for **survey, question, read, reflect, recite, and review** (Tomas & Robinson, 1972). An explanation of the different components of the SQ4R follows:

Survey During the **survey (S)** part, readers examine the headings, illustrations, bold letters, and major components of the text in order to develop predictions and generating **questions (Q)** about the topic.

Question The student may wish to devise some questions that the chapter will probably answer. Through these questions, students establish the purpose for reading and the questions serve as a reading guide. If the chapter has questions at the end, the student can also study these before reading the chapter.

Read (1R) During the next stage, students read while looking for answer to the questions previously generated and/or those questions written by the publishers, which are usually located at the end of the section.

Write (2R) Students monitor their comprehension as they write a summary of the story or text. Creating a summary allows students opportunities to internalize and make their own interpretation of the content.

Recite (3R) The student attempts to answer orally, or in writing, the student-developed questions or the questions at the end of the chapter.

Review (4R) Finally, students **review** the text to evaluate the accuracy of their answers and to show how much they learned about the content.

Reciprocal Teaching

Reciprocal teaching is an instructional activity designed for struggling readers in which the teacher engages students in a dialogue about specific portions of a text (Palincsar, 1986). The main purpose of this activity is to guide children to construct meaning and to monitor reading comprehension. The dialogue is structured to elicit four components:

1. summarizing the content of a passage
2. asking a question about the main idea
3. clarifying difficult parts of the content
4. predicting what will come next

DRTA

The acronym **DRTA** stands for Directed Reading/ Thinking Activity. This teacher-directed strategy helps students to establish a purpose for reading a story or

reading expository writing from a content book (Reuzel & Cooter, 1992). The teacher models the process of creating and correcting predictions as the story progresses to strengthen comprehension. DRTA has three main steps:

- Sample the text to develop background. Children are guided to read the title, pictures or any kind of visual representations, and read some sample lines from the text to develop hypothesis about the content of the text.

- Make Predictions: Students make predictions based on a sample of the text.

- Confirm or correct predictions: Children read the text and engage in follow-up activities to corroborate if the predictions were correct. The steps are: establish background, allow for oral or silent reading and study, and follow-up activities.

Reading Comprehension in the Content Areas

To assist children and especially ELLs in reading material that may be beyond their reading level, teachers can incorporate the following strategies.

Tape-record selected passages that students can listen to while reading along in the text. Teachers can use adult volunteers and fluent readers in the group to read to children unable to read it for themselves.

Pair children off into a tutor/tutee arrangement or in a small group reading format. Teachers should pair children of different linguistic levels and degree of achievement to create a peer-support system.

Introduce the technical vocabulary of the content areas prior to reading. Introduce elements such as connotation (implied meaning) and denotation (literal meaning), and idioms in the way they are used in text. For example, the word *right* can have multiple meanings depending on the content area or the activity. In mathematics, *right* is an angle of 90 degrees, but in social studies *right* can be used to provide directions or to declare correctness.

Teach content vocabulary through direct, concrete experiences as opposed to definitions. Definitions can lead to misinterpretations since additional words are required to define the term. Teaching vocabulary in a contextualized situation is particularly important for ELLs because they often rely on translations that do not always represent the intended concept. For example, in English, the word *bayou* is used extensively in Texas and Louisiana. However, *bayou* is very difficult to define for someone who has never seen one. What is the difference between a bayou, a creek, a swamp, or a marshland? How big is a bayou? If an adult has difficulty answering these questions, imagine how young children may struggle!

Introduce instructional strategy for self-monitoring reading comprehension. In this kind of strategy, students read aloud a passage and then pause to question themselves about the meaning of the passage.

Representations of Information for a Variety of Purposes

Charts, tables, graphs, pictures, and print and non-print media are examples of materials used to present information. Readers should realize that these representations are important. Their purpose is to present information and to encourage interpretation. A graphic can expand a concept, serve as an illustration, support points, summarize data, organize facts, add a dimension to the content (such as a cartoon adding humor), compare information, demonstrate change over time, or furnish additional information. Through graphics, the reader can interpret, predict, and even apply information with some careful observation. The questions that teachers use can make a difference in the ability of students to focus on and clarify the information derived from graphics.

Many students initially skip over graphics, or may just notice their presence without reading them. These students may not have been taught how to use multiple representations of information. Even students who have some training in the use of graphic information may not be able to transfer that knowledge to other content areas, or may have trouble going from print to graphic and then back to print.

Adults can help students use multiple representations of information by using open-book and guided reading. A teacher can demonstrate how to use a chart or graph by using an overhead projector. Even a graphic that appears uncomplicated may challenge a reader's interpretive skills. Many inferences may be necessary for

even the simplest visual aid or graphic. Modeled reading may also be an effective technique to use.

Pictures and other graphics can arouse interest and stimulate thinking. Additionally, graphics can add clarity; prevent misunderstandings; show step-by-step developments; exhibit the status of things, events, and processes; and demonstrate comparisons and contrasts (Vacca and Vacca 1989).

Strategies for Developing Critical Thinking Skills

Critical thinking skills include analysis, synthesis, and evaluation. Benjamin Bloom (1956) created a taxonomy for categorizing levels of thinking processes typical in school children. The taxonomy presents a structure to categorize the levels of thinking required in order to ask and answer questions. These questions have traditionally been used to guide children from the basic recalling of information (**knowledge**) and understanding information (**comprehension**) to use higher order thinking skills such as analysis, synthesis, and evaluation. Recalling and understanding are important parts of reading comprehension; however, it is a teacher's responsibility to help children move from literal comprehension and explicit ideas to a more figurative comprehension and implicit ideas. Teachers have to guide children to analyze (**analysis**) the ideas presented in text and then to make inferences (**analysis**), to assess their inferences (**evaluation**), to draw conclusions about the ideas (**synthesis**), and perhaps to apply the ideas to new situations (**application**). Children who are able to go beyond the literal and explicit information in text develop a deeper understand of the content areas and are able to manipulate the content at higher levels of thinking.

Linguistic Accommodation Testing for ELLs and Special Education Students

The State of Texas provides for linguistic accommodation for ELLs and special education children taking the content portion of the TAKS examination in grades 3–8 and 10 in order to ensure that reading comprehension does not interfere in assessing content mastery. Based on specific recommendations from the Admission, Review, and Dismissal (ARD) and/or the Language Proficiency Assessment Committee (LPAC), districts can allow linguistic accommodations for special education and ELL students when taking the basic skills test (TAKS). A list of allowed linguistic accommodations follows (TEA, 1005).

1. Presenting the information in two languages side by side

2. Allowing the test administrator to read the questions or translate words, phrases, and sentences

3. Using dictionaries to find translations

4. Allowing the use of bilingual or English-language glossaries

5. Allowing the test administrator to present the information using simple language

6. Using visual and non-verbal communication to make content clear

Strategies like the linguistic accommodation testing (LAT) can be used to enhance reading comprehension of special populations in the content areas.

Competency 009 (Writing Conventions)

The teacher understands the conventions of writing in English and provides instruction that helps children develop proficiency in using writing conventions.

Connection Between Spelling and Phonological and Alphabetic Awareness

The transition from oral language development to written communication requires students to develop an awareness of the following concepts (Peregoy and Boyle, 2005):

1. Print carries meaning and it conveys a message

2. Spoken words can be written and preserved

3. English reading/writing follows a specific direction; that is, from left to right, and top to bottom

4. Spoken language is composed of phonemes and these sounds can be represented by specific letters of the alphabet (alphabetic principle)

5. As an alphabetic language, English has a sound-symbol correspondence but often it is inconsistent

6. Spoken language can be used as a foundation for spelling (phonics)

Spoken and Written English

The productive skills of language—speaking and writing—are interconnected. A strong oral development can facilitate the development of written communication. However, because spoken language is generally more informal that written language, teachers need to be sure that students use formal language when writing.

English favors the use of active voice as opposed to passive voice in both oral and written communication. For example the sentence *Katrina devastated the city of New Orleans*, is stronger and more effective than a sentence using the passive voice such as *The city of New Orleans was devastated by Katrina*. To provide support in this area, guide students to work with a partner in converting passive sentences to active sentences; then guide them to discuss how these changes affect the tone and meaning of the sentences. If a student is having problems connecting sounds to written text, teachers can provide phonics instruction. Guiding students to "sound out" words as a foundation for spelling can improve written performance.

Developing Readiness for Writing

A visit to an early childhood classroom shows that children spend the bulk of the time singing, playing with blocks and puzzles, cutting figures with scissors, playing with clay, drawing, and painting. By looking at this picture, lay people might question the value of instruction in early childhood. However, the reality is that children are doing intensive work on developing the fine motor skills needed to master pre-reading skills such as pencil grip, appropriate paper position, and the first strokes of representing the shapes of letters and words.

Stages of Spelling

As children begin to name letters and read print, they also begin to write letters and words. Writing development seems to occur at about the same time as reading development—not afterward, as traditional reading readiness assumed. Whole language seeks to integrate the language arts rather than sequencing them. Just as change has marked educators' beliefs about reading instruction and the way that reading develops, change has also marked the methods and philosophies behind the teaching of writing in the schools.

Drawing is the beginning of children's attempt to convey a message in written form. Teachers can use this interest to introduce writing skills by guiding them to add words to drawings to supplement the information. Initially, the children can dictate the story to teachers until they feel comfortable enough to write it on their own. The development of written communication generally follows a predictable sequence beginning with scribbling, then developing pseudo letters and invented words until conventional spelling is achieved. An analysis of the stages of spelling follows.

Scribbling

In this phase, children pretend that they are writing. Eventually, they develop letter-like symbols. This stage represents an awareness of the difference between writing and drawing to communicate. Scribbling is different from drawing because in scribbling, the child purposely scribbles from left to right and often also follows the top to bottom progression.

Pseudo letters

In this phase, the child attempts to create forms that resemble letters but these forms cannot always be identified as such. The child becomes aware that the alphabet contains characters of different shapes and attempts to reproduce these in a random way resulting in some form of invented spelling.

Random letters

In this phase, a child creates individual letters from the alphabet in an attempt to create words. The letters are randomly selected with no clear connection with the phonemes that they are to represent. That is, children are not producing phonetic spelling at this stage. They write letter strings and often leave a space between strings, which suggest that they are beginning to understand word boundaries.

Invented spelling

At this stage, the child tries to connect the sounds (phonemes) and the letters (graphemes) to create words resulting in non-standard writing. This phonetic spelling is often represented by a single letter or a series of letters, which represent the phonemes contained in the intended word. A child can write an *M* to represent the word mother and often they can point to the word. They can also use strings of letters, mostly consonants, to represent a word. For example, a kindergartener wrote the word *park* as *Prk*, producing the three consonants and omitting the vowel. Because the phoneme-grapheme correspondence of vowels is not consistent, children generally have problems writing them.

Transitional spelling

Eventually, children discontinue over-reliance on phonetic spelling and begin noticing visual clues and developing a knowledge of word structure. Sight word training becomes very important at this stage. Students begin producing more standard spelling and attempt self-correction. Writing samples might become difficult to read because students erase continuously in an attempt to self-correct. Some inflectional endings (plurals, comparative, superlative, past tense, and present progressive) may appear in writing samples. Students may continue having problems with words with double vowels, like *book* and *feed*, and words containing consonant diagraphs like *through* or *eight*.

Conventional spelling

At this stage, children spell most words using conventional spelling. They still may have problems with consonant digraphs, homonyms, contractions, compound words, as well as prefixes, suffixes, and more difficult letter combinations.

In addition to the traditional spelling stages, students also go through specific stages of writing. Lapp et al., divided the process into three stages: emerging, early writer, and newly fluent writers. A summary of these stages follows (Lapp et al., 2001).

Characteristics of Emerging Writers

Students at the emerging stage of writing development are generally able to:

- Dictate an idea or a complete story
- Use initial sounds in their writing
- Use picture, scribbles, symbols, letters, and/or known words to communicate a message
- Understand that writing symbolizes speech

Educational Implications

Read stories to children and ask them to retell the story while you record it. Then, read the story back to the child to emphasize the connection between speech and print. When children begin writing words or pseudo words, ask them to read it to you, and if necessary, provide conventional spelling as an alternative. Use the *Language Experience Approach* to guide children to connect spoken words with their written representations. That is, guide children to dictate words and sentences while you record them on the board. Read the words while pointing to them. Then, ask students to copy the sentences. The next day, review the sentences written and use them for additional language development. Introduce writing for functional tasks like labeling objects and places in the classroom, writing the plan of the day, taking notes, and listing names or things to remember.

Early Writers

Typically, children at the early stage of writing exhibit the following behavior:

- Understand that a written message remains the same each time it is read
- Utilize their knowledge of sounds and letters as they progress through the stages of spelling development
- With modeling and assistance, incorporate feedback in revising and editing their own writing

- Begin to use conventional grammar, spelling, capitalization, and punctuation

Educational Implications

Guide children to read and reread the same information to establish a connection between letters and sounds. Identify specific words and divide them into syllables to establish a connection between the sounds within a syllable. Take expressions that are commonly used in children's literature and oral communication and guide them to hear word boundaries. For example, children at this stage might write the statement "Once upon a time" as "Oncesoponditim," which represents the way the expression is produced orally without appropriate word boundaries. Model the writing process using a LCD projection system or the traditional chalkboard. Think aloud while you are writing and ask for guidance from students, e.g., Do we need a comma here or a final period? Do we need a capital A in the word "american"? In the writing samples of children, use peer input for editing and guiding students to conduct self-corrections. Instead of making direct error corrections, ask questions leading children to examine the grammaticality of the sentences and to make their own corrections.

Characteristics of Newly Fluent Writers

Newly fluent writers are generally able to:

- Use prewriting strategies to achieve their purposes
- Address a topic or write to a prompt creatively and independently
- Organize writing to include a beginning, middle, and end
- Consistently use conventional grammar, spelling, capitalization, and punctuation
- Revise and edit written work independently and/or collectively
- Produce many genres of writing

Educational Implications

Use prewriting activities to plan for writing using an outline that indicates the sequence of ideas. This activity is especially important for children whose native language does not require the use of the linear progression required in English writing. The outline will guide children to comply with this linear rhetorical pattern. Provide interesting writing prompts to children to guide their writing. You may use the prompt used on the TAKS released tests available on line. Traditionally, the Texas Education Agency releases the tests used in its yearly examinations. For information on TAKS-released tests, see the Texas Education Agency, Student Assessment Division, at *www.tea. state.tx.us/student.assessment/resources/release/taks/ index.html*). Continue using peer editing and encourage self-corrections. Guide students to produce different kinds of writing such as response to literature, journal writing, writing to convince someone, or writing to argue a point.

Writing Expectations

Children in kindergarten through fourth grade are expected to progress through stages of writing and develop conventional spelling and coherent compositions. The fourth-grade TAKS examinations require students to develop a coherent piece of writing free of major errors. It is also expected that children produce and refine compositions for general and specific audiences. Children are required to edit their work and the work of others based on clarity of ideas, and coherence and the conventions of writing.

Strategies for Using Writing Conventions

The main objective of writing is to put ideas in writing in a logical pattern. Once this is accomplished, students have to check for writing conventions—grammar, punctuation, and capitalization. Some of the strategies to introduce writing conventions are listed below.

1. Modeling is one of the best tools to introduce effective writing. To model effective writing, teachers can introduce writing samples where conventions are used appropriately. A variant of this activity is to present a writing sample to the whole class that contains typical errors in English conventions and ask them to provide corrective feedback.

2. One of the typical problems found in the writing samples produced by children is the use of sentence fragments. To guide children to produce complete sentences, teachers can use a technique called "sentence builders." In this technique, the teacher provides students with a list of words by syntactic categories (articles, adjectives, nouns, verbs, and conjunctions), and guides children to produce sentences using each component. As a follow-up activity, children are asked to identify the subject and the predicate, and specifically the verb. They are also asked to read the sentence to see if it contains a complete idea.

3. To teach the importance of punctuation, teachers can use sentences where commas or periods are necessary to deliver the intended ideas and guide students to use punctuation to clarify the intended message. For example, in the sentence *Mary, a student from Italy, requested bread, coffee and olive oil for breakfast*, it is not clear if Mary wants coffee mixed with olive oil or just coffee and also olive oil. In this case a comma is needed for clarification.

4. Assess students' writing to identify common problems across the group, and design lesson to address identified problems. For example, if students are producing words like *bred* and *sale boat* in place of *bread* and *sailboat*, provide training in vowel digraph and compound words. A vowel digraph occurs when we have two vowels together that produce one sound, e.g., be<u>a</u>ch. A consonant digraph is more than one consonant that produces only one sound, e.g., thou<u>gh</u>t.

Connecting Discourse

Connecting discourse is a definite challenge to students in the early grades. Children generally produce choppy sentences without transition words or phrases to connect ideas or paragraphs. Most of these connectors are not used in daily speech unless students have had some speech training or an academic preparation in the area; thus, teachers need to teach connectors directly. When writing a composition, teachers can provide a list of possible connectors to guide students to use them. Examples of connectors are presented in Table 1-5.

Dependent and Independent Clauses

Another way to minimize the use of choppy sentences in compositions is by guiding children to combine sentences in one of the following ways:

1. Using conjunctions such as *and, but, or, nor, or yet*. For example, *My car is beautiful, but it is getting old.*

Table 1-5. Connectors Used in Writing

Writing Task	Sample Connectors
Sequencing	First, second, after, meanwhile, then, lastly, finally, at the beginning, next, following that, before, in conclusion…
Result	Therefore, consequently, then, as a result, thus, hence, as a consequence…
Conclusion	To conclude, in conclusion, as a final point, lastly, finally, at the end, bring to a close, terminate, finish…
Contrast	On the other hand, instead, on the contrary, as opposed to, as an alternative, in its place, conversely, then again, in contrast…
Opinion	According to, as far as I know, in my opinion, I believe, from my point of view…
Condition	Unless, provided that, as soon as, so that, except, only if, given that, as long as, if…
Adding Information	Besides, also, even, additionally, moreover, furthermore, likewise, further, as well…

Notice that in the sentence, there are two independent clauses joined by a coordinate conjunction, *but*. A comma is required before the conjunction.

2. Joining two complete sentences with a semicolon. For example, the sentence *Maricela is a highly intelligent student; she was the Valedictorian of the 2006 class*. Notice that lower case is used after the semicolon.

3. Using dependent and independent clauses. For example, the sentence *Although Dora is my friend, she did not vote for me*. Notice that in this case, the use of a dependent linking word *although* at the beginning clause made the second clause necessary to complete the whole idea. The last statement makes sense by itself, but it becomes a more complete sentence when used together.

Strategies to Promote Written Communication

Reading to Students

Reading to students can provide multiple benefits to children. It develops print awareness and understanding of the intonation pattern of the language. A discussion on the content of the story allows students opportunities to enhance comprehension and practice speaking. It also provides a model of fluent reading together with the appropriate intonation pattern of the language. Reading together can be enjoyable. Students laugh and talk about the story and the characters. Children can also be exposed to different kinds of writing (genre) like prose fiction, biography, tables, and short stories. Finally, they are exposed to the story framework, which is the setting, characters, plot, climax, and resolution.

Dictated Materials—The Language Experience Approach

Children's individual or group-dictated stories, which can be written on experience charts, guide children to connect spoken language with its written representation. The teacher can record student's dictation or ask them to talk into a tape recorder. When the teacher is recording the stories, saying each word aloud while writing it down can be helpful to the students. Following the writing of the story, teachers read the story in a natural sounding tone of voice, pointing to each word as it is pronounced. To assist students in developing the knowledge of clauses and phrases, read the story placing a hand under each phrase as it is read. Students can also read the story in choral reading, by pairs, or individually.

Interactive Journals

Writing in journals provides students opportunities to use language authentically in literary contexts. Teachers and students can have a designated time for journal writing to communicate on a daily basis. This gives students the freedom to use their own mechanics and invented spelling. Because the purpose of written journals is to communicate, teachers should not correct children's journal writing, but should write comments on content and provide encouragement and reassurance. Some of the key advantages of interactive journals for children and teachers follow.

Advantages of Journal Writing for Children

- Students learn that written language communicates

- Students experience making choices about topics and develop a sense of ownership of the written product

- Students develop their writing within meaningful context

- Students develop a personal interaction with the teacher and with peers;

- Students can use this safe environment to experiment with language

Advantages of Journal Writing for Teachers

- Teachers learn about each child's interest, ideas, and everyday concerns

- Teachers interact and communicate on an individual basis with each child

- Teachers model standard convention or writing in the context of authentic communication

Using Routines as Literacy Events

Several routine activities can be modified to promote reading and writing development. Some of these activities are:

- Taking attendance: Using a chart with students' names on it. In the morning, students get their card and move it to the chart showing that they are present. The names of the students can also be placed in alphabetical order, which uses indirect teaching to deal with that concept.

- The daily weather report: Use pictures and words representing the climatic conditions, i.e., cloudy, clear, raining. Students will move the cards showing the prevailing weather conditions for the day.

- Today's day: Student select the appropriate card showing the days of the week.

- Organize a calendar of events for the day or for the month. Review the plan of the day in the morning.

- Use notes to communicate with students. Praise them or discuss behavior in written form.

Competency 010 (Development of Written Communication)

The teacher understands that writing to communicate is a developmental process and provides instruction that promotes children's competence in written communication.

Writing Process

The writing process includes the knowledge and use of prewriting strategies like:

- brainstorming, semantic mapping, outlining, reading and research;

- factors to consider in writing for various audiences and purposes (e.g., expressive, informative, persuasive);

- knowledge and use of text genres and structures (e.g., letter, poem, story, play); and strategies (e.g., peer conferences);

- skills for drafting, editing, revising, proofreading, and publishing materials.

Children also need knowledge of English grammar and mechanics to revise their writing. It includes revising given texts in terms of sentence construction like:

- revising run-on sentences and misplaced modifiers;

- revising subject-verb and pronoun-antecedent agreement;

- revising verb forms, pronouns, adverbs, adjectives, and plural and possessive nouns;

- revising capitalization, punctuation, and spelling.

Students also need to analyze and revise written work in relation to style, clarity, organization, intended audience, and purpose. This includes revising text prepared for a given audience or purpose, and improving

Table 1-6. Process Writing

Phase	Purpose	Strategies
Prewriting	To generate and gather ideas for writing; to prepare for writing; to identify purpose and audience for writing; to identify the main ideas and supporting details; to write more coherently	Talking and discussing the topics; brainstorming, clustering, questioning, reading, keeping journal in all content areas; to discuss experiences with partner
Drafting	Getting ideas in writing; getting first draft that can be evaluated according to purpose and audience for paper	Fast writing; daily writing; journal of all types: buddy journals, dialogue journal and learning journals
Revising	Reordering arguments or reviewing scenes in a narrative; reordering supporting details; reviewing or changing sentences	Shortening sentences; combining sentences; peer response groups; teacher conferences
Editing	Correcting spelling, grammar, punctuation, mechanics…	Peer editing groups; proofreading; computer programs for spelling; mini-lessons
Publishing	Sharing writing with one another, with students and parents; showing that writing is valued; creating a classroom library; motivating writing	Writing may be shared in many formats; paper placed on bulletin boards, papers published with computers, paper shared in school book fairs…

organization and unity. This can be done by adding transition words and phrases, reordering sentences or paragraphs, deleting unnecessary information, and adding a topic sentence. Another strategy is to increase text clarity, precision, and effectiveness through word choices.

Dr. Donald Graves, a professor of education at the University of New Hampshire, developed an approach to writing instruction called *process writing* (1983). His notion was simple—teach children to write the way real writers write. What do writers do? They tend to write about what they want to write about. Then they may read about the subject, talk about the subject, take notes, or generally fool around with the topic before they compose. Then they may write a draft, knowing up-front that they are not done at this point. Writers may share the draft with others, and end up writing all over it. They may also go over every sentence, thinking about word choice, and looking for vague spots, or spots where the piece falls off the subject. Writers may then revise the draft again, share it again, revise it again, and so on, until they are satisfied with the product. Then they publish it. Often, writers receive feedback before and after the piece is published, which may lead to a new writing effort. Some writers save scraps of writing in a journal. They may save a turn of phrase, a comment overheard on a bus, a new word, good quotes, or an interesting topic.

Another aspect of process writing is celebration. Children are invited to share their work with the class. After young authors read their piece, classmates ought to offer affirmations and suggestions. Able teachers should have children save each piece of paper generated in the writing process, and store them in a personal portfolio for review. A summary of process writing together with strategies for each phase is presented in Table 1-6 (Peregoy & Boyle, 2005).

New Trends in Writing

In addition to process writing, there is a new trend emphasizing specific elements of the writing process. The best known system is called the 6+1 Writing Traits. This system, which was developed by the Northwest Regional Education Laboratory (NREL), emphasizes seven elements of the writing process (2006). These elements are described below.

1. **Organization**—the internal structure of the sample

2. **Ideas**—how ideas are presented in the sample

3. **Voice**—the uniqueness of the author and how ideas are projected

4. **Word Choice**—the vocabulary used to convey meaning

5. **Sentence Fluency**—the flow of ideas and the use of connectors

6. **Conventions**—the use of capitalization, punctuation, and spelling

7. **Presentation**—how the final product looks in print.

The Texas Education Agency developed a similar writing program emphasizing similar components:

1. **Focus and Coherence**—how the main idea is introduced and supported in the composition

2. **Organization**—the organization of ideas, including connectors

3. **Development of Ideas**—how the ideas are presented and supported in writing

4. **Voice**—the uniqueness of the author and how ideas are projected

5. **Conventions**—the use of capitalization, punctuation, and spelling

Both the 6+1 Writing Traits and the TAKS writing program guide children to demonstrate knowledge of writing traits. To assess their performance, both programs develop a four-point rubric for each of the writing traits (see Table 1-7).

Identifying the Characteristics of Modes of Writing

Writing serves many different functions. The main functions are to narrate, to describe, to explain, and to persuade. Students need to be aware of each of these functions. In any event, these four categories are neither exhaustive nor mutually exclusive.

The **narrative** is a story or an account. It may recount an incident or a series of incidents. The account may be autobiographical to make a point. The narrative may be fiction or nonfiction.

The purpose of **descriptive** writing is to provide information about a person, place, or thing. Descriptive writing can be fiction or nonfiction. Description is a powerful tool in advertisement. Advertisements describe items using factual information, but the way the information is presented can become a persuasive type of writing for prospective buyers.

The purpose of **expository** writing is to explain and clarify ideas. Students are probably most familiar with

this type of writing. While the expository essay may have narrative elements, the storytelling or recounting aspect is minor and subservient to the explanation element. Expository writing is typically found in many textbooks; for instance, a textbook on the history of Texas would likely be expository in nature.

The purpose of **persuasive** writing is to convince the reader of something. Persuasive writing fills current magazines and newspapers, and permeates the World Wide Web. The writer may be trying to push a political candidate, to convince someone to vote for a zoning ordinance, or even to promote a diet plan. Persuasive writing usually presents a point, provides evidence, which may be factual or anecdotal, and supports the point. The structure may be very formal, with counterpositions and counterarguments. Whatever the organizational pattern, the writer's intent is to persuade readers of the validity of some claim. Nearly all essays have some element of persuasion.

Authors choose their form of writing not necessarily just to tell a story but also to present an idea. Whether writers choose the narrative, descriptive, expository, or persuasive format, they have something on their minds that they want to convey to their readers.

Writing for a Variety of Occasions, Purposes, and Audiences

The writer must consider the audience, the occasion, and the purpose when choosing the writing mode. The writer's responsibility is to write clearly, honestly, and cleanly for the reader's sake and so the **audience** is very important. The teacher can designate an audience for students' writing. Knowing who will read their work, students can modify their writing to suit the intended readers. For instance, a fourth-grade teacher might suggest that the class take their compositions about a favorite animal to second graders and allow the younger children to read it. The writers soon will realize that they need to use manuscript and not cursive writing, to employ simple vocabulary, and to omit complex sentences when they write for their young audience.

The **occasion** also helps to determine the elements of writing. The language should fit the occasion. Students should keep in mind that particular words may have certain effects, such as evoking sympathy or raising questions about an opposing point of view. The

Table 1-7. Rubric for the TAKS Writing (TEA, 2004)

Focus and Coherence: Point 1	Focus and Coherence: Point 4
1. Individual paragraphs and/or composition as a whole are not focused. It may shift abruptly from idea to idea, making it difficult for the reader to understand how the ideas included in the composition are related.	1. Individual paragraphs and the composition as a whole are focused. This sustained focus enables the reader to understand and appreciate how the ideas included in the composition are related.
Organization: Point 1	**Organization: Point 4**
1. The writer's progression of thought from sentence to sentence and/or paragraph is not logical. Sometimes weak progression results from an absence of transition or from the use of transitions that do not make sense. At other times, the progression of thought is simply not evident even if appropriate transitions are included.	1. The writer's progression of thought from sentence to sentence and/or paragraph is smooth and controlled. The writer's use of meaningful transitions and the logical movement from idea to idea strengthen this progression.
Development of Ideas: Point 1	**Development of Ideas: Point 4**
1. The writer presents one or more ideas but provides little or no development of those ideas.	1. The writer's thoughts and specific development of each idea creates depth of thought in the composition, enabling the readers to truly understand and appreciate the writer's ideas.
Voice: Point 1	**Voice: Point 4**
1. The writer does not engage the reader, therefore failing to establish connection.	1. The writer engages the reader and sustains this connection throughout the composition.
Conventions: Point 1	**Conventions: Point 4**
1. There is little or no evidence in the composition that the writer can correctly apply the conventions of the English language. Severe and/or frequent errors in spelling, capitalization, punctuation, grammar, usage, and sentence structure may cause the writing to be unclear or difficult to read. These errors weaken the composition by causing an overall lack of fluency.	1. The overall strength of the conventions contributes to the effectiveness of the composition. The writer demonstrates a consistent command of spelling, capitalization, punctuation, grammar, usage, and sentence structure. When the writer attempts to communicate ideas through sophisticated forms of expression, he/she may make minor errors as a result of these compositional risks. These types of errors do not detract from the overall fluency of the composition.

students and teacher might try to determine the likely effect on an audience of a writer's choice of a particular word or words.

The **purpose** helps to determine the format (narrative, expository, descriptive, or persuasive) and the language of the writer. The students, for instance, might consider the appropriateness of written material for a specific purpose such as a business letter, a communication with residents of a retirement center, or a thank-you note to parents. The teacher and students might try to identify persuasive techniques used by a writer in a passage.

In selecting the mode of writing and the content, the writer might ask the following:

What would the audience need to know to believe you or to accept your position? Imagine some-

one you know (visualize her or him) listening to you declare your position or opinion and then saying, "Oh yeah? Prove it!" What evidence do you need to prove your idea to this skeptic? With what might the audience disagree? What common knowledge does the audience share with you? What information do you need to share with the audience? The teacher might wish to have the students practice selecting the mode and the language by adapting forms, organizational strategies, and styles for different audiences and purposes.

Types of Writing

Teachers need to encourage children to write for meaningful purposes. Meaningful writing can be easily incorporated as part of daily classroom activities and can enhance not only writing skills, but also content area mastery. Some of the types of writing that can be incorporated follow.

1. Functional writing describes activities where writing is used to achieve a specific purpose. For example, labeling areas and objects in the classroom is a meaningful and useful activity for all students, especially ELLs. Note taking, developing a grocery list, or list of holiday gifts becomes a meaningful activity and will motivate children to write.

2. Journal Writing

    *   **Personal journals** are used to record personal information and to encourage self-analysis of their experiences. This is a personal document and it is up to the child to make it available to others.

    *   **Dialogue journals** promote written communication among students and between the teacher and students. The main purpose is to communicate not to teach writing skills. Teachers can model writing when they reply to children.

    *   **Reflective journals** are used to respond in writing to specific situations or problems. It is often shared with the teacher for input.

    *   **Learning logs** are commonly used in the content areas to record elements discussed in class. In this logs, students describe what they have learned and elements where they have difficulties. Teachers read the document and act on request for assistance.

Integrating Technology with Language and Content

Teachers should feel encouraged to use state-of-the-art technology to motivate children to write and monitor their writing. **Word processing** programs have features that can help children with editing. Elements like spell check, definitions of terms, thesaurus, and even suggestions for sentence constructions, are commonly available in programs like Microsoft Word. However, teachers have to teach children how to use and take advantage of these features. For example, the real function of a spell checker is not only to identify misspelled words, but to free students from the pres-

sure of spelling. Students are encouraged to put their ideas in writing without stopping to check for spelling. Once they finish the content of the writing, they can take care of superficial elements like spelling. However, children should be guided to pay attention to corrections and to learn from them.

Electronic Dialogue Journals

The Internet can be used to expand the use of dialogue journals. Teachers can contact schools in other states or countries to initiate an electronic "pen pal" system involving more mature or advanced writers.

Projection Systems

Computers with the appropriate projection system can be used to display work and to model writing.

Competency 011 (Assessment of Developing Literacy)

The teacher understands the basic principles of literacy assessment and uses a variety of assessments to guide literacy instruction.

Knowledge and Use of Literacy Assessment

The two main types of assessment are formal and informal. Both have a place in the classroom, particularly in the literacy classroom. The effective teacher understands the importance of ongoing assessment as an instructional tool and uses both informal and formal assessment measures. There is never an occasion to group children permanently on the basis of one assessment, either formal or informal. Any grouping of students should come about after the consideration of several assessments, and the grouping should be flexible enough to consider individual differences among the students in each group.

Informal Assessments

Teachers can learn valuable information by simply observing their students at work. Many school districts use a type of inventory/report card to inform adults at home about the progress that children are making. Experienced teachers usually develop, through trial and error, their own means of assessing the skills of students in their classes. Almost every book on teaching reading and writing contains its own informal tests. Teachers can also develop their own informal reading assessment. The purpose of these assessments is to collect meaningful information about what students can and cannot do. A **running record** is a way to assess students' word identification skills and fluency in oral reading. In a running record, the teacher uses a copy of the page to mark each word the child mispronounces as the teacher listens to a student read a page. The teacher writes the incorrect word over the printed word, draws a line through each word the child skips, and draws an arrow under repeated words.

Reading Levels

Reading specialists have identified three reading proficiency levels—independent, instructional, and frustration. If the student reads 95% of the words correctly, the book is at the child's **independent level**. If the student reads 90% to 94% of the words correctly, the book is at the child's **instructional level**, which means the child can perform satisfactorily with help from the teacher. If the student reads 89% or fewer words correctly, the book is probably at the child's **frustration level**. These reading levels are determined based on the ability of children to answer comprehension questions after reading passages. Reading levels are generally assessed through reading informal reading inventories.

Informal Reading Inventories

Informal reading inventories are informal assessment instruments designed to identify the reading levels of children. Most basal reader books contain some type of informal reading inventory. These are graded (by reading levels) passages that include comprehension questions. Teachers begin with a passage at the reading level of the child and continue increasing the complex-ity until the child is not able to respond to the comprehension questions.

Asking a child to retell a story is another type of informal assessment. The ability to retell a story is an informal type of assessment that is useful to the teacher, parent, and eventually, the child. Informal assessment measures can also include observations, journals, written drafts, and conversations.

The teacher may make **observations** during individual or group work. Usually, the teacher makes a **checklist** of competencies, skills, or requirements, and then uses the list to check off the ones a student or group displays. A teacher wishing to emphasize interviewing skills could devise a checklist that includes personal appearance, mannerisms, confidence, and addressing the questions asked. A teacher who wants to emphasize careful listening might observe a discussion with a checklist that includes paying attention, not interrupting, summarizing the ideas of other members of the group, and asking questions about others.

Checklists give teachers the potential for capturing behaviors that cannot be accurately measured with a paper-and-pencil test, such as following the correct sequence of steps in a science experiment, or including all important elements in a speech in class. One characteristic of a checklist that is both an advantage and a disadvantage is its structure, which provides consistency but inflexibility. However, an open-ended comment section at the end of a checklist can help overcome this disadvantage.

Anecdotal records are helpful in some instances, such as capturing the process a group of students uses to solve a problem. This anecdotal records can be useful when giving feedback to the group. Students can also be taught to write explanations of the procedures they use for their projects or science experiments. One advantage of an anecdotal record is that it can include all relevant information. Disadvantages include the amount of time necessary to complete the record and difficulty in assigning a grade. If the anecdotal record is used solely for feedback, no grade is necessary.

Portfolios

Portfolios are collections of students' best work. They can be used in any subject area where the teacher wants students to take more responsibility for planning, carrying out, and organizing their own learning. Like a portfolio created by an artist, model, or performer, a student portfolio provides a succinct picture of the child's achievements over a certain period. Portfolios may contain essays or articles swritten on paper, videotapes, multimedia presentations on computer disks, or a combination of these. Language arts teachers often use portfolios as a means of collecting the best samples of student writing over an entire year.

Teachers should provide, or assist students in developing, guidelines for what materials should go in their portfolios because it would be unrealistic to include every piece of work in one portfolio. Using portfolios requires that the students devise a means of evaluating their own work. A portfolio should not be a scrapbook for collecting handouts or work done by other individuals, but it can certainly include work by a group in which the student was a participant.

Some advantages that portfolios have over testing are that they provide a clear picture of students' progress, they are not affected by one inferior test grade, and they help develop students' self-assessment skills. One disadvantage of portfolios is the amount of time required to teach students how to develop meaningful portfolios. However, the time is well spent if students learn valuable skills. Another concern is the amount of time teachers must spend to assess portfolios. However, as students become more proficient at self-assessment, the teacher can spend more time in coaching and advising students throughout the development of their portfolios. Another concern is that parents may not understand how the teacher will grade the portfolios. The effective teacher devises a system that the students and parents understand before work on the portfolios begins.

Miscue Analysis

Miscue analysis is an assessment procedure to assess oral reading. Miscues refer to any deviation from text made during oral reading. The procedure for its implementation follows.

1. Select reading material a little bit above the current reading level of the child. The complete story should be about 500 words in length.

2. Provide a copy of the selection to the child.

3. Get a copy of the selection that is triple spaced to allow room to write comments.

4. Audiotape the reading.

5. Provide instructions to the child, and tell the student that you cannot help him/her during the reading

6. Ask questions about the story.

7. Let the reader listen to the tape recording and then analyze it.

8. Look for consistent miscues and pay special attention to initial and final clusters/blends and diagraphs.

Running Records

Running records is a form of ongoing assessment designed to identify early reading difficulties in children. The teacher evaluates the reading performance of individual children based on checklists.

Through informal observations and through the use of inventories (formal and informal), teachers should be able to determine the **learning styles** of their students. Student learning styles play an important role in determining classroom structure.

Formal Assessments

Formal measures may include teacher-made tests, district exams, and standardized tests. Both formative and summative evaluations are part of effective instruction. **Formative evaluation** occurs during the process of learning when the teacher or the students monitor progress while it is still possible to modify instruction. **Summative evaluation** occurs at the end of a specific time or course of study. Usually, a summative evaluation applies a single grade or score to represent a student's performance.

The effective teacher uses a variety of formal assessment techniques. Teacher-made instruments are ideally developed at the same time as the planning of goals and outcomes, rather than at the last minute after the completion of the lessons. Carefully planned objectives and assessment instruments serve as lesson development guides for the teacher. Paper-and-pencil tests are the most common method for evaluating student progress.

Criterion-Referenced Tests

In **criterion-referenced tests (CRTs)**, the teacher attempts to measure each student against uniform objectives or criteria. CRTs allow the possibility that all students can score 100 percent on the test because they understand the concepts being tested. Teacher-made tests should be criterion-referenced because the teacher should develop them to measure the achievement of predetermined outcomes for the course. If teachers have properly prepared lessons based on the outcomes and, if students have mastered the outcomes, then scores on CRTs should be high. In this type of test, students are not in competition with each other for a high score, and there is no limit to the number of students who can score well. Some commercially developed tests are criterion-referenced; however, most are norm-referenced.

The **Texas Assessment of Knowledge and Skills** (TAKS) is a basic skills test for children in grades 3 to 12. This criterion-referenced test assesses the implementation and the mastery of the Texas Essential Knowledge and Skills (TEKS)—the Texas state curriculum.

Norm-Referenced Tests

The purpose of a **norm-referenced test (NRT)** is to compare the performance of groups of students. This type of test is competitive because a limited number of students can score well. A plot of NRT scores resembles a **bell-shaped curve**, with most scores clustering around the center, and a few scores at each end. The **midpoint** is the average of test data; and therefore, half of the population will score above average and half below average. The bell-shaped curve is a mathematical description of the results of tossing coins. As such, it represents the chance or normal distribution of skills, knowledge, or events across the general population. A survey of the height of sixth-grade boys will result in an average height, with half the boys being above average height, and half below. There will also be a very small number with heights far above average and a very small number with heights far below average; but, most heights will cluster around the average. A **percentile score** (not to be confused with a percentage) is a way of reporting a student's NRT score. The percentile score indicates the percentage of the population whose scores fall at or below the student's score. For example, a group score at the eightieth percentile means that the group scored as well as or better than 80 percent of the students who took the test. A student with a score at the fiftieth percentile has an average score. Percentile scores rank students from highest to lowest. By themselves, percentile scores do not indicate how well the student has mastered the content objectives. **Raw scores** indicate how many questions the student answered correctly and are, therefore, useful in computing a percentage score.

The Texas Education Agency (TEA) has a comprehensive list of approved norm-reference tests that districts can choose from to assess achievement of students in the state. This list includes the California Achievement Test (CAT), Stanford Achievement Test, and the Iowa Test of Basic Skills (ITBS), among others.

Performance-Based Assessment

Some states and districts are moving toward performance-based tests, which assess students on how well they perform certain tasks. Students must use higher-level thinking skills to apply, analyze, synthesize, and evaluate ideas and data. For example, a content-based performance-based assessment might require students to read a problem, design and carry out a laboratory experiment, and then write summaries of their findings. The performance-based assessment would evaluate both the processes students used and the output they produced. An English performance-based test might ask students to first read a selection of literature and then write a critical analysis. A mathematics performance-based test might state a general problem, require students to invent one or more methods of solving the problem, use one of the methods to arrive at a solution, and write the solution and an explanation of the processes they used.

Performance-based assessment allows students to be creative in solutions to problems or questions, and it requires them to use higher-level skills. During these assessments, students work on content-related problems and use skills that are useful in various contexts. There are weaknesses in this approach, however. This type of assessment can be time consuming. Performance-based assessment often requires multiple resources, which can be expensive. Teachers must receive training in applying the test. Nonetheless, many schools consider performance-based testing to be a more authentic measure of student achievement than traditional tests.

Classroom Tests

Teachers must consider fundamental professional and technical factors when constructing effective classroom tests. One of the first factors to recognize is that test construction is as creative, challenging, and important as any aspect of teaching. The planning and background that contribute to effective teaching are incomplete unless evaluation of student performance provides accurate feedback to the teacher and the student about the learning process.

Good tests are the product of careful planning, creative thinking, hard work, and technical knowledge about the various methods of measuring student knowledge and performance. Classroom tests that accomplish their purpose are the result of the development of a pool of items and refinement of those items based on feedback and constant revision. It is through this process that evaluation of students becomes valid and reliable.

Tests serve as a valuable instructional aid because they help determine student progress and also provide feedback to teachers regarding their own effectiveness. Student misunderstandings and problems that the tests reveal can help the teacher understand areas of special concern in providing instruction. This information also becomes the basis for the remediation of students and the revision of teaching procedures. Consequently, the construction, administration, and proper scoring of classroom tests are among the most important activities in teaching.

Authentic Assessments

Paper-and-pencil tests and essay tests are not the only methods of assessment. Other assessments include projects, observations, checklists, anecdotal records, portfolios, self-assessments, and peer assessments. Although these types of assessments often take more time and effort to plan and administer, they can often provide a more authentic measurement of student progress.

Essay Tests

There are advantages and disadvantages to essay tests. Advantages of essay questions include the possibility for students to be creative in their answers, the opportunity for students to explain their responses, and the potential to test for higher-level thinking skills. Disadvantages of essay questions include the time students need to formulate meaningful responses, and the time teachers need to evaluate the essays. In addition, language difficulties can make essay tests extremely difficult for some students, including ELLs. Consistency in evaluating essays can also be a problem for some teachers, but an outline of the acceptable answers—a scoring rubric—can help a teacher avoid inconsistency. Teachers who write specific questions and know what they are looking for are more likely to be consistent in grading. Also, if there are several essay questions, the effective teacher grades all student responses to the first question, then moves on to all responses to the second, and so on.

Using Rubrics for Assessment

A **rubric** is a checklist with assigned point values. To construct a rubric, a teacher uses the lesson objectives. Students should receive an explanation of the rubric *before* starting to work on their writing assignment, and they can use the rubric as a guideline while they are preparing their writing assignment. The teacher can use the rubric to evaluate the completed assignment.

When teachers can provide clear, well-planned instructions and guidelines for activities, they can significantly decrease student frustration. Rubrics can provide this valuable guidance. When teachers model what they expect and state clear objectives or goals for each assignment, students perform better. Accordingly, there should be a clear and obvious link between the assignment's goals and the students' achievement.

Scoring Compositions

Holistic scoring is used to evaluate the composition and writing performance of students in Texas. The whole writing sample is scored based on a pre-established criterion contained in a rubric. The writing rubric used to score the performance on TAKS is based on four levels. Students need to score at level three or four to pass the test.

Table 1-8. Criteria for Evaluation Compositions Based on a Four-Point Scale

Point Scale

4. An excellent paper that is well organized and displays facile use of language, content, and mechanics.

3. A paper that demonstrates adequate organization, content, language use, and handling mechanics. It may lack imagination and creativity.

2. A lower-half paper that is weak in content, organization, style, and/or mechanics.

1. An unacceptable paper that addresses the topic but is weak in organization, content, and language use and is full of errors in mechanics.

Educator's Guide to TEKS-Based Assessment (TEA, 2004)

The writing portion of the fourth grade TAKS test is assessed based on two objectives:

1. The student will, within a context, produce an effective composition for a specific purpose.

2. The student will produce a piece of writing that demonstrates command of the conventions of spelling, capitalization, punctuation, grammar, usage, and sentence structure.

These objectives are integrated into the five components of effective writing approved by the TEA and used for scoring the writing component of TAKS, which are focus and coherence, organization, development of ideas, voice, and conventions. (See competency 10 for detailed explanations of these components.) The rubric has a four-point scale based on the five components of the writing process and is used to assess the writing performance of children. Table 1-8 presents a description of the four levels of performance where four is the maximum scored possible.

Ongoing Assessment

Ongoing assessment provides teachers with updated information about the progress and challenges that children are facing in writing. This information can then be easily incorporated in daily instruction.

Assessing English Language Learners

Texas English Language Proficiency Assessment System (TELPAS) was designed to comply with the accountability system required in the No Child Left Behind (NCLB) legislation (TEA, 2006). The legislation requires that ELLs are assessed yearly in all language skills—listening, speaking, reading, and writing. Students begin taking TELPAS in kindergarten and only stop participating when they are exited from the program.

This system is composed of two testing components: the Reading Proficiency Tests in English (RPTE) and the Texas Observation Protocols (TOP). Both assessment instruments were especially developed for ELLs. The RPTE is an assessment that measures reading skills of ELLs, which are word meaning, supporting idea, summarization, analyzing, and evaluating. RPTE is given in a booklet in a multiple-choice format. The TOP is an assessment that measures four language skills through classroom observation and daily interactions. It is graded holistically. Both assessments are broken down into four levels: beginning, intermediate, advanced, and advanced high.

Listening, speaking, reading, and writing are assessed with the TOP in kindergarten to second grade. In grades 3 and up, listening, speaking, and writing are assessed by the TOP, and reading is assessed with the RPTE. To assess the writing component, at least five writing samples a year are collected for ELLs in grades 2 through 12, and assessed holistically to comply with the four language levels mentioned earlier—beginning, intermediate, advanced, or advanced high level. ELLs stop taking the RPTE when they reach the advanced high level of the combined TOP and RPTE scores.

Diversity in the Classroom

The effective teacher appreciates human diversity. An empowered instructor recognizes how diversity in the classroom creates an environment in which everyone accepts and celebrates both the diversity and the uniqueness of individuals. In that environment, the teacher and the students view race, ethnicity, religion, national origin, learning style, and gender of learners as strengths that foster learning with and from each other.

Assessing Diverse Learners

The purpose of both formal and informal assessments in the classroom is to improve the instruction and the learning of all students. It is important for the teacher to (1) analyze and interpret the information gathered through informal and formal means, (2) to use test results professionally to help all students in the classroom to learn to the best of their ability, and (3) to take into account diversity when teaching and assessing children. The use of criterion-referenced, norm-referenced, performance-based, classroom, and authentic assessments is essential to giving the child, the teacher, and the parents a complete picture of the child's progress.

References

Anderson, P. F. 1995–2005. The Mother Goose Pages *http://www.personal.umich.edu/~pfa/dreamhouse/nursery/rhymes.html*

Bloom, B. S. ed. 1956. Taxonomy of educational objectives: The classification of educational goals: *Handbook I, cognitive domain*. New York; Toronto: Longmans, Green.

Browning Schulman, M. & Payne, C. D. (2000). *Guided reading: Making it work*. New York: Scholastic, Inc.

Clay, M. M. 2002. *An observation survey of early literacy achievement* 2nd ed. Portmouth, NH: Heinemann.

Ehri, L. 1998. Grapheme-phoneme knowledge is essential for learning to read words in English. In *Word recognition in beginning literacy*, eds J. Metsala and L. Ehri, 3–40. Mahwah, NJ: Erlbaum.

Goudvis, A. and Harvey, S. 2000. *Strategies that work*. Portland, ME: Stenhouse.

Graves, D. H. 1983. *Writing: Teachers and children at work*. Portsmouth, NH: Heinemann Educational Books.

Lapp, D., Fisher, D., Flood, J. and Cabello, A. 2001. An integrated approach to the teaching and assessment of language arts. In *Literacy assessment of second language learners*, eds S. Rollins Hurley and J. Villamil Tinajero, 1–24. Boston, MA: Allyn and Bacon, 1–24.

Martin, K. and Doris, D. 2006. Cinderella stories. *The Children's Literature http://www.ucalgary.ca/~dkbrown/cinderella.html*

Northwest Regional Education Laboratory. 2006. 6+1 Writing Trait. *http://www.nwrel.org/assessment/definition*

Palincsar, A. S. 1986. Reciprocal teaching. In *Teaching reading as thinking*. Oak Brook, IL: North Central Regional Educational Laboratory.

Peregoy, S. F. and Boyle, O. F. 2005. *Reading, writing, and learning in ESL: A resource book for K-12 teachers*. 4th ed. New York: Pearson.

Peregoy, S. F. & Boyle, O. F. 2005. *Reading, writing, and learning in ESL: A resource book for K-12 teachers* 4th ed. New York: Pearson.

Piper, T. 2003. *Language and learning: The home school year*. 3rd ed. Columbus, Ohio: Merrill Prentice Hall.

Progressive Phonic Book (2006). The Genki, English, website. *http://www.genkienglish.net/phonics.htm*

Reuzel, R. D., & Cooter, R. 1992. *Teaching children to read: From basals to books*. New York: Macmillan Publishing Co.

Snow, C. E., Burns, M. S., & Griffin, P. Eds. 1998. *Preventing reading difficulties in young children*. Washington, DC: National Academy Press. *http://books.nap.edu/html/prdyc*

Stewig, J. W. and Jett-Simpson. 1995. *Language arts in the early childhood classroom*. Belmont, CA: Wadsworth.

TAKS 2005. Chapter 110. 3 English Language arts and reading. Subchapter A. *Elementary. Texas Education Code, §28.002.*

TEA 2002. *Guidelines for examining phonics and word recognition programs, Texas Reading Initiative. http://www.tea.state.tx.us/reading/products/products.html*

TEA 2004. TAKS Scoring Guide for 4th Grade Writing Composition. Released tests. *http://www.tea.state.tx.us/student.assessment/resources/release/taks/2004/g4sg.pdf*

TEA 2005. Linguistically Accommodated Testing (LAT) Supplement to the TAKS and SDAA II. Test Administrator Manuals. Student Assessment Division. *http://www.tea.state.tx.us/student.assessment/admin/rpte/LAT_TA_supp.pdf#xml= http://www.tea.state.tx.us/cgi/texis/webinator/search/xml.txt?query=Linguistic+accommodations&db=db&id=f8b138c3acf474d6*

TEA 2006. Texas Observation Protocol (TOP). *Rater Manual Grades K-12. Texas English Language Proficiency Assessment System (TELPAS).* Austin, TX: Texas Education.

TEA 2006. Texas English Language Proficiency Assessment System (TELPAS). Texas Student Assessment Program Coordinator Manual. *http://www.tea.state.tx.us/student.assessment/resources/guides/coormanual/telpas06.pdf#xml=http://www.tea.state.tx.us/cgi/texis/webinator/search/xml.txt?query=TELPAS&db=db&id=a890725020c9a8c0*

Texas Education Agency. 2004. Division of Student Assessment. TAKS Released test. *http://www.tea.state.tx.us/student.assessment/resources/release/taks/index.html*

Tomas, E., & Robinson, H. 1972. *Improving reading in every class: A source book for teachers*. Boston: Allyn and Bacon.

U.S. Department of Education 2006. A closer look at the five essential components of effective reading instruction. *http://www.tea.state.tx.us/reading/readingfirst/readingfirst.html*

UT System/TEA. 2002. Effective fluency instruction and progress monitoring. *http://readingserver.edb.utexas.edu/downloads/primary/guides/Fluency_Presentation.PDF#search='Reading%20fluency'*

Vacca, R. T., and Vacca, J. A. 1989. *Content area reading*. 3rd. Glenview, IL: Scott Foresman.

Domain II: Mathematics

Competency 012 (Mathematics Instruction)

The teacher understands how children learn mathematical skills and uses this knowledge to plan, organize, and implement instruction and assess learning.

In 2000, the National Council of Teachers of Mathematics (NCTM) published the *Principles and Standards for School Mathematics*. In this publication, the association outlined the components of effective mathematics programs. The document identified six principles and ten standards that children in K–12 ought to master. A description of the principles and standards for mathematics follows.

Principles of Mathematics

The NCTM identified six principles for school mathematics—equity, curriculum, teaching, learning, assessment, and technology (2000).

1. **Equity**. Excellence in mathematics education requires equity—high expectations and strong support for all students.

2. **Curriculum**. A curriculum must be coherent, focused on important mathematics, and well articulated across grades.

3. **Teaching.** Effective mathematics teaching requires understanding of what students know and need to learn, and then challenging and supporting them to learn it well.

4. **Learning.** Students must learn mathematics with understanding, actively building new knowledge from experience and previous knowledge.

5. **Assessment.** Assessment should support the learning of important mathematics concepts, and furnish useful information to both teachers and students.

6. **Technology.** Technology is essential in teaching and learning mathematics; it influences the teaching of mathematics and enhances students' learning.

Standard for Mathematics

The standards for mathematics are divided into two sections—content and process.

Content Standards

In addition to the six principles, the NCTM introduced five standards for effective mathematics teaching as it applies to children in grades K–4.

1. **Number and operations.** These components include the concept of number, and fraction, and basic computation.

2. **Algebra.** This component includes elementary algebraic reasoning involving patterns and sets of numbers.

3. **Geometry.** This encompasses the study of geometric shapes and spatial reasoning.

4. **Measurement.** This component includes the units of measurements (standard and metric) and the process for measurement in general.

5. **Data analysis and probability.** These two components cover the collection, analysis, and display of mathematics information.

Process Standards

1. **Problem solving.** In this component students are guided to formulate and solve mathematics problems that can be used in real-life situations.

2. **Reasoning and proof.** These two components allow student opportunities to examine problems, find solutions, and justify them using logical and mathematics principles.

3. **Communication.** This component teaches children to use precise and appropriate mathematics vocabulary to explain processes and outcomes.

4. **Connections.** This component emphasizes the importance of mathematics and the connection to other content areas and life in general.

5. **Representations.** This component teaches how mathematics information can be presented in various ways—numbers, letters, tables, graphs, and so on.

The Texas Essential Knowledge and Skills

The Texas Essential Knowledge and Skills (TEKS) requires a well-balanced curriculum beginning in kindergarten and continuing through grade 12 (TEA, 2006). For children in pre-kindergarten, the state developed curriculum guides to help educators implement a standardized curriculum. The curriculum guides provide a means to align the pre-kindergarten content with the TEKS. You can view the Texas Pre-Kindergarten Curriculum Guides at *www.tea.state.tx.us/curriculum/early/prekkguide.html*. Both the TEKS and the Pre-kinder guides incorporate the principles and standards of the NCTM and introduces these in a sequential manner that reflects the cognitive development of children. Children in kindergarten begin exploring number concepts using concrete objects and mastering one-to-one

Table 2-1. Mathematics Curriculum for K–4

Grade Level	Primary Focal Point
Kindergarten	Whole-number concepts and using patterns and sorting to explore numbers, data, and shapes
First	Adding and subtracting whole numbers and organizing and analyzing data
Second	Comparing and ordering whole numbers, applying addition and subtraction, and using measurement processes
Third	Multiplying and dividing whole numbers, connecting fraction symbols to fractional quantities, and standardizing language and procedures in geometry and measurement
Fourth	Comparing and ordering fractions and decimals, applying multiplication and division, and developing ideas related to congruence and symmetry

correspondence. In first and second grades, they continue exploring number concepts and begin studying basic computations skills. In third through fifth grades, they continue expanding number concepts to include multiplication, division, fractions, decimal representations, geometric principles, and algebraic reasoning.

Table 2-1 presents the focal points for kindergarten through grade 4.

Children in Texas are required to demonstrate mastery of mathematics TEKS in grades 3 through 12. Every year students take the math portion of the state basic skills examination—the Texas Assessment of Knowledge and Skills (TAKS).

Cognitive Development and Mathematics

The cognitive development of children in prekindergarten (PK) through grade 4 represents a special challenge when attempting to learn the symbolic and abstract representations used in mathematics. Piaget classified students in PK through grade 4 into two broad stages—Preoperational (2–7 years) and Concrete Operational (2–11 years) (cited in Sperry Smith, 2001). Children in the preoperational stage of cognitive development (2–7 years/PK through grade 2) experience problems with at least two perceptual concepts— centration and conservation (Sperry Smith, 2001).

Centration—Four- and five-year-old children focus attention on one characteristic of an object and ignore the others. They might notice that the objects are round, but fail to notice that they have different colors and texture. Children at this age play with blocks in a very simplistic and systematic way— linear fashion. They do not become more creative because they are emphasizing one feature at time. Based on cognitive development, children at this age generally experience problems developing and recognizing patterns in mathematics.

Conservation—Four- and five-years-olds might not understand that changes in the appearance do not necessarily change characteristics of the object (Conservation). This limitation can affect children's ability to measure volume and to understand the value of money. That is, children might get confused when liquid is moved between containers of different shapes or when trying to determine the value of a quarter versus five nickels. These perceptual limitations can affect children's ability to understand measurement and the value of money.

During the Concrete Operational stage of cognitive development—second to seventh grades—children experience rapid growth in cognitive development. This stage is characterized by the ability to think logically about concrete objects or relationships. Some of the accomplishments of students at this stage are as follows:

- Can form conclusions based on reason rather than perception

- Can arrange objects based on characteristics (Classification)

- Can organize objects based on multiple criteria (Ordering or Seriation)

- Can understand that changes in appearance do not necessarily affect the substance (Conservation)

- Can conceptualize what would have happened if an action is reversed (Reversibility)

Despite the cognitive growth of this stage, teachers have to structure lessons to provide students with a concrete foundation to support their thinking. For example, a teacher can introduce the concept of graphing by asking students to follow the growth of a plant for a period of time and document the growth using a *line graph*, or to compare how one plant grows versus another plant using a *bar graph*. Teachers should also break down a task into manageable components with the use of graphic organizers (charts, diagrams, webs, time lines, etc.).

Developmentally Appropriate Instruction

A basic understanding of numbers is developed at a very early age—younger than 2. Infants and toddlers understand the concepts of "one" and "more," usually in relation to food. Rote counting, or the repetition of a verbal chain of numbers, begins at the age of 2 or 3, for which children receive positive reinforcement. This rote memorization of the names and order of those

The Use of Blocks in Mathematics

names can be used as a foundation on which to build an understanding of what those names and order mean. This is known as rational counting. It is at this time, in kindergarten through grade 2, that using concrete objects such as blocks or other analogous items is most effective.

Basic computation can be presented using concrete objects. In kindergarten this concept can be introduced with blocks, figures such as toys, coins, and beads. For example, a simple addition problem can be introduced by putting beads on a string and asking students to add or subtract them. For more advanced students, the number line can be used to add, subtract, and even multiply. For example, in a problem of subtraction, like $6 - 4 = 2$, teachers can guide students to follow simple instructions to arrive at the correct answer.

Step 1: Since the 6 is a positive number, move from zero to the 6.

Step 2: From the 6, move four digits to the left (negative) to find the answer = 2.

$$-5 \quad -4 \quad -3 \quad -2 \quad -1 \quad 0 \quad 1 \quad 2 \quad 3 \quad 4 \quad 5 \quad 6$$

Mathematics concepts can be very abstract and difficult to grasp. However, teachers have the option of teaching these abstract concepts beginning with concrete representations and working until the mathematics concepts make sense to the child.

Manipulatives in Mathematics

Children in elementary school can benefit from group instruction and the use of concrete objects and manipulatives. Manipulatives can be used from kinder-

garten to high school. However, these are mostly used in elementary education. Some of the most common manipulatives found in the early childhood classrooms are *play money, buttons, paper clips, tooth picks, playing cards, rulers, blocks, dice, empty egg cartons, measuring cups, thermometers, pattern blocks, dominoes, teddy bear counters,* and *games.* These objects can be used to teach a variety of concepts and processes in the mathematics classroom.

Games are highly motivational for children in prekindergarten through grade 4. A simple game with dice can be used to teach counting and even probabilities; blocks and tri-dimensional figures can be used to teach sequencing, patterns, and even geometric concepts (Bellonio, 2006). Children learn best when they can link and convert what they are learning into real-life, concrete experiences; for example, they may learn fractions by cutting and putting back together things like an apple, an orange, or a pizza. They can talk in a very concrete and real situation about eating $\frac{1}{8}$ of a pizza or $\frac{1}{16}$ of an apple.

Numbers and fractions represent a challenge to elementary education children. Through the use of manipulatives, teachers can provide a concrete representation of abstractions like numbers and fractions. For example, the mixed number 2½ can be represented concretely by using basic blocks or pictures representing the numbers, as shown in the figure above. By analyzing the concrete representation of 2½, the child can be led to identify equivalent fractions (e.g., 2, 5/10).

In addition to the manipulatives used in the mathematics, the typical mathematics classroom contains a variety of tools and instructional supplies to support children in the learning process. Some of these instructional tools are as follows:

- **Protractor** is a semicircular instrument for measuring and constructing angles.

- **Calculators** are generally used to calculate large numbers when the main focus of the activities goes beyond simple computations.

- **Stopwatches** can be used to introduce the concept of time (e.g., how long is a minute?).

- **Scales are** used to measure mass.

Mathematics and English Language Learners

Contrary to popular belief, mathematics is not a universal language. It is a language with special nomenclature and unique concepts. Even the way that people perform mathematical processes is often different. For example, in Mexico and the Dominican Republic the processes used for division differ from the process used in the United States. In Mexico the problem is set up in a similar fashion but most of the steps are done mentally, as opposed to the American way, where students write every single step as part of the process. For example, in the problem, 11 divided by 2, children in Mexico are taught to multiply 5 by 2 and get 10, but they do not write the 10 under the 11; they do it mentally and write the remainder below the 11. In the Dominican Republic, children do not use the traditional division bracket used in the United States and Mexico; instead, they use a bracket similar to an elongated **L**, and they place the *divisor* inside the bracket and the *dividend* outside. Children from Mexico and the Dominican Republic might experience confusion when asked to perform division the "American way." **Table 2-2** illustrates the three different processes used to perform division.

The use of Arabic numbers does not present problems for English language learners (ELLs). The real challenge

Table 2-2. Processes of Division

American	Mexican	Dominican
$\begin{array}{r}5\\ 2\overline{)11}\\ -10\\ \hline 1R\end{array}$	$\begin{array}{r}5\\ 2\overline{)11}\\ 1R\end{array}$	$\begin{array}{r}11\ \lfloor\ 5\\ -10\quad 2\\ 1R\ \ 10\end{array}$
Result: **5**^{1r}	Result: **5**^{1r}	Result: **5**^{1r}

Table 2-3. Terminology of Mathematics

Terminology	Generic Meaning	Mathematical Meaning
plane	flat surface or aircraft	a two-dimensional surface or space
right	true, proper, a direction	perpendicular forming a 90° angle
foot and feet	part of a leg	unit of length
faces	front of the human head	surface of an object (geometry)
natural numbers	occur naturally in nature	whole number greater than 0
even numbers	equal in amount, not owning	number divisible by 2
odd number	unusual, irregular	not divisible by 2
volume	loudness of sound	quantity of liquid
mass	Catholic ceremony	body of matter for measurement
property of 0	something owned	traits or attributes

is to comprehend the explanation of the process in a language that ELLs have not mastered yet. Providing examples of mathematics process and modeling while describing them can definitely improve comprehension. Students who enjoy *inductive teaching*—learning through examples—will definitely benefit from this approach. However, children who enjoy the *deductive approach*—learning step by step—might experience comprehension problems.

The Nomenclature of Mathematics

In addition to the obvious English communication problems, ELLs still face another dilemma: the technical vocabulary or the nomenclature of mathematics. They need to learn the English language plus the specialized language of mathematics. Table 2-3 shows mathematic terminology that can be confusing not only to ELLs but to all children.

Mathematics in Real-Life Situations

The U.S. Department of Labor (2005) developed a list of the top professions that require a strong knowledge in mathematics. Some of the most prominent jobs are *accountants and auditors, computer programmers, computer scientists, computer engineers and system analysts, economists and marketing research analysts, managers, mathematicians, operations research analysts, statisticians,* and *financial planners.*

The preceding list is useful for emphasizing the importance of mathematics in our lives; however, most children in early childhood might not be aware and cannot relate to these kinds of jobs. The best way to link mathematics to real jobs or activities is to guide students to develop a list of jobs available in their community. For example, a unit about community helpers will yield a large list of occupations, such as *nurses, physicians, sanitary workers, home builders, landscaping, plumbers, carpet and tiles installers,* among others. Teachers can assign readings about these professions and invite community sources to describe and demonstrate how they use mathematics in their profession. The interactive and concrete approach can easily present the need for mathematics in our daily lives.

One of the key challenges in promoting interest in mathematics is to convince children that mathematics plays an important role in their lives. Based on this assumption, teachers need to introduce mathematics concepts in a problem-solving format using real-life situations. Some examples for PK through grade 4 follow:

- Purchase inexpensive items in the dollar store and set up a "classroom store" where students can go to purchase items using play money. Children can earn money as part of the classroom management program, which can reward students with play money for good behavior.

- Organize cooking activities at home or in school using recipes requiring specific units of measurement; this activity can also be linked to science and chemistry.

- Guide students to identify the most appropriate measuring system to compute the size of objects and the area of spaces in the classroom or school.

- Plan a field trip where students have to estimate the cost of the trip. Children have to use computations skills to determine the cost of the activity.

- Plan a road trip using mapquest.com or any other program to calculate distance from one place to the other. Then use the distance to calculate travel time and gas expenses based on mileage.

For additional information about activities to link mathematics to real-life situations, visit the *On-line Math Applications* website: *http://library.thinkquest. org/4116.*

Competency 013 (Number Concepts, Patterns, and Algebra)

The teacher understands concepts related to numbers and number systems and demonstrates knowledge of patterns, relations, functions, and algebraic reasoning.

Number Concepts and Algorithms

One of the key challenges in mathematics education is the teaching of technical vocabulary and concepts. Teachers as well as students need to understand and use this vocabulary to communicate effectively in the mathematics classroom. A summary of key mathematics vocabulary and concepts follows.

The number system used in the United States and most nations in the word is the **Arabic** number system. This system uses a 10-number system beginning with 0 and ending with 9. The system contains whole and rational numbers. **Whole numbers** are positive or negative complete numbers that begin with zero (0) and continue until infinity. **Rational numbers** are numbers that can be represented as a fraction or a ratio. A whole number can be divided among equal parts to create **fractions**. For example, a number can be divided into two halves, three thirds, four fourths, and so forth.

Integers

Integers are positive and negative numbers. On a number line, integers to the left of the zero are negative and those on the right are positive.

Natural Numbers

Natural or counting numbers begin with 1 and continue until infinity (i.e., 1, 2, 3, 4, 5, . . .).

Prime Numbers

Prime numbers are number greater that 1 whose only divisors are 1 and the number itself (e.g., 2, 3, 5, 7, 11, 13, 17, 19, 23, 29). For example, 7 is a prime number because it has only two factors, 1 and 7.

Composite Numbers

A composite number is a whole number that has three or more whole number factors. For example, 8 is a composite number because it has four different factors: 1, 2, 4, and 8.

Even and Odd Numbers

Even numbers are whole numbers that have 2 as a factor (e.g., 2, 4, 6, 8, 10, 12, 14. . .). Odd numbers are whole numbers that **do not** have 2 as a factor (e.g., 1, 3, 5, 7, 9 . . .).

Exponential Notation

Exponential notation is a way to show repeated multiplication. For example, the notation 4^3 is equivalent to $4 \times 4 \times 4 = 64$. People often get confused with this kind of notation and believe that 4^3 is equivalent to 4×3.

Scientific Notation

Scientific notation provides a method for representing any numbers using exponents. A number is a notation when it is shown as a number between 1 and 10 times a power of 10. For example, the number 1956 in scientific notation is shown as 1.956×10^3.

Algorithm

An **algorithm** is a step-by-step problem-solving procedure and recursive computational procedure for solving a problem in a finite number of steps.

Basic Operations

The four basic operations with whole numbers are addition, subtraction, multiplication, and division.

Addition

Addition in mathematics refers to the process of combining two or more digits into one number. In addition of whole numbers, the key element is to align the numbers based on place value—ones, tens, hundreds, thousands, and so forth. Following the alignment, proceed to add beginning with the ones—right to left progression.

25 (addend)   Step 1: Add the two ones (5 + 2 = 7).
+32   Step 2: Add the tens (2 + 3 = 5).
57 (sum)   Answer

Subtraction

Subtraction is the process of removing objects from a larger group, or the inverse process for addition (Graeme, 2006). Like addition, subtraction is a process that children can master with simple demonstrations. However, when children and especially ELLs are given *word problems*, the complexity of the language can create comprehension problems. See the following word problem.

From a group of 25 cars, 20 were sold. How many are left?

The child might know the operation but he/she might not understand that the word *left* in the problem calls for subtraction. Teachers need to develop a list of key words linked to each of the four basic operations. See the following operation.

$$25 \text{ (minuend)}$$
$$\underline{-20} \text{ (subtrahend)}$$
$$05 \text{ (remainder)}$$

Step 1: Beginning with the ones, subtract the bottom numbers from the top numbers.

Step 2: Subtract the tens using the same process to get the results.

Multiplication

Multiplication is a faster way to addition. It requires students to memorize the multiplication facts and the steps in the process (e.g., 95×7).

$$95 \text{ (factor)}$$
$$\underline{\times 7} \text{ (factor)}$$
$$665 \text{ (product)}$$

Step 1: Multiply the two ones first—$7 \times 5 = 35$.

Step 2: Since the number has more than one digit (i.e., 3 tens and 5 ones), place the 3 on top of the tens column and the 5 in the ones column.

Step 3: Multiply the digit in the tens place (9)—$7 \times 9 = 63$.

Step 4: Add the 63 to the 3 placed in the tens place; this equals 66.

Step 5: Place the 66 on the left of the ones to obtain the final result—665.

Division

Division is a process that requires students to master subtraction and multiplication.

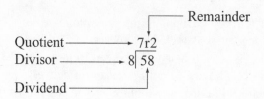

Step 1: Place the divisor outside the bracket on the left-hand side and the dividend inside the bracket.

Step 2: Examine the first digit of the dividend. If this is smaller than the divisor, then take both numbers of the dividend.

Step 3: Identify how many times the divisor (8) can fit into the dividend (58).

Step 4: Place the result on top of the bracket (i.e., 7).

Step 5: Multiply the quotient (7) with the divisor (8)–56.

Step 6: Subtract 56 from 58 to identify a possible remainder.

Step 7: Place the remainder on the quotient (i.e., R2)

Numbers and their Properties

1. **Commutative Property.** The order of the **addends** or **factors** do not change the result.
$$a + b = b + a$$
   Addition: $6 + 8 = 14$ is the same as $8 + 6 = 14$
   Multiplication: $5 \times 8 = 40$ is the same as $8 \times 5 = 40$

2. **Associative Property of Multiplication and Addition.** The order of the addends or product will not change the sum or the product. $(a + b) + c = a + (b + c)$
   Addition: $(2 + 3) + 5 = 10$ $2 + (3 + 5) = 10$
   Multiplication: $(2 \times 3) \times 5 = 30$ $3 \times (2 \times 5) = 30$

3. **Property of Zero.** The sum of a number and zero is the number itself, and the product of a number and zero is zero.
   Addition: $8 + 0 = 8$
   Multiplication: $8 \times 0 = 0$

distributive Property

4. **Distributive Property**. You can add and then multiply or multiply then add.

$$a(b + c) = (a \times b) + (a \times c)$$
$$8 \times (5 + 2) = (8 \times 5) + (8 \times 2) = 56$$

Order of Operations

In mathematics, we encounter many problems in which the solution involves a series of calculations. When doing more than one operation, we need to follow a set of rules regarding which calculations to do first. For example, what is the right answer to **3 + 2 × 6 = ?** Should we go "left to right" and just do the + first and get 30, or do we do the multiplication first and get 15? Well, in order to avoid confusion and get the correct answer, mathematicians decided long ago that all calculations should be done in the same order. You may have learned the order of operations as being: *Please Excuse My Dear Aunt Sally!* where the words stand for *Parentheses, Exponentiation, Multiplication, Division, Addition*, and *Subtraction*. So what is the correct answer for our problem? The order of operations would say that in the absence of parentheses, you would multiply 2×6 first, then add 3, so the result should be 15.

Rounding Numbers

Another issue we need to deal with when we perform operations is how to state the answer (SEF, 2006). For example, if we are dividing a 20-centimeter wire into 3 equal pieces, we would divide 20 by 3 to get the length of each piece. If we took the time to work this division out by hand, we would get

$$\frac{20}{3} = 6.666666666666666666\ldots$$

The 6 repeats forever. How do we report this number? We **round** to some usually pre-determined number of digits or decimal places. By "digits" we mean the total number of numbers both left and right of the decimal point. By "decimal places" we specifically refer to the number of numbers to the **right** of the decimal point.

For comparison, let's try rounding this number to two **decimal places**—two numbers to the right of the

point. To round, look at the digit *after* the one of interest—in this case the third decimal place—and use these rules:

- If the digit is 0, 1, 2, 3, or 4, round down.

- If the digit is 5, 6, 7, 8, or 9, round up.

In our example, 6.666666666666 . . . , the next digit is 6, so we round up, giving 6.67 as the desired answer.

Sometimes rounding is the result of an approximation. If you had 101 or 98 meters of some wire, in each case you would have "about 100 meters."

Time, Temperature, and Money

Time

There are two kinds of clocks—analog and digital. The digital presents the time using Arabic numbers separating the hours from the minutes with colon—12:45—which makes it relatively easy to read it. However, the analog clock uses two hands to represent the hours and minutes based on 60 minutes for an hour and 60 seconds for a minute. The analog clock represents a challenge since students must have a mathematical understanding of each of the numbers on the clock face.

Temperature

Temperature is measured with a thermometer, an instrument that generally uses mercury—a liquid metallic element that expands with heat—to measure temperature. Thermometers in the United States uses the **Fahrenheit** scale, which uses a system from 0 to 212 degrees to represent temperature. The **Celsius** scale is used in most other countries in the world, and it is specifically useful in scientific experimentation. This system measures heat based on a system from 0 to 100 degrees. Water boils at 212°F or 100°C, and it freezes at 32°F or 0°C.

Money

The American monetary system is based on the dollar, which was based on the amount of gold reserves available in the nation at one point. In 1971, President Richard Nixon decided to depart from the gold standard (Wheat, 2006). Now, the money of the United States is backed by the government itself, without a direct connection with U.S. gold reserves. The U.S. monetary system uses a paper and metal coin system based on dollars, half dollars, quarters, dimes, nickels, and pennies.

Basic Computation and Place Value

Estimating is generally done by rounding the numbers to the nearest tenth. For example, a sum 23 + 35 can be solved easily by rounding 23 to **20** and 35 to **40** to obtain the estimation 20 + 40 = 60.

Place values are the basic foundation for understanding mathematic computation. A simple number like 1984 can be explained based on the positions of the numbers in the value scale. See the example in the following table

Thousand	Hundred	Ten	One
1000	900	80	4
1	9	8	4

Graphs and Symbolic Representations

Use of graphs and lists

In addition to pictorial graphs—representation of objects with a picture—bar graphs are one of the most concrete ways to represent information for students in PK through grade 4. Bar graphs can easily be used to integrate mathematics and other content areas. See the following example.

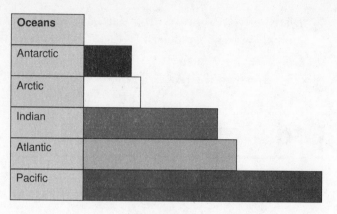

Graph

The Oceans of the World in Square Miles	
Indian	28,300,500
Pacific	64,186,300
Antarctic	4,000,000
Arctic	5,125,000
Atlantic	33,420,000

Use this graph to guide children to visualize and compare the size of the oceans. What is the smallest ocean? What is the largest ocean? What oceans are similar in size?

Patterns

Patterns are used to teach logical relations and mathematical reasoning. Simple patterns like the one that follows can guide children to see the relationship and predictability of the pattern's components. Complete the pattern: △◊◊◊△◊◊◊△◊◊◊△_ _ _ _

The teaching of patterns can be difficult for children in PK and kindergarten because they might not be able to compare simultaneously multiple characteristics of the pattern to see how it is created.

Operations with Algebraic Expressions

Operations with algebraic expressions are governed by various rules and conventions.

- In **addition and subtraction**, *only like algebraic terms (same exponent) can be added or subtracted* to produce simpler expressions. For example, $2x^3$ and $3x^3$ can be added together to get $5x^3$, because the terms are *like* terms; they both have a base of x^3. You cannot add, say, $7m^3$ and $6m^2$ because they are *unlike* bases. (*Note*: To *evaluate* an algebraic expression means to simplify it using conventional rules.)

- When **multiplying exponential terms** together, the constant terms are multiplied, but the *exponents of terms with the same variable bases are added together*, which is somewhat counterintuitive. For example, $4w^2$ multiplied by $8w^3$ gives $32w^5$ (not $32w^6$, as one might guess).

- When like algebraic terms are **divided**, exponents are subtracted. For example,

$$\frac{2x^7}{5x^3} \quad \text{becomes} \quad \frac{2x^4}{5}$$

Algebraic Expressions

An algebraic expression is an expression using letters, numbers, symbols, and arithmetic operations to represent a number or relationship among numbers. A *variable*, or unknown, is a letter that stands for a number in an algebraic expression. *Coefficients* are the numbers that precede the variable to give the quantity of the variable in the expression. Algebraic expressions are comprised of terms, or groupings of variables and numbers. An algebraic expression with one term is called a *monomial*; with two terms, a *binomial*; with three terms, a *trinomial*; with more than one term, a *polynomial*.

For example, $2ab - cd$ is a binomial algebraic expression with variables a, b, c, and d, and terms $2ab$ and $(-cd)$. 2 is the coefficient of ab and -1 is the coefficient of cd. $x^2 + 3y - 1$ is a trinomial algebraic expression using the variables x and y, and terms x^2, $3y$, and (-1); $z(x - 1) + uv - wy - 2$ is a polynomial with variables z, x, u, v, w, and y, and terms $z(x - 1)$, uv, $(-wy)$, and (-2).

Multiplication of Binomials

In algebra, it is frequently necessary to multiply two *binomials*. Binomials are algebraic expressions of two terms. The FOIL method is one way to multiply binomials. FOIL stands for "first, outer, inner, last": Multiply the first terms in the parentheses, then the outermost terms, then the innermost terms, then the last terms, and then add the products together. For example, to multiply $(x + 3)$ and $(2x - 5)$, you multiply x by $2x$ (the first terms), x by -5 (outer terms), 3 by $2x$ (inner terms), and 3 by 5 (last terms). The four products ($2x^2$, $-5x$, $6x$, and -15) add up to $2x^2 + x - 15$. If the polynomials to be multiplied have more than two terms (*trinomials*, for instance), make sure that *each* term of the first polynomial is multiplied by *each* term of the second. The opposite of polynomial multiplication is factoring. Factoring a polynomial means rewriting it as the product of factors (often two binomials). The trinomial $x^2 - 11x + 28$, for instance, can be factored into $(x - 4)(x - 7)$. (You can check this by "FOILing" the binomials.) When attempting to factor polynomials, it is sometimes necessary to factor out any factor that might be common to all terms first. The two terms in $5x^2 - 10$, for example, both contain the factor 5. This means that the expression can be rewritten as $5(x^2 - 2)$.

Fractions

1. **Finding equivalent fractions or simplification of fractions.** To identify an equivalent fraction, follow these steps using the example 2/4:

   - Find a number that can divide the numerator and the denominator. For example, in the fraction 2/4, the number 2 can divide the numerator (2) and the denominator (4).

   - Divide the number (2) by the denominator and the numerator to get the result—2/4 = ½.

2. **Adding and subtracting homogeneous fractions.** When adding or subtracting fractions with the same denominator, add or subtract the numerators—the denominator remains the same. For example, 2/5 + 1/5 = 3/5; 7/9 − 5/9 = 2/9.

3. **Changing improper fractions to mixed numbers.** To change an improper fraction like 5/2 to mixed num-

bers, divide the numerator by the denominator and represent the remainder as a fraction, such as 2½.

4. **Adding and subtracting mixed numbers.** To add and subtract mixed numbers, see the examples and follow the rule provided.

$$2\frac{5}{10}$$
$$+1\frac{4}{10}$$
$$3\frac{9}{10}$$

$$7\frac{9}{12}$$
$$-5\frac{4}{12}$$
$$2\frac{5}{12}$$

Add or subtract the fractions and then the whole number.

5. **Changing mixed numbers to fractions.** To change a mix number, multiply the denominator (4) by the whole number (2) □ 8; then take the result and add it to the numerator (3) to get the result: **11/4.**

$$2\frac{3}{4}=\frac{11}{4}$$

6. **Adding fractions with different denominators.** To work with these kinds of fractions, it is necessary to *rename fractions* using a *common denominator*. For example, to rename the fractions ½ and 2/3, it is necessary to find the common denominator between the 2 and 3. In this case the lowest common denominator is 6, because both of the original denominators can be divided by 6. That is, ½ can be written as 3/6, and 2/3 can be written as 4/6. 3/6 □ 4/6 now can be added—7/6.

7. **Multiplying fractions.** Multiplying fractions involves multiplying the numerator together and the denominators together (horizontally), then simplifying the product.

$$\frac{2}{3}\times\frac{3}{4}=\frac{6}{12}\frac{1}{2}$$

If the numbers to be multiplied are mixed fractions, first rewrite them as "improper" fractions like 6/2 and then proceed to multiply as described earlier.

8. **Dividing fractions**. To perform this operation, invert the second fraction (the one doing the dividing) and multiply the numbers as described earlier. In the case of 1/5 divided by 3/8, follow these steps:

- Invert the second fraction 3/8 to 8/3.
- Proceed to multiply.

$$\frac{1}{5}\times\frac{8}{3}=\frac{8}{15}$$

9. **Adding, subtracting, and dividing decimals.** Decimal numbers are fractions whose denominators are powers of 10 (i.e., 10, 100, 1000, and so forth). For example, 0.098 is equivalent to 98/1000. To add or subtract decimal numbers, arrange them vertically, aligning decimal points, then add or subtract as for whole numbers. See the following example.

23.5   The decimal point remains in the same
20.5   location.
44.0

10. **Multiplying decimals.** Multiplication of decimals does not require aligning decimal points; the numbers can be arranged vertically, with right *justification*. The numbers can then be multiplied as if they were whole numbers. The numbers of digits to the right of the decimal point in the product should be equal to the total number of digits to the right of the two factors. See the following example.

  1.25   Count the number to the right of the
× 0.6   period and place it accordingly.
0.750   In this example the period will go to the place value of the thousands.

11. **Dividing decimals.** Division of decimals is done like traditional whole number division. The number of digits to the right of the decimal point in the **divisor** is how far the decimal point in the answer (quotient) should be moved to the right. See the following example:

$$0.3\overline{)1.44}\quad 4.8$$

Percent

Percent is another way of expressing a fractional number. Percent always expresses a fractional number in terms of $\frac{1}{100}$ or 0.01s. Percents use the "%" symbol.

$$100\% = \frac{100}{100} = 1.00$$

$$25\% = \frac{25}{100} = 0.25$$

As shown in these examples, a percent is easily converted to a common fraction or a decimal fraction. To convert a decimal to a common fraction, place the percent in the numerator and use 100 as the denominator (reduce as necessary). To convert a percent to a decimal fraction, divide the percent by 100, or move the decimal point two places to the left. For example,

$$25\% = \frac{25}{100} = \frac{1}{4} \text{ and } 25\% = 0.25$$

To convert a *common fraction to a percent*, carry out a division of the numerator by the denominator of the fraction to three decimal places. Round the result to two places. To convert a decimal fraction to a percent, move the decimal point two places to the right (adding 0's as placeholders, if needed) and round as necessary. For example,

$$\frac{1}{4} = 1 \div 4 = 0.25 = 25\%, \qquad \text{and}$$

$$\frac{2}{4} = 2 \div 4 = 0.50 = 50\%$$

If you wish to find the *percentage* of a known quantity, change the percent to a common fraction or a decimal fraction, and multiply the fraction times the quantity. The percentage is expressed in the same units as the known quantity. For example, to find 25% of 360 books, change 25% to 0.25 and multiply times 360, as follows: $0.25 \times 360 = 90$. The result is 90 books. (*Note*: The known quantity is the base, the percent is the rate, and the result is the percentage.)

Performing Operations with Negative and Positive Numbers

When performing operations on negative and positive whole numbers, the key component is to pay atten-

tion to the sign—the positive or negative value. Rules for multiplication and division are the same—two positives and two negatives make a positive, and mixing negative with positive makes a negative. See the following examples.

- negative − negative = positive $(-6 \times -5 = 30)$
- positive − positive = positive $(6 \times 5 = 30)$
- positive − negative = negative $(5 \times -5 = -25)$

Competency 014 (Geometry, Measurement, Probability, and Statistics)

The teacher understands concepts and principles of geometry and measurement and demonstrates knowledge of probability and statistics and their applications.

Principles and Properties of Geometry

A fundamental concept of geometry is the notion of a *point*. A point is a specific location, taking up no space, having no area, and frequently represented by a dot. A point is considered to have no dimensions. In other words, it has neither length nor breadth nor depth.

Through any two points there is exactly one straight line; straight lines are one dimensional—they have infinite length but no breadth nor depth. Planes (think of flat surfaces without edges) are two dimensional, meaning they have infinite length and breadth but no depth. From these foundational ideas you can move to some other important geometric terms and ideas.

- A segment is any portion of a line between two points on that line. It has a definite start and a definite end. The notation for a segment extending from point *A* to point *B* is $\overline{AB}$.

- A ray is like a line segment, except it extends forever in one direction. The notation for a ray originating at point *X* (an *endpoint*) through point *Y* is $\overrightarrow{XY}$.

Angles

When two rays share their endpoints, an *angle* is formed. A *degree* is the unit of measure of the angle created. If a circle is divided into 360 even slices, each slice has an angle measure of 1 degree.

- If an angle has exactly 90 degrees it is called a **right angle**.

- Angles of less than 90 degrees are *acute* **angles**.

- Angles greater than 90 degrees are *obtuse* **angles**.

- If two angles have the same size (regardless of how long their rays might be drawn), they are *congruent*. Congruence is shown this way: $\angle m = \angle n$ (read "angle *m* is congruent to angle *n*").

Polygons

A polygon is a closed plane figure bounded by straight lines or a closed figure on a circle bounded by arcs. These figures are described based on the number of sides. Some of the most common are the following:

- Three-sided polygons are *triangles*.

- Four-sided polygons are *quadrilaterals*.

- Five-sided polygons are *pentagons*.

- Six-sided polygons are *hexagons*.

- Eight-sided polygons are *octagons*.

(Note that not all quadrilaterals are squares.) If two polygons (or any figures) have exactly the same size and shape, they are *congruent*. If they are the same shape, but different sizes, they are *similar*.

Lines of Symmetry

Polygons may have lines of symmetry, which can be thought of as imaginary fold lines that produce two congruent, mirror-image figures. Squares have four lines of symmetry, and non-square rectangles have two, as shown in the following figures. Circles have an infinite number of lines of symmetry.

Diameter and Radius

The *diameter* of a circle is a straight line segment that goes from one edge of a circle to the other side, passing through the center. The *radius* of a circle is half of its diameter (from the center to an edge). A *chord* is any segment that goes from one spot on a circle to any other spot (all diameters are chords, but not all chords are diameters).

Finding the Perimeter

The *perimeter* of a two-dimensional (flat) shape or object is the distance around the object (think of a fence, for example). Perimeter is measured in linear units (e.g., inches, feet, and meters).

The **perimeter of a rectangle** is found by adding twice the length of the rectangle to twice the width of the rectangle. This relationship is commonly given by the formula

$P = 2l + 2w$, where *l* is the measure of the length and *w* is the measure of the width. For example, if

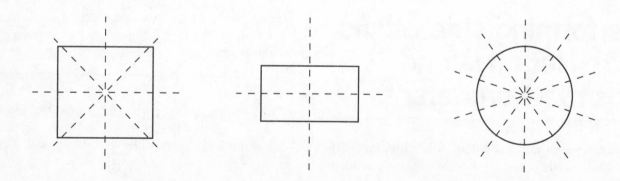

a rectangle has $l = 10$ m and $w = 5$ m, then the perimeter of the rectangle is given by $P = 2(10$ m$) + 2 (5$ m$) = 30$ m.

The **perimeter of a square** is found by multiplying four times the measure of a side of the square. This relationship is commonly given by the formula $P = 4s$, where s is the measure of a side of the square. For example, if a square has $s = 5$ feet, then the perimeter of the square is given by $P = 4(5$ feet$) = 20$ feet.

The **perimeter of a triangle** is found by adding the measures of the three sides of the triangle. This relationship can be represented by $P = s1 + s2 + s3$, where $s1$, $s2$, and $s3$ are the measures of the sides of the triangle. For example, if a triangle has three sides measuring 3 inches, 4 inches, and 5 inches, then the perimeter of the triangle is given by $P = 3$ inches $+ 4$ inches $+ 5$ inches $= 12$ inches.

Finding the Area

The **area of a rectangle** is found by multiplying the measure of the length of the rectangle by the measure of the width of the triangle. This relationship is commonly given by $A = l \times w$, where l is the measure of the length and w is the measure of the width. For example, if a rectangle has l = 10 m and w = 5 m, then the area of the rectangle is given by $A = 10$ m $\times 5$ m $= 50$ m^2.

The **area of a square** is found by *squaring the measure* of the side of the square. This relationship is commonly given by $A = S^2$, where s is the measure of a side. For example, if a square has $s = 5$ ft, then the area of the square is given by $A = (5$ ft$^2) = 25$ ft^2.

Volume

Volume refers to how much space is inside of three-dimensional, closed containers. It is useful to think of volume as how many cubic units could fit into a solid. If the container is a rectangular solid, multiplying width, length, and height together computes the volume.

If all six faces (sides) of a rectangular solid are squares, then the object is a cube.

Cube

A **cube** is a three-dimensional solid figure. This figure has 6 faces, 12 edges, and 8 vertices. The number of faces, edges and vertices can be identified visually, or through the application of the following formula:

Formula for the figure: $F + V = E + 2$

Vertex: A vertex is the union of two segments or point of intersection of two sides of a polygon.

Faces: Each of the plain regions of a geometric body is a face.

Edge: An edge is a line segment where two faces of a three-dimensional figure meet.

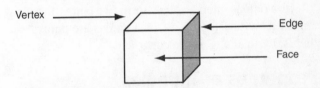

Parallel and *perpendicular* are important concepts in geometry. Consider the two parallel lines that follow, and the third line (a *transversal*), which crosses them.

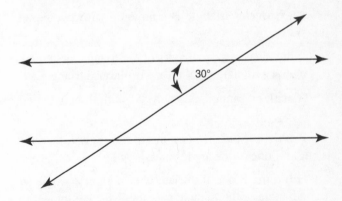

Note that among the many individual angles created, there are only two angle measures: (30° noted in the figure) and 150° (180° − 30°).

Angle Measure

Angles are usually measured in degrees. A circle has a measure of 360°, a half-circle 180°, a quarter-circle 90°, and so forth. If the measures of two angles are the same, then the angles are said to be congruent as stated earlier. Three types of angles are commonly identified—right, acute, and obtuse.

- Right angles measure 90°.
- Acute angles measure less than 90°.
- Obtuse angles measures more than 90°.

In addition to the traditional type of angles, combinations of two angles are classified as complementary and supplementary.

- Supplementary angles measure 180°.
- Complementary angles measure 90°.

Vertical Angles

If two lines intersect, they form two pairs of vertical angles. The measures of vertical angles are equivalent; that is, vertical angles are congruent.

Properties of Triangles

The sum of the measures of the angles of a triangle is 180°. Triangles are three-sided polygons. There are three kinds of triangles—isosceles, equilateral, and scalene.

- An **isosceles** triangle is a polygon with two equal sides.
- If the measures of all sides of the triangle are equal, then the triangle is called an **equilateral** triangle.
- A **scalene** triangle is a polygon with three unequal sides.

Problem: Find the measures of the angles of a right triangle if one of the angles measures 30°.

Solution: Since the triangle is a right triangle, a second angle of the triangle measures 90°. We know the sum of the measures of a triangle is 180°, so that 90° + 30° + x° = 180°. Solving for x°, we get x° = 60°. The measures of the angles of the triangle are 90°, 60°, and 30°.

Formulas for Basic Polygons

The following are formulas for finding the areas of basic polygons (formally defined as closed, copla-

nar geometric figures with three or more straight sides). Abbreviations used are as follows: *A* stands for area, *l* stands for length, *w* stands for width, *h* stands for height, and *b* stands for length of the base.

- **Triangle** (a three-sided polygon): $A = \dfrac{b \times h}{2}$

(Note that, as shown in the figure that follows, the height of a triangle is not necessarily the same as the length of any of its sides.)

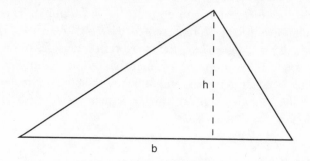

- **Rectangle** (a four-sided polygon with four right angles): $A = l \times w$
- **Parallelogram** (a four-sided polygon with two pairs of parallel sides): $A = l \times h$ (Note that, as with triangles, and as shown in the figure below, the height of a parallelogram is not necessarily the same as the length of its sides.)

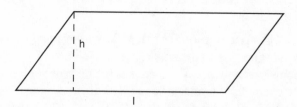

- **Circle** The area of a circle can be found by squaring the length of its radius, then multiplying that product by π. The formula is given as $A = \pi r^2$ (pi is the ratio of a circle's circumference to its diameter).

The value of π is the same for all circles; approximately 3.14159. (The approximation 3.14 is adequate for most calculations.) The approximate area of the circle shown below can be found by squaring 6 (giving 36), then multiplying 36 by 3.14, giving an area of about 113 square units.

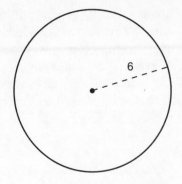

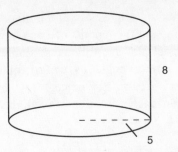

Here are several commonly used **volume formulas**:

The volume of a rectangular solid is equal to the product of its length, width, and height; $A = l \times w \times h$. (A rectangular solid can be thought of as a box, wherein all intersecting edges form right angles.)

A prism is a polyhedron—a three-dimensional solid consisting of a collection of polygons—with two congruent, parallel faces (called bases) and whose lateral (side) faces are parallelograms (Weisstein, 2006). The volume of a prism can be found by multiplying the area of the prism's base by its height. The volume of the triangular prism shown hereafter is 60 cubic units. (The area of the triangular base is 10 square units, and the height is 6 units.)

A property of all triangles is that the sum of the measures of the three angles is 180°. If, therefore, the measures of two angles are known, the third can be deduced using addition, then subtraction. Right triangles (those with a right angle) have several special properties. A chief property is described by the Pythagorean theorem, which states that in any right triangle with legs (shorter sides) a and b, and hypotenuse (the longest side) c, the sum of the squares of the sides will be equal to the square of the hypotenuse ($a^2 + b^2 = c^2$). Note that in the following right triangle, $3^2 + 4^2 = 5^2$.

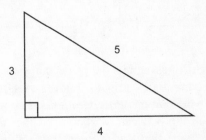

Apply Reasoning Skills

Reasoning skills include drawing conclusions using the principles of similarity, congruence, parallelism, and perpendicularity; and using inductive and deductive reasoning. Geometric figures are *similar* if they have the exact same shapes, even if they do not have the same sizes. In transformational geometry, two figures are said to be similar if and only if a similarity transformation maps one figure onto the other. In the figure that follows, triangles A and B are similar.

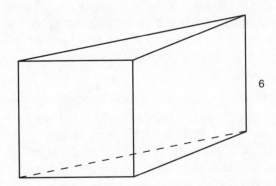

A cylinder is like a prism in that it has parallel faces, but its rounded "side" is smooth. The formula for finding the volume of a cylinder is the same as the formula for finding the volume of a prism: the area of the cylinder's base is multiplied by the height. The volume of the cylinder in the following figure is approximately 628 cubit units ($5 \times 5 \times \pi \times 8$).

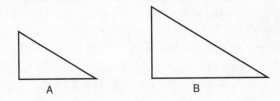

Corresponding angles of similar figures have the same measure, and the lengths of corresponding sides are proportional. In the following similar triangles, $\angle A \cong \angle D$ (meaning "angle A is congruent to angle D") $\angle B \cong \angle E$, and $\angle C \cong \angle F$. The corresponding sides of the following triangles are proportional, meaning that

$$\frac{AB}{DE} = \frac{BC}{EF} = \frac{CA}{FD}$$

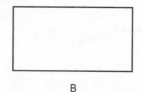

Figures are *congruent* if they have the same shape *and* size. (Congruent figures are also similar.) In the following figure, rectangles A and B are congruent.

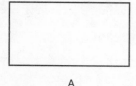

Straight lines within the same plane that have no points in common (that is, they never cross) are parallel lines. Note that the term *parallel* is used to describe the relationship between two coplanar lines that do not intersect. Lines that are not coplanar—although they never cross—are not considered to be parallel. Coplanar lines crossing at right angles (90°) are perpendicular.

When presented with math or logic problems, including geometry problems, *deductive reasoning* may be helpful. Deductive reasoning is reasoning from the general to the specific, and it is supported by deductive logic. Here is an example of deductive reasoning:

All humans who have walked on the moon are males (a general proposition). Neil Armstrong walked on the moon, therefore he is a male (a specific proposition).

Note that conclusions reached via deductive reasoning are only sound if the original assumptions are actually true. With *inductive* reasoning, a general rule is inferred from specific observations (which may be limited). Moving from the statement, "All fish that I have ever seen have fins" (specific but limited observa-

tions) to "All fish have fins" (a general proposition) is an example of inductive reasoning. Conclusions arrived at via inductive reasoning are not necessarily true. An example of how logical reasoning can be used to solve a geometry problem is given hereafter. (In this case *deductive* reasoning is used to find the measure of $\angle J$.)

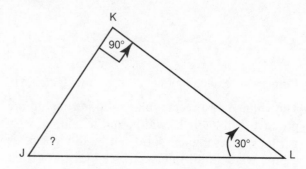

The sum of the measures of the three angles of any triangle is 180° (a general proposition). The sum of the measures of $\angle K$ and $\angle L$ is 120°, therefore the measure of $\angle J$ is 60° (a specific proposition).

Graphic Representations

On the TExES, teacher candidates are required to study graphs, charts, and tables and answer questions based on the information presented. Four kinds of graphs are generally used in grades PK to grade 4—pictorial, bar, pie, and line.

Pictorial graphs are the most concrete representation of information. They represent a transition from the real object graphs to symbolic graphs (Sperry Smith, 2001). These are usually used to introduce children to graphing in PK through grade 1. For example, the teacher can use pictures of pizzas and hot dogs to represent the number of children that prefer one food over the other.

Bar graphs are used to represent two elements of a **single** subject. For example, the bar graphs that follows presents the number of books read by a group of students. This graph presents in a concrete fashion that child E was the top reader with 5 books, while child A is the one with the lowest number of books read.

Number of Books Read in April

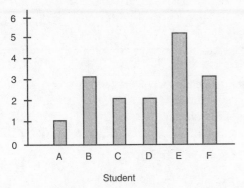

Student

Line graphs present information in a similar fashion as the bar graphs, but it uses points and lines. This type of representation is more abstract for children and is therefore more challenging for them. A line graph tracks one or more subjects. One element is usually time, over which the other element increases, decreases, or remains static. The following line graph depicts U.S. immigration statistics from 1820 to 2000.

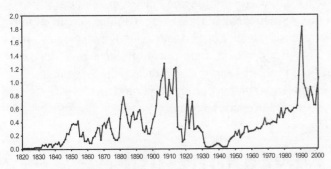

Pie charts are used to help visualize relationships based on percentages of a subject. The figure is divided based on the percentages out of a possible 100%. This graph appears to be easy to read, which is deceptive. It requires an understanding of percentages, which makes it inappropriate for children in the early grades. A pie graph representing food preferences follows.

Food Preferences

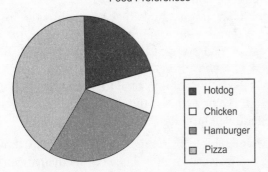

- Hotdog
- Chicken
- Hamburger
- Pizza

Units of Measurement

TEKS require that students in kindergarten through grade 4 become familiar with and apply knowledge of measurement using both U.S. Customary (standard) and metric systems.

Customary Units

- Customary units of length include inches, feet, yards, and miles.

- Customary units of weight include ounces, pounds, and tons.

- Customary units of capacity (or volume) include teaspoons, tablespoons, cups, pints, quarts, and gallons.

Metric Units

- Metric units of length include millimeters, centimeters, meters, and kilometers. The centimeter is the basic metric unit of length, at least for short distances. There are about 2.5 centimeters to 1 inch. The kilometer is a metric unit of length used for longer distances. It takes more than 1.5 kilometers to make a mile. A very fast adult runner could run a kilometer in about three minutes.

- Metric units of weight include grams and kilograms. The gram is the basic metric unit of mass (which for many purposes is the same as *weight*). A large paper clip weighs about 1 gram. It takes about 28 grams to make 1 ounce.

- Metric units of capacity include milliliters and liters. The liter is the basic metric unit of volume (or capacity). A liter is slightly smaller than a quart, so it takes more than four liters to make a gallon.

Table 2-4 presents an overview of these two systems of measurement.

Table 2-4. Units of Measurement

U.S. Customary	Metric System
Linear 12 inches = 1 foot 3 feet = 1 yard 1760 yards = 1 mile 5280 feet = 1 mile	Linear 10 millimeter = 1 centimeter 100 centimeter = 1 meter 1000 meters = 1 kilometer
Liquid 1 gallon = 4 quarts 1 quart = 2 pints 1 pint = 2 cups 1 pint = 16 ounces 1 cup = 8 ounces	Liquid 1 liter = 1000 milliliters (ml) A liter is more than 1 quart.
Weight 1 ton = 2000 pounds 1 pound = 16 ounces	Weight 1 kilogram = 1000 grams (paper clip) 1 gram = 1000 milligrams (grain of salt)

Competency 015 (Mathematical Process)

The teacher understands mathematical processes and knows how to reason mathematically, solve mathematical problems, and make mathematical connections within and outside of mathematics.

The National Council of Teachers of Mathematics (NCTM) and the Texas Essential Knowledge and Skills (TEKS) have emphasized the importance of teaching mathematical reasoning for children from kindergarten through grade 12. TEKS requires children to explore mathematical reasoning as early as kindergarten. This requirement presents a challenge for teachers since the ability to perform operations involving logical reasoning requires some level of cognitive maturity and the ability to think abstractly. From kindergarten to grade 2, children must understand the principles and patterns of the number system and the symbols used to represent numbers. Principles of measurement and basic geometry are also introduced early in the process. In grades 1 and 2, children begin using quantitative reasoning and basic algorithms for addition and subtraction.

Beginning in grade 3 and continuing throughout elementary school, students continue improving their basic knowledge of the number system and the abstraction of mathematical reasoning. Children begin exploring basic algebraic, geometric, and spatial reasoning. They also master multiplication facts and division. Word problems and mathematical reasoning are heavily emphasized in third-grade preparation for TEKS, which is offered in grades 3 to 12.

Developmental Considerations

Children in PK through kindergarten might have problems understanding basic number systems and how numbers are presented symbolically. They might have difficulties dealing with measurement activities that require them to master the principle of *conservation*. They might think that an apple split in half is more than a single apple, or a soda drink in a tall and narrow glass might be more than the same liquid poured in a shorter and wider glass. These cognitive and reasoning limitations tend to disappear as children develop. By first grade, the principle of conservation is generally acquired.

Mathematics instruction in kindergarten through grade 4 involves not only knowing mathematical processes but also being able to determine when a given process is required. Children must develop the ability to reason through word problems and understand the type of answer required. Most third graders can do addition, subtraction, multiplication, and even division. However, they might have difficulties with word problems and problem-solving activities that require them to identify the appropriate mathematical process. They might also have problems understanding questions involving multiple steps and deciding on the appropriate answer. The word problem that follows represents an example of this challenge.

> *Joe can place a maximum of 5 apples in a paper sack. If he needs to put 32 apples in sacks, how many sacks does he need?*

In this example, most students will know that the problem calls for division—32 divided by 5, which will yield the expected number of 6.4. Some students will provide 6.4 as the answer, but the real question is, How many sacks does Joe need? Children will have to reason that paper sacks cannot be divided; thus the answer cannot be 6.4 but 7 paper sacks.

Mathematical reasoning is crucial for understanding and using mathematics. This type of contextual or situational reasoning is certainly important, and questions such as the preceding one have a solid place in the curriculum and on state tests. Logical reasoning is the foundation for understanding mathematics and its use in life.

Promoting Reasoning Skills

Teachers must create opportunities to motivate children to engage in exploratory mathematics to develop logical thinking. For the early grades this exploration can be done in *learning centers*, where children have the opportunity to work with blocks, shapes, and other manipulatives (Lowery, Schull, and Lamb, 2004). The mathematics learning centers are designed to allow children exposure to carefully selected manipulatives. These manipulatives are selected to teach mathematics concepts in an indirect fashion through fun and relaxing activities. To enhance the value of this activity, teachers can guide children in the use of manipulatives through the use of questions to guide them in the mastery of the intended instructional objective.

In addition to exposure to mathematics concepts in learning centers, teachers should guide children to apply mathematics concepts in real-life situations. Role play involving problem solving can be used to guide children in the application of mathematics concepts in real-life situations. For example, a role-play activity involving ordering food in a restaurant can be easily organized for third- or fourth-grade students. A group of children can be given a budget to order food in a restaurant. They have to read the menu and determine how much food they can buy and stay within the budget. In making this decision, the group must estimate the cost of the meals, the taxes, and possible tips. These types of activities can guide children to understand basic mathematical concepts, including the value of money, the tax system, and the use of mathematics in daily life.

Mathematics in Daily Living

Mathematical concepts are an integral part of our daily life. Children should be encouraged to pay attention to daily activities and identify the mathematical principles used to perform the activity or the task. A simple visit to the local supermarket requires some level of mathematical development to communicate effectively. For instance, reading product labels requires an understanding of weight and measurements. It also requires knowledge of the standard and metric systems and the value of money. Without this kind of knowledge, it would be practically impossible to make intelligent decisions. Consider the following situation. A consumer is trying to decide between two products—a kilogram of coffee for $3.99 or 2 pounds of the same coffee for $3.99. What item represents the best value? In order to make this decision, the consumer must have an understanding of the *standard* and *metric* systems of measurement. Most consumers in the United States will probably go with 2 pounds because they are familiar with the *standard* system of measurement. However, this option is not the best value for the money because 1 kilogram is equivalent to 2.2 pounds. Parents can present this kind of problem to children and ask them to help in the decision-making process. When mathematics is used in real-life situations, it becomes more meaningful and easier to internalize.

Integration of Mathematics in Content Areas

Mathematics is a significant component of content area instruction. It is practically impossible to teach a content area without addressing mathematical concepts in some form or shape. For example, a lesson on the American flag can be easily expanded to introduce geometry and the concept of symmetry or the lack of symmetry. Children can probably notice that the flag represents a rectangle and that rectangles are symmetrical figures. This fact can lead children to develop faulty assumptions like the one presented in the following syllogism:

> *Rectangles are symmetrical figures;*
> *the American flag is a rectangle;*
> *thus, the American flag is symmetrical.*

An explanation on the concept of symmetry can lead children to understand the fallacy represented in the syllogism. The design of the flag and the distribution of the stars and the stripes within the rectangle make it asymmetrical. Children can also compare the original flag with 13 stars—made by Betsy Ross—with the current version with 50 stars. They can count the number of stars and compare them with the number of stripes. Simple computation can be done with the number of stars, white stripes, and red stripes. Finally, children can be led to identify the age of the flag (i.e., the age of the flag from its official adoption in 1777 to the present). These types of activities can lead children to understand the interconnectedness of the content area and, most importantly, the value of mathematics.

Thematic Units

Thematic instruction is the organization of curriculum content based on themes or topics. Thematic instruction integrates basic disciplines like reading, math, music, art, and science with the exploration of broad subjects like *American Indians*, *Flags over Texas*, *State symbols*, *river systems in Texas*, *the rain forest*, *recycling resources*, and so on. The selection of the theme can be done schoolwide, by grade, or by individual teacher.

Thematic planning provides opportunities for the students to hear similar information in various instructional segments and from a variety of sources. Additionally, it allows students opportunities to apply cognitive processes and creativity through content area instruction based on real-life situations. For example, a theme for fourth graders can be "Native American groups." Students can discuss different aspects of the lives and accomplishments of native peoples, emphasizing important components from each of the content areas, such as how many tribes there were or what was the population of a specific tribe (mathematics), where they lived (geography), when they lived there (history), and what stories they told (reading/language arts).

Planning and Organization of Thematic Units

There are several important elements that teachers must consider when planning thematic units. The basic steps are as follows (Fredericks, Blake-Kline, and Kristo, 1997).

Selecting the Theme Identify a theme, taking into account the interest to children, relevance of the topic, and the connection to the state curriculum. The theme should be broad enough to allow the integration of content areas. For example, a topic like "our solar system" is broad enough to cover every content area in the curriculum. However, a topic like "gold fish" might be too limited in scope to allow the easy integration of subjects.

Designing the Integrated Curriculum The state curriculum (TEKS) should be the guiding force in the organization of the integrated curriculum. Once this connection is established, teachers must identify the main principles or generalization about the theme. Using the generalizations, teachers need to identify the key objectives to involve each content area and the materials needed to implement instruction.

Gathering Materials for the Unit Gathering materials for the unit can be challenging for first-year teachers. They should request input from veteran teachers and from the school librarian. Some of the key considerations when selecting materials are as follows:

- The materials should focus on the same set of generalizations/principles and each of the content areas.

- Materials should include narratives, expositions, drama, poems, and a variety of materials and resources —books, magazines, newspapers, movies, Internet materials, videotapes, and audiotapes, and so on.

- Materials should also represent a range of thinking abilities and literacy development, including materials written in a language other than English.

- Materials should represent the home as well as the school culture and language of the students.

Designing Instruction Thematic instruction minimizes the artificial boundaries created through traditional course scheduling. The fixed course scheduling for the content areas can now be combined into larger segments where multiple content areas are delivered in an integrated manner. When designing instruction for children in the early grades, teachers must take into account the developmental characteristics of the children to keep them focus and engaged.

Arranging Thematic Materials and Activities Traditionally, thematic units are organized into three main segments—introduction to the unit, presentation of the content, and a closing activity. The opening activity is designed to motivate children and to get them interested in the theme. Children are exposed to the goals and the steps in the presentation of the theme. The presentation of the content is done through various coordinated lessons and activities. The closing activity is designed to review and draw together the concepts learned and to celebrate the mastery of the content.

Historical Development of Mathematics

Every culture has developed some form of functional mathematical concept. In most cases, the accomplishments of these civilizations have been transmitted to and enhanced by other groups. This transmission of knowledge and its cumulative effects have resulted in the creation of the modern-day mathematics used around the world. Some of the key civilizations that impacted the development of mathematics in the Western world are discussed next.

Egyptians and Babylonians

The first mathematicians that impacted the development of modern-day mathematics were from the ancient civilizations of Babylon and Egypt around the third millennium BCE (Joyce, 2006). The ancient Egyptians wrote numbers using hieroglyphs to represents the numbers 1, 10, 100, 1,000, 10,000, and 1,000.000 (Sperry Smith, 2001). They used numbers into the millions for practical purposes like managing resources and for building large-scale public structures like temples and pyramids.

The Babylonians made great advances in science, math, and specifically in astronomy. They also developed tables for multiplication, division, and square and cube roots. One of the greatest accomplishments of Babylonian civilization was the development of a number system with a base of 60. This number system constituted the foundation for the advanced mathematics evolution that followed the Egyptians and Babylonians.

Greeks

The Greeks built on the accomplishments of the Egyptians and Babylonians and further developed the field of mathematics. Most historians believe that the formal study of mathematics as a discipline began with the Athenian Greek school of Thales and Pythagoras (Bailey, 2006). Thales (640–550 BCE) was a merchant who traveled extensively and became acquainted with Egyptian mathematics. Some of his contributions include the notions that a circle is bisected by the diameter, angles at the base of an isosceles triangle are equal, and the angle in a semicircle is right (Joyce, 2006). Pythagoras, his former pupil, followed Thales's ideas and eventually became one of the leading figures of Greek mathematics. Pythagoras taught that there is a basic relation between harmony and mathematics. He was also a pioneer in linking geometry with numbers, as exemplified by the Pythagorean theorem. Some authorities label Thales and Pythagoras as the founders of Greek mathematics.

It was after the early Athenian Greeks that the Alexandrian Greeks emerged as the leaders in the study of science and mathematics. Around 300 BCE, Ptolemy founded the university at Alexandria, Egypt, which became the center of learning for the Western world. This institution became the leading force in the study of mathematics, contributing multiple discoveries and some of the greatest thinkers of the time. Two of the leading figures that emerged during this period were Archimedes and Euclid.

Archimedes calculated the distances of the planets from the Earth and constructed a spherical planetarium imitating the motions of the sun, moon, and six then-known planets. He also made multiple discoveries with scientific and military applications.

Euclid was one of the most influential Greek mathematicians in the world. He is believed to have learned geometry from the students of Plato. He is famous for providing a complete record of the mathematics accomplishments of Ancient Greece (Gustafson & Frisk, 1991). He wrote several books on the elements of geometry. His mathematics knowledge has served as the standard mathematics textbook for over two thousand years (Lewis, 2006).

The Greeks also discovered that real numbers could not accurately express all mathematical values. Based on this need, they developed the concept of irrational numbers (Joyce, 2006). An irrational number cannot be expressed as a fraction. In decimal form, numbers do not repeat in a pattern or terminate; they continue to infinity. Some examples of irrational numbers are as follows:

$$\pi = 3.141592654\ldots \text{ and } \sqrt{2} = 1.414213562\ldots$$

Hindus

Around the fifth century CE, the Hindus developed a system of mathematics that allowed astronomical calculations. They also developed a technique of computation into modern-day algebra (Crystalink, 2006).

The Concept of the Zero

Some historians believe that the concept of zero used today originated in India around 650 CE (Crystalink, 2006; Joyce, 2006; Smith, 1953). Others suggest that it was perfected from the work of Greek astronomers (O'Connor & Robertson, 2000). However, all seem to agree that eventually, the Arabs used the concept of the

zero to develop the current system of enumeration used in the world.

The concept of zero was also developed separately by the Mayans in 700 CE; however, there is no evidence to suggest that the Mayan concept of zero impacted the development of mathematics beyond the Maya empire in Central America. The zero that we know today came from the Hindu tradition (Crystalink, 2006; Joyce, 2006).

Around the thirteenth century, the Arab and other Islamic groups invaded the Hindu regions. They collected the mathematic knowledge of the Hindus and translated this into Arabic. Perhaps as a result of contacts during the Crusades of the tenth through the thirteenth centuries, Christian kingdoms from Western Europe learned about the mathematic accomplishment of the Hindus and Arabs.

Arab Contributions

The Arabs were the first civilization to solve sophisticated algebraic equations currently used in science and engineering—quadratic equations. They also developed and perfected geometric algebra. Arab mathematicians used the work of the Greeks in geometry and improved the development of the field. They founded the *non-Euclidian* geometry and made advances in trigonometry (Arabic News, 1998). The greatest contributions of the Arabs were the development of the numeric system and the diffusion of the cumulative knowledge of mathematics to the world.

The Number System

The number system used in modern days is described as Hindu-Arabic numeration system. It uses numbers from 1 to 9 and the zero. Historians seem to agree that the Hindus contributed to the development of the base-10 digit system and the Arabs perfected it and spread it through the world (Sperry Smith, 2001).

The cumulative knowledge the Babylonians, Egyptians, and Greeks was translated from Greek into Arabic. At the same time, the mathematic accomplishments of the Hindus were also translated into Arabic. The collective knowledge of these civilizations and the improvement and innovations developed in the Arab world became the mathematics of Western Europe and, over a period of several hundred years of further development, became the mathematics of the world.

Contributions from Other Civilizations

Other civilizations, like the Mayans and the Aztecs, made significant progress in mathematics. The Mayan civilization around 700 CE developed an elaborate calendar and the mathematical concept of zero. The Mayans also had highly advanced knowledge of astronomy, engineering, and the arts.

The Aztec civilization flourished around 1325 BCE. The Aztecs were also skilled builders and engineers, accomplished astronomers, and mathematicians. Like the Egyptians, they used mathematic principles for functional purposes like engineering to build pyramids, palaces, plazas, and canals.

There are other places in the world that developed significant mathematic accomplishments. China, Japan, and several kingdoms from Africa are examples of civilizations that made sizeable progress in mathematics; however, their accomplishments did not have a direct impact on the development of mathematics in the Western world. For a detailed analysis of the historical development of mathematics and the contribution of various civilizations, see the "History of Mathematics" website, maintained by David E. Joyce of Clark University in Worcester, Massachusetts.

References

Arabic News. (1998). Arab contribution to mathematics and the introduction of the zero. Retrieved on May 29, 2006, from *http://www.arabicnews.com/ansub/daily/day/980422/199042208.html*

Bailey, E. C. (2006). *A brief history of mathematics*. Retrieved on May 29, 2006, from *http://www.oxford.emory.edu/oxford/restricted/university/Classes/Chen/Calculus/History/HistorybyECB.pdf*

Bellonio, J. L. (2006). *Multi-sensory manipulatives in mathematics: Linking the abstract to the concrete*. Yale-New Haven Teachers Institute. Retrieved on January 3, 2006, from *http://www.yale.edu/ynhti/curriculum/units/2001/6/01.06.12.x.html#f*

Crystalinks (2006). Ancient and lost civilizations. Retrived July 10, 2006, from *http://www.crystalinks.com/ancient.html*

Fredericks, A. D., Blake-Kline, B., & Kristo, J. V. (1997). *Teaching the integrated language arts: Process and practice*. New York: Longman.

Graeme, M. (2006). *Properties of equality*. Mathematic help. Retrieved on June 2, 2006, from *http://mcraefamily.com/MathHelp/BasicArithmetic.htm*

Gustafson, R. D., & Frisk, P. D. (1991). *Elementary geometry*. New York: John Wiley & Sons, Inc.

Joyce, D. E. (2006). *History of mathematics*. Department of Mathematics and Computer Science at Clark University. Retrieved on May 29, 2006, from *http://aleph0.clarku.edu/~djoyce/mathhist/mathhist.html*

Lewis, G. (2006). *Euchild's mathematics*. Freedom in Education. Retrieved on June 6, 2006, from *http://www.freedom-in-education.co.uk/Euclid/euclid.htm*

Lowery, N. V., Schull, R. M., & Lamb, C. E. (2004). *Preparing to teach mathematics*. In Janice L. Nath and John Ramsey. Preparing for the Texas PreK-4 teacher certification: A guide to the comprehensive TExES content areas exam, 88–147. Boston: Allyn and Bacon.

NCTM. (2000). *Principles and Standards for School Mathematics*. National Council of Teachers of Mathematics. [online version] Retrieved on May 24, 2006, from *http://www.nctm.org/standards/*

O'Connor, J. J., and Robertson, E. F. (2000). *A history of zero*. Retrieved on May 29, 2006, from *http://www.groups.dcs.st-andac.uk/history/HistTopic/Zero.htm*l

Shodor Education Foundation, Inc.—SEF. (2006). *Numbers and their properties*.

Department of Chemistry. The University of North Carolina at Chapel Hill.

Smith, D. E. (1953). *History of mathematics*. Boston: Ginn.

Sperry Smith, S. (2001). *Early childhood mathematics*. 2nd ed. Boston: Allyn and Bacon.

TEA. (2006). Texas Essential Knowledge and Skills. Texas Administrative Code (TAC), Title 19, Part II Chapter 111. Texas Essential Knowledge and Skills for Mathematics. Retrieved on May 24, 2006, from *http://www.tea.state.tx.us/teks/*

U.S. Department of Labor. (1998–1999). Occupational outlook handbook. Bureau of Labor and Statistics. Bulletin 2500-4. Retrieved on January 3, 2006, from *http://www.pueblo.gsa.gov/cic_text/employ/compnmath/oohmath.htm*

Weisstein, E. W. (2006). *Polyhedron*. Math World Web Site. Retrieved on June 2, 2006, from *http://mathworld.wolfram.com/Polyhedron.html*

Wheat, T. (2006). *A state of clear and present danger: A history of American foreign policy during the Cold War* [online]. Retrieved on June 5, 2006, from *http://www.geocities.com/s011023/coldwar9.htm*

Domain III:
Social Studies

Competency 016 (Social Science Instruction)

The teacher uses social science knowledge and skills to plan, organize, and implement instruction and assess learning.

Social Studies Curricula

Social studies is an umbrella term used to encompass the disciplines of history, geography, civics and government, economics, and psychology. All five components have been intertwined with the standards or strands shown in Figure 3-1, which were developed by the National Council for the Teaching of Social Studies in 1997 (NCTSS 2006).

These strands and curriculum standards were used by the Texas Education Agency (TEA) as a foundation to develop the state social studies curriculum for kindergarten through grade 12.

Texas Essential Knowledge and Skills (TEKS) in Social Studies

The Texas Essential Knowledge and Skills (TEKS) is the state curriculum for kindergarten to grade 12. The TEKS organizes the social studies content inductively, from the known to the unknown. Children begin learning about the self in kindergarten and expand their knowledge with each successive grade, eventually encompassing the community, the state, the nation, and the world. A summary of the key components of the social studies curriculum covered in kindergarten through grade 4 follows.

Kindergarten—Child, Home, Family, and Classroom

- The child as an individual
- Home and families
- State and national heritage
- Patriotic holidays and the contribution of historical characters

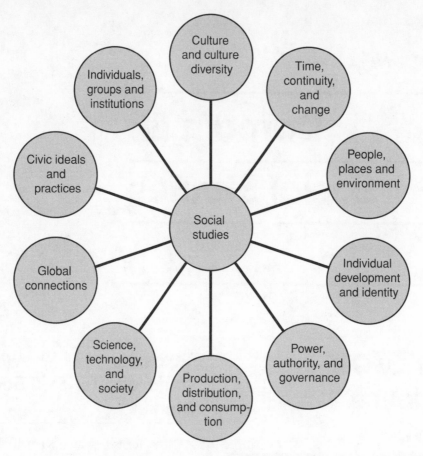

Figure 3-1. Social Studies Strands

Grade 1—Child's Relationship to the Classroom, School, and Community

- The concept of chronology developed by distinguishing among past, present, and future
- Anthems and mottoes of Texas and the United States

Grade 2—Local Community

- Impact of significant individuals and events in the history of the community, state, and nation
- Concepts of time and chronology by measuring calendar time by days, weeks, months, and years
- Relationship between the physical environment and human activities
- Functions of government and services that they provide

Grade 3—How Individuals Change Their Communities and the World

- Past and present heroes and their contributions
- People who overcame obstacles
- Economic, cultural and scientific contributions made by individuals

Grade 4—History of Texas

- History of Texas from its beginning to the present
- Events and individuals of the nineteenth and twentieth centuries
- Human activity and physical features of regions in Texas and the Western Hemisphere
- Native Americans in Texas and the Western Hemisphere

- European exploration and colonization
- Types of Native American governments
- Characteristics of Spanish and Mexican colonial governments

Using Maps and Globes

Symbolic representation can pose challenges for children in kindergarten through grade 4. Maps and globes are tools for representing space symbolically. In the early grades, the main purpose for using globes is to familiarize children with the basic roundness of the earth and to begin developing a global perspective. It can also be used to study the proportion of land and water. In kindergarten through third grade, teachers should use a simplified 12-inch globe. Generally, this type of globe uses no more than three colors to represent land elevation and no more than two to represent water depth. For this age group, the globe should include only the largest rivers, cities, and oceans. In grades 4 through 6, students can use a 16-inch globe containing additional details. Generally, seven colors are used to represent land elevation and three colors to represent water depth.

Activities for Students in Kindergarten through Grade 4

Teaching map concepts in kindergarten through grade 4 should include the following activities:

- Stress that the globe is a very small representation of the earth.
- Show children how land areas and water bodies are represented on the globe.
- Identify major land and water bodies.
- Show the location of the North Pole and the concept of the Northern Hemisphere, where most of the world's land is located.
- Show the location of the South Pole and the concept of the Southern Hemisphere, where most of the world's water is located.

- Show the relationship and location of the earth in the solar system.
- Use the globe to find the continent, the country, and the city where the children live.
- Encourage children to explore the globe to find places by themselves.
- Compare the size of the continents represented on a globe with their representation on a Mercator's projection—the flat representation.

Latitude and Longitude

The concepts of latitude and longitude are generally covered in fourth grade and up. However, even fourth graders may have difficulty understanding the mathematics involved in the grid system. Children might get confused with these concepts:

- The sizes of the meridians of longitude and the parallels of latitude are not the same. The meridians of longitude have a consistent size, but the parallels of latitude vary in size, becoming smaller as they move away from the equator.
- They might have problems conceptualizing and separating the Western Hemisphere and the Eastern Hemisphere, or the Northern and Southern hemispheres.

  Teachers should use concrete materials like a pumpkin to represent these concepts.

Using Technology Information in Social Studies

Research in social studies involves the use of systematic inquiry. Engaging children in inquiry involves the ability to acquire information from various resources. Inquiry involves the ability to design and conduct investigations, which requires students to develop an understanding of key information in social studies content.

To gather content information, students should become familiar with the various resources used in social sciences research. Those resources include primary and secondary sources, encyclopedias, almanacs, atlases, government documents, artifacts, and oral histories. Information about social studies is available from the Internet; however, students need to evaluate the scholarship of the many sources available and use only those known to be reliable. In addition to sources available electronically, students can use commercially developed programs like *Oregon Trails* and *Where in the World Is Carmen San Diego?* These kinds of interactive programs can expose students to problem-solving skills and social studies content in a fun and supportive environment.

Integration of Social Studies

As mentioned earlier, the teaching of social studies by definition implies integration of content from five disciplines: history, geography, civics and government, economics, and psychology. However, teachers can go beyond this integration and add components from other content areas. The use of a **literature-based approach** is an ideal way to integrate social studies with language arts. Through the use of authentic multicultural literature, teachers can expose children to quality reading and the cultures of the many ethnic and linguistic groups living in the United States.

The use of **thematic units** can also help teachers to integrate the content areas. In this approach, a teacher or teachers select a theme and organize content area instruction around it. Thematic instruction can be done in a self-contained classroom or in a departmental format in which content is taught by several teachers.

Thematic instruction is ideal for English language learners (ELLs) because the use of a common theme in multiple content areas makes content more cognitively accessible for them. For example, in a unit on the *solar system*, the names of the planets and the terminology used to describe the system can be introduced and repeated in several subjects through the duration of the unit. The presentation and repetition of content in different subjects and conditions allows students the opportunity to develop English vocabulary while learning content.

Graphic Representations of Historical Information

Information in social studies can be presented in a graphic form through the use of graphs and charts to make content accessible to all children, including ELLs.

Graphs

The most commonly used graphs are the pictorial graph, the bar graph, the pie or circle graph, and the line graph. The pictorial graph is the most concrete type of graph because it uses a picture of the object being represented. Bar graphs are more concrete than pie graphs. Although the pie graph appears to be simple enough for children in the elementary grades, students need to understand the concept of percentages to correctly interpret the meaning of this type of graph, and the concept of percentages is not acquired until late in the elementary grades. At first, teachers can use real-life situations to guide students in the construction of graphs. For example, teachers can create a simple graph showing information about students in the classroom, like the number of boys and girls in the classroom or their color or food preferences. Figure 3-2 shows the results of a poll on the favorite foods of first-grade students.

Teachers can use more sophisticated graphs like the pie to represent research information. For example,

Food Preference for 1st Graders

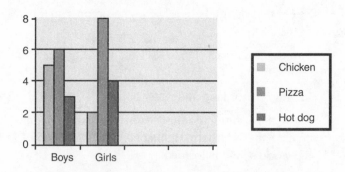

Figure 3-2. Bar Graph—Food Preferences for First Graders

children can take 5 to 10 minutes a day to observe the types of transportation used by people in the neighborhood and prepare a graph similar to the one presented in Figure 3-3. Teachers can use this information to guide children to make inferences about the information contained in the graph. Why are so many people using pickup trucks as a mode of transportation? Why are only a small number of people walking?

Charts

Charts can be used to record information and present ideas in a concise way. Charts are ideal for promoting concept formation in a concrete fashion. **Data retrieval charts** are used to gather and keep track of data gathered from research, observation, or experimentation. The chart is constructed to allow the easy comparison of two or more sets of data. For example, students could use the chart shown in Table 3-1 to record information about the foods of the ethnic groups represented in their classroom.

Narrative charts are used to show events in a sequence. For example, students can develop charts showing the steps in making their favorite dishes. A narrative chart can also be used to present a time line of historical events. An example of a simple time line is one that shows a child's personal history. Because children in kindergarten through grade 2 might have problems conceptualizing time, initial exposure to time lines should begin with things that they did yesterday, things that they are doing today, and things that will be done tomorrow. Starting in third grade, children can begin introducing

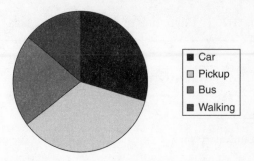

Figure 3-3. Pie Graph—Methods of Transportation

> **I was born (1990)—I moved to Dallas (1995)—I came to Ms. Perk's class (1995)**
>
> **—Brother Mike was born (1996)—I got my first bike—Met my best friend, Mary . . .**

Figure 3-4. A Time Line—My History

more challenging components, like the ones listed in Figure 3-4.

A tabulation or classification chart provides an orderly columnar display information for comparison. For example, Table 3-2 compares data from the 2000 U.S. census.

Using developmentally appropriate vocabulary, teachers can guide students to recall or infer data from the chart.

A **pedigree chart** shows the origin and development of something. Examples are a person's family, the

Table 3-1. Data Retrieval Chart—Ethnic Foods

Ethnic Group	Foods Served for Breakfast	Foods Served for Dinner	Foods served on Special Days
Mexican American			
Puerto Rican			
African American			
Italian American			

Table 3-2. A Tabulation or Classification Chart—U.S. and Texas Populations by Ethnic Group

Ethnic Group	Percentage of U.S. Population	Percentage of Texas Population
White	75.1%	71%
African American	12.3%	11.5%
Asian American	3.8%	0.6%
Hispanic	12.5%	32.0%
Native American	0.1%	0.6%
Population Totals	**281,421,906**	**20,851,820**

Source: U.S. Census Bureau, 2000

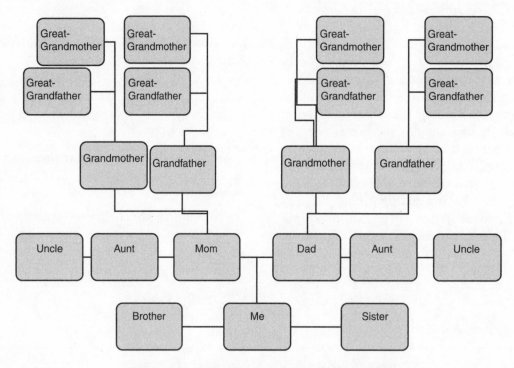

Figure 3-5. A Pedigree Chart—My Family Tree

pedigree line of a purebred dog, and the development of a political party. Figure 3-5 presents a pedigree chart.

An **organizational chart** shows the structure of an organization, like a school or business. Figure 3-6 is a chart showing the typical organization of an elementary school.

A **flowchart** shows a process involving changes at certain points—for example, the process used to complete an academic degree.

Figure 3-7 presents a typical program sequence for bilingual education students.

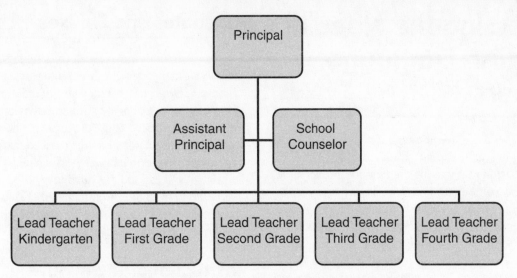

Figure 3-6. Organizational Chart—Elementary School

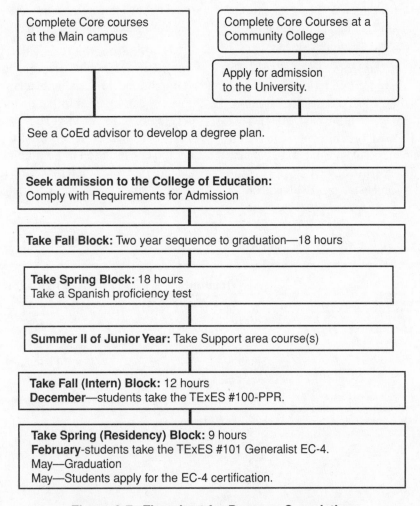

Figure 3-7. Flowchart for Program Completion

Addressing the Needs of English Language Learners

English language learners can find social studies instruction quite challenging; thus, teachers need to modify instruction to make the content comprehensible for this group. Some textbooks have been written with ELLs in mind. These books use numerous visual and graphic representations to make the content cognitively accessible to children learning English. For example, *Adventure Tales of America*, written by Jody Potts (1994), is an American history book that uses cartoons and illustrations to explain complex concepts like the processes of electing the president and making a bill into law. It also uses concrete time lines to represent the historical development of the nation. The illustrations give ELLs the fundamental meanings of important concepts from which teachers can develop lessons.

Other books integrate language instruction with content to deliver both components in a contextualized format. One example is the ESL series titled *Avenues*, published by Hampton Brown (Schifini et al. 2004). This set of books presents ESL lessons in conjunction with content from other disciplines. The integration of content and language is one of the most effective strategies to promote content area mastery and language development.

Cognates and Suffixes

English and most Western languages have been heavily influenced by the Greek and Roman civilizations. The association has resulted in the creation of multiple cognates—words that are similar in two languages. Most of the sophisticated English words in the content areas and especially in social studies are cognates of Spanish and other Western languages. Teachers can use these similarities to expand the vocabulary of students and enhance content area comprehension. Table 3-3 presents examples of the connection between English and Spanish words (Rosado and Salazar 2002–2003).

Instructional Techniques to Support ELLs

Teachers need to implement a variety of activities to teach the state curriculum to ELLs at the **grade level** and **complexity** required of native English speakers.

Scaffolding was originally used to describe the way in which adults support children in their efforts to communicate in the native language (L1). The same concept can be used to facilitate language and content development for ELLs. The term *scaffolding* alludes to the provisional structure used to provide support during the construction of a building and eliminated when the structure is complete. Following this analogy, ELLs receive language support to make content cognitively

Table 3-3. Common Greek and Latin Roots and Affixes

Roots/Affixes	Meaning	English/Spanish Cognates
phobia (fobia) Xeno	Fear of Foreigners or strangers	Xenophobia / Xenofobia
Phono (Fono) logy(ía)	Sound Study of	Phonology / Fonología
Photo (Foto) graphy (grafia)	Light Graph, form	Photography / Fotografía
Homo sapiens	Same, man Able to think	Homo sapiens / Homo sapiens
Democracy (cracia)	People Government	Democracy / Democracia

accessible to them until they achieve mastery in the second language (L2); once that mastery is accomplished, the language support is eliminated.

Graphic organizers are visuals used to show relationships. These are the most common graphic organizers:

- A **semantic web or tree diagram** shows the relationship between main ideas and subordinated components.

- A **time line** presents a visual summary of chronological events and is ideal for showing historical events or events in a sequence.

- A **flowchart** shows cause-and-effect relationships and can be used to show steps in a process, like the process for admission to a school or program.

- A **Venn diagram** uses circles to compare common and unique elements of two or three distinct components, such as properties of numbers, elements of stories, or events or civilizations (like the Maya, Inca, and Aztec shown in Figure 3-8).

The **SQ4R** is a study strategy in which the learner is engaged in the entire reading process. The acronym stands for **survey**, **question**, **read**, **reflect**, **recite**, and **review**. During the **survey** part, readers examine the headings and major components of the text to develop predictions and generate questions. Through these **questions**, students establish the purpose for reading. As they **read**, students look for answers to the questions they generated. They monitor their comprehension as they **reflect**, write a summary, and **recite** the content they learned. Finally, they **review** to evaluate how much they learned about the content.

Reciprocal teaching is an instructional activity designed for struggling readers, with the teacher engaging students in a dialogue about a specific portion of a text. The dialogue is structured to encourage students to follow these steps:

1. Summarize the content of a passage

2. Ask a question about the main idea

3. Clarify difficult parts of the content

4. Predict what will come next

Strategies to Integrate Language Arts and Social Studies

Sheltered English

Sheltered English is an instructional approach designed to make content comprehensible for ELLs (Echevarria, Vogt, and Short 2000). In the program, children are "sheltered" from the pressure of competing with native English learners. To deliver comprehensible input, content instruction is linguistically simplified through contextualized instruction, visual aids, hands-on activities, and body language. Some strategies teachers can use to modify language to make it comprehensible are listed here:

- Control the length and complexity of the sentences. Children respond better to short, simple sentences.

- Introduce technical vocabulary before beginning the lesson.

- Use repetition, restatement, and paraphrasing to clarify concepts.

- Control the speed of delivery, and use a different type of intonation to emphasize important concepts.

- Supplement oral presentations with diagrams, graphic organizers, and manipulatives to make content easier to understand.

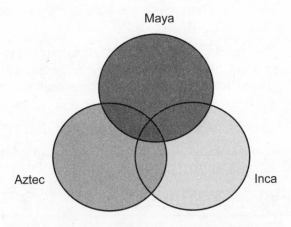

Figure 3-8. Venn Diagram to Compare Three Civilizations

- Help students use drawings and graphic organizers to visualize word problems and experiments, and as tools for communication.

- Guide students in using role-play to represent important concepts.

- Use linguistic modifications, such as repetition and pauses during speech (Parker 2001).

- Make the presentation of content more interactive with comprehension checks.

- Use cooperative learning strategies.

- Organize of content around thematic units.

- Use graphic organizers to simplify and chunk content.

- Emphasize the gist of concepts instead of details.

Sheltered English is most effective in a classroom with students from many language groups who are at least at the intermediate level of English language development (Schifini 1985).

Cooperative learning is a teaching strategy designed to create a low-anxiety learning environment in which students work together in small groups to achieve instructional goals. As a result of this instructional arrangement, students with different levels of ability or language development work collaboratively to support each other to ensure that each member masters the objectives of the lesson. This approach can easily be used to deliver content and language instruction. Traditionally, the strategy is delivered in specific steps (Arends 1998):

1. **Present Goals**—The teacher goes over the objectives of the lesson and provides the motivation.

2. **Present Information**—The teacher presents information to students either verbally or with text.

3. **Organize Students into Learning Teams**—The teacher explains to students how to form learning teams and helps groups make an efficient transition.

4. **Assist Teamwork and Study**—The teacher assists learning teams as they do their work.

5. **Test Students on the Content**—The teacher tests students' knowledge of learning materials as each group presents the results of their work.

6. **Provide Recognition**—The teacher finds ways to recognize both individual and group efforts and achievement.

To emphasize the cooperative nature of the strategy, specific methods were developed to enrich the lessons. These specialized methods are described in the sections that follow.

Student Teams Achievement Divisions (STAD)

1. The teacher presents new academic information to students.

2. Students are divided into four- or five-member learning teams.

3. Team members master the content and then help each other learn the material through tutoring, quizzing one another, or carrying on team discussions.

4. Each student receives an improvement score that helps show the growth he or she has made.

5. Daily or weekly quizzes are given to assess mastery.

6. Each week, through newsletters or a short ceremony, groups and individual students are recognized for showing the most improvement (Slavin 1986).

Group Investigation

1. Students select a subtopic within a general area.

2. The teacher divides the class into small groups, each composed of two to six students. Group composition should be ethnically and academically heterogeneous.

3. The students and the teacher plan specific learning procedures, tasks, and goals.

4. Students carry out the plan using various sources. The teacher monitors the process and offers assistance as needed.

5. The students analyze and evaluate information and plan how they can summarize it in an interesting fashion for possible display or presentation to the class as a whole.

6. The students present their final product.

7. The teacher conducts individual or group evaluation (Thelen 1981).

Think-Pair-Share

This activity was developed as a result of the wait-time research. Wait time research suggest that pausing for few seconds to allow children to reflect on the question can improve the quality of the response and the overall performance of children (Rowe 1986).

1. **Think**—The teacher poses a question and asks students to spend a minute thinking alone about the answer. No talking or walking is allowed.

2. **Pair**—Students pair off and discuss what they have been thinking about, sharing possible answers or information.

3. **Share**—Students share their answers with the whole class. The teacher goes around the classroom from pair to pair until a fourth or a half of the class has a chance to report (Lyman 1981)

Numbered Heads Together

This activity was designed to involve more students in the review of materials covered in class.

1. **Number**—The teacher divides the students into teams with three to five members each and assigns a number to each member.

2. **Question**—The teacher asks a question.

3. **Heads Together**—Students put their heads together to figure out the answer and to be sure *everyone* knows the answer.

4. **Answer**—The teacher calls a number, and students from each group with that number raise their hands and provide the answer (Kagan 1985).

Competency 017 (History)

The teacher demonstrates knowledge of significant historical events and developments and applies social science skills to historical information, ideas, and issues.

World History

The *World History Encyclopedia* divides the history of the world into five periods: Ancient World, Middle Ages, Age of Discovery, Revolution and Industry, and the Modern World (Ganeri Martell, and Williams 1999). A summary of key events in each period is presented here.

The Ancient World (4 Million Years Ago to 500 CE)

Study of the ancient world focuses on the development of the first humans, the first farmers, and the first civilizations. It emphasizes the history of the ancient civilizations of Mesopotamia, Sumeria, Assyria, Babylon, Egypt, the Indus Valley, megalithic Europe, ancient China, Phoenicia, ancient America, ancient Greece, the Celts, the Romans, and empires in Africa and India. Following is a time line of key historical events in the period.

Time Line of the Ancient World

4000 BCE	*Homo sapiens* appear in various regions in the world
3500 BCE	The Sumerians of Mesopotamia invent writing and the wheel
3100 BCE	Egypt becomes unified
2800 BCE	Building begins in Stonehenge, England
2500 BCE	Indus civilization flourishes in India
1600–1100 BCE	Mycenaean control of Greece
1200–400 BCE	Olmec civilization flourishes in western Mexico
1000–612 BCE	New Assyrian Empire flourishes
753 BCE	Foundation of Rome
605–562 BCE	King Nebuchadnezzar rebuilds the city of Babylon
476–431 BCE	Golden age of Athens
336–323 BCE	Alexander the Great rules the world
27 BCE to 14 CE	Augustus rules as the first Roman emperor
476 CE	Western Roman Empire falls

The Middle Ages (500–1400 CE)

This period includes the Byzantine civilization, the rise of Islam, civilizations of the Americas, the Vikings, the feudal system, the Crusades, Genghis Khan and China, the African kingdoms, and the Hundred Years' War. Here is a time line for the Middle Ages.

Time Line for the Middle Ages

500	Eastern Roman (Byzantine Empire) at its peak
600	Teotihuacan civilization flourishes in Mexico
600	Rise of Islam
700	Mayan civilization at its height in Central America
700	Feudal system begins in Europe; peasants serve a lord in exchange for protection
711	Moors invade Spain
750	Abbasid dynasty is founded; Arab Empire at its peak
800	Charlemagne crowned emperor of the Holy Roman Empire
900	Rise of Toltec civilization in Mexico
1000	Vikings land in North America
1095	Muslim Turks take Jerusalem and ban Christian pilgrims from the city
1096–1270	Crusades try to rescue the Jerusalem from the Muslims
1215	Genghis Khan and the Mongols invade China
1271	Marco Polo travels to China from Italy
1300	Renaissance begins in Europe
1325	Aztec found Tenochtitlan near modern-day Mexico City
1453	Fall of the eastern Roman Empire (Constantinople)
1368	Foundation of the Ming dynasty in China
1454	Gutenberg invents the printing machine
1500	Inca Empire at its peak in Peru

Age of Discovery (1400–1700)

This period includes the Renaissance, the development of the Aztec and Inca civilizations, voyages of discovery from Spain and Portugal, African empires, the Reformation, the Ottoman Empire, the Ming dynasty in China, the Dutch Empire, colonization of America, and the slave trade.

Time Line for the Age of Discovery

1441	Portuguese begin slave trade from Africa to Europe
1488	Portuguese explorers reach the southern part of Africa
1492	Columbus sails from Spain to America
1492	Spain becomes unified and expels the Moors
1497	Portuguese reach India
1517	Martin Luther begins the religious Reformation in Europe
1520	Suleiman rules the Ottoman Empire
1522	Magellan travels around the world
1535	Spain completes the conquest of the Aztecs in Mexico and the Incas in Peru
1543	Copernicus suggests that the sun is the center of the universe, not the earth
1571	Europeans defeat the Muslim Ottomans in the battle of Lepanto
1588	England defeats the Spanish Armada and becomes the greatest naval power in the world
1609	Galileo uses a new invention, the telescope, to study the universe
1618	Thirty Years' War begins
1607	England begins the colonization of North America

Revolution and Industry (1700–1900)

This period includes the Russian Empire, the Manchu dynasty in China, the period of Enlightenment in Europe, the growth of Austria and Prussia, the birth of the United States, the French Revolution, the Napoleonic era, the Industrial Revolution, the British Empire, the American Civil War, and the unification of Italy and Germany.

Time Line for the Age of Revolution and Industry

1644	The Manchu overthrow the Ming dynasty of China

1682–1725	Peter the Great rules Russia
1740	Frederick the Great becomes king of Prussia—Domination of Europe
1756–1763	Seven Years' War ensues, with France, Austria, and Russia clashing against Prussia and England
1768	James Cook visits regions in the Pacific
1776	America declares independence from England
1789	French Revolution begins with the fall of the Bastille in Paris
1791	As part of the Enlightenment period, Thomas Paine publishes *The Rights of Man*
1804	Napoleon declares himself emperor of France, beginning the Napoleonic era
1808	Wars for independence begin in Spanish America
1837–1901	British Empire at its peak under Queen Victoria
1848	Year of revolution in all Europe
1869	Union Pacific Railroad links the East and West coasts of the United States
1861–1865	American Civil War

The Modern World (1900–2006)

This period includes the struggle for equal rights for women, World War I, the Russian Revolution, the Great Depression, the rise of fascism, revolution in China, World War II, Israel versus Palestine, the Cold War, the space race, the Korean and Vietnam wars, and globalization.

Time Line for the Modern World

1914	World War I begins when Austria declares war on Serbia and Germany on Russia
1917	Russian Revolution starts when the Bolsheviks, led by Lenin, seize power from the czar
1918	World War I ends; Europe is in ruins, and Germany is heavily punished
1929	Great Depression begins in the United States.

1933	Adolf Hitler achieves power in Germany
1936–1939	Spanish Civil War brings Francisco Franco to power
1939	World War II begins with the invasion of Poland and Czechoslovakia
1941	United States enters World War II
1945	Germany surrenders to the Allied Forces, and Japan surrenders after the United States detonates two atomic bombs in Hiroshima and Nagasaki
1947	Pakistan and India obtain independence from Great Britain
1948–1949	State of Israel is founded in Palestine, and the Arabs declare war
1949	Communist Mao Zedong (Tse-tung) gains control of China
1960	Many countries in Africa gain independence
1965–1972	America participates in the Vietnam War
1969	Neil Armstrong lands on the moon
1990	Germany is reunited
1991	Soviet Union collapses, and the Cold War ends
1994	Free elections in South Africa and the end of apartheid
2001	9/11 Terrorist Attack in New York City and Washington, D.C.
2001	War in Afghanistan against the Taliban
2003	War in Iraq

For details about these historical periods, go to these Web sites: Kidipede—History for Kids: *www.historyforkids.org* and Ancient Mesoamerican Civilizations, created and maintained by Kevin L. Callahan of the University of Minnesota Department of Anthropology: *www.angelfire.com/ca/humanorigins*.

The Industrial Revolution and Modern Technology

The Industrial Revolution began in England in the mid-eighteenth century. Inventions that made mining of fossil fuel (charcoal) easier provided the energy needed to expand and promote industrial development. Improvement on the steam engine and industrial machines led to the mass production of goods and a better distribution system. The economic growth motivated people to leave the rural areas and move to the cities. The following time line highlights inventions that supported the industrial revolution and modern life:

Time Line for Industrial and Technological Development

1769	Richard Arkwright patents the spinning machine powered by a waterwheel
1810	A German, Frederick Koenig invents an improved printing press
1831	An American, Cyrus H. McCormick invents the reaper
1836	Samuel Colt invents the first revolver
1837–1938	Samuel Morse invents the telegraph and Morse code
1846	Ascanio Sobrero, an Italian chemist, invents nitroglycerin
1856	Louis Pasteur invents the process of pasteurization
1858	Jean Lenoir invents an internal combustion engine
1866	Albert Nobel invents dynamite.
1876	Alexander Graham Bell patents the telephone
1885	Gottlieb Daimler invents the first gas engine motorcycle
1900	Ferdinand Von Zeppelin invents a hot air balloon called the zeppelin
1903	The Wright brothers invent the first gas-powered airplane
1905	Albert Einstein publishes the theory of relativity: $E = mc^2$
1914	Henry Ford introduces the assembly line and begins building the first American cars
1928	Biologist Alexander Fleming discovers penicillin
1930	Vannevar Bush at the Massachusetts Institute of Technology in Boston invents the analog computer
1940	Peter Goldmark invents modern color television
1946	The atomic bomb is invented
1952	The hydrogen bomb is invented
1955	The antibiotic tetracycline is invented
1959	Jack Kilby and Robert Noyce invent the microchip
1969	The predecessor of the Internet, called the ARPAnet, is invented
1971	Ray Tomlinson invents Internet-based e-mail
1985	Microsoft invents the Windows program
1988	Digital cellular phones are invented
1990	Tim Berners-Lee created the Internet protocol HTTP and the World Wide Web language HTML

Ancient Civilizations of the Americas

Among the most developed ancient civilizations in the Americas were the Mayas, Toltecs, Olmecs, Aztecs, and Incas.

Mayas

One of the earliest civilizations of Mesoamerica was the Mayan, from regions of Mexico's Yucatan Peninsula, Guatemala, and Honduras. The Mayas developed a highly integrated society with elaborate religious observances for which they built stone and mortar pyramids. The center of the Maya civilization was the city of Chichen Itza and its religious centers, where human victims were sacrificed. The Mayas developed an elaborate calendar, a system of writing, and the mathematical concept of zero. They also had highly advanced knowledge of astronomy, engineering, and art. By the time the Spanish conquerors arrived, most of the Mayan religious centers had been abandoned and the civilization was in decline.

Zapotecs, Olmecs, and Toltecs

Farther north in Mexico, three highly sophisticated civilizations emerged: the Olmecs, Zapotecs, Teotihuacan, and Toltecs. Beginning with the Olmecs, who flourished around 1200 BCE and followed by the Toltecs and Zapotecs, these groups developed highly sophisticated civilizations. They had already begun to use a ceremonial calendar and had built stone pyramids on which they performed religious observances. **Teotihuacan** is the best-known example of religious ceremonial sites built by these civilizations. They developed a partly alphabetic writing system and left codices describing their history, religion, and daily events.

Aztecs

The Aztec civilization achieved the highest degree of development in Mexico. They had a centralized government headed by a king and supported by a large army. The Aztecs were also skilled builders and engineers, accomplished astronomers and mathematicians. They built the famous city of **Tenochtitlan**, with many pyramids, palaces, plazas, and canals. At the peak of their civilization, the Aztecs had a population of about five million.

For information about the civilizations that emerged in Mexico, go to the Web site titled "Teotihuacan: The City of the Gods," hosted by the Arizona State University, at *http://archaeology.la.asu.edu/teo/intro/intrteo.htm* and the National Indian Education Association web site at *www.xmission.com/~amauta/index.htm*.

Incas—Children of the Sun

The Inca civilization covered the modern countries of Ecuador, Peru, and central Chile. Although they were not as advanced in mathematics and the sciences as the Mayans and Aztecs, the Incas had a well-developed political system. They also built a monumental road system to unify the empire. Their civilization was at its peak when the Spanish conquerors arrived in Cuzco, the capital of the empire.

Mound Builders in North America

In North America, two major groups, known as the Woodland and Mississippian peoples, lived in the Great Lakes and Mississippi area. These people built burial mounds dated as early as 500 CE. The Mississippian people built flat-topped mounds as foundations for wooden temples dating from 500 CE. The chiefs and the priests of these groups lived in residences built on the top of the mounds, while the rest of the population lived in houses below. These mound-building civilizations declined gradually and disappeared by the fourteenth century.

Inhabitants of the South and Southwest

In the southwestern United States and northern Mexico, two ancient cultures developed: the Anasazi and the Hohokam. The Anasazi developed adobe architecture consisting of individual apartments, storage areas, and a central plaza. They worked the land extensively, had a highly developed system of irrigation, and made cloth and baskets. The Hohokam built separate stone and timber houses around a central plaza. Neither group developed a written language. Drought and attacks from rival tribes contributed to the decline of these civilizations. Historians believe that the Anasazis built the cliff dwellings at Mesa Verde, Colorado, during the fourteenth and fifteenth centuries to protect themselves from these attacks.

Pueblo Indians

There is evidence to suggest that the Anasazis settled along the Rio Grande and intermarried with the local population, leading to the emergence of the Pueblo people. The Pueblo culture continued and improved on the architectural tradition and farming techniques of their predecessors. They were able to produce drought-resistant corn and squash, which became the foundation of their diet. The Pueblo Indians managed to survive the Spanish conquest and colonization period.

Iroquois

The Iroquois inhabited the area of Ontario, Canada, and Upstate New York for at least 4,500 years before the arrival of Europeans. They hunted and fished, but farming became the main economic activity for the group. The Iroquois had a matrilineal line of descent, with women doing most of the farming to support the community. They developed the Iroquois Confederation to discourage war among the groups and to provide for a common defense.

American History

Colonization

In 1565, the Spaniards established the first successful European settlement in North America near the current city of Jacksonville, Florida. Following the Spaniards, the English attempted to establish a permanent colony on Roanoke, an island off the coast of North Carolina. This colony eventually disappeared. Further north, the Dutch settled colonies in the region of present-day New York and New Jersey. Following the Dutch, numerous private companies received royal charters, or patents, permitting them to begin the colonization process in North America. Three of the first and most successful companies were the Plymouth Company, the Massachusetts Bay Company, and the London Company. The London Company was the first to exercise this patent.

Virginia (1607)

The London Company established the first English colony in Jamestown, Virginia. The leader of the colony was Captain John Smith. Natives of the area captured Smith and sentenced him to death. Pocahontas, daughter of the tribe's chief, intervened and saved his live. Contrary to popular belief, John Smith did not marry Pocahontas; instead, Pocahontas married John Rolfe, a tobacco farmer from the same colony.

Massachusetts (1620)

Plymouth was founded by the Puritans, who fled England to avoid religious persecution. The group obtained a patent from the London Virginia Company. Before arriving at their destination, they wrote the Mayflower Compact, a document containing rules to guide life in the community. This compact established the first type of government in North America.

New Hampshire (1623)

The colony of New Hampshire was founded by two groups. The first group was lead by Captain John Mason, who established a fishing village in 1623. In 1638, a group led by John Wheelwright founded a second settlement called Exeter. That colony began as a proprietorship but eventually became a royal colony.

New Jersey (1623)

The Dutch founded the New Jersey colony in 1623. After taking over the Dutch territory between Virginia and New England in 1664, King George II of England gave these possessions to his brother, the Duke of York. The duke then gave the territory as a proprietary grant to Sir George Carteret and Lord Berkeley. In 1702, New Jersey became an English colony.

New York (1624)

The area of New York was part of New Amsterdam, a possession of the Dutch government. In 1674, the British took control of the territory, and in 1685 New York officially became a royal colony.

Maryland (1633)

In 1632, King Charles I granted a Maryland Charter to Lord Baltimore (George Calvert). In 1633, the colony was established as a refuge for freemen, especially Catholics.

Rhode Island (1636)

The Rhode Island colony was founded by Roger Williams in 1636, and in 1638 an additional part of the colony was settled by Anne Hutchinson. Both Williams and Hutchinson had been banned from Massachusetts for their religious and political views and were looking for sanctuary. The colony was initially a corporation and eventually became a royal colony.

Connecticut (1636)

As early as 1633, Dutch traders had established a permanent settlement near Hartford. After the decline of the Dutch influence in the area, Thomas Hooker established the colony of Connecticut. Hooker and his followers were also seeking religious freedom after being expelled from Massachusetts. In 1662, Connecticut obtained a Royal Charter under the leadership of John Winthrop Jr.

Delaware (1638)

This colony was initially settled by the Dutch and Swedish. With the decline of the Dutch influence in the area, the English took control. In 1682, Delaware was awarded to William Penn.

North Carolina (1653)

By 1653, Virginia colonists began moving south and settling in the North Carolina region. In 1691, the region was officially recognized as a colony, and Charles I granted a royal charter in 1729.

South Carolina (1663)

In 1663, King Charles II created the colony of Carolina by granting the territory, of what is now the region of present-day North Carolina, South Carolina, and Georgia, to loyal supporters. It began as proprietary colony and became a royal colony in 1719. The city of Charleston was founded in 1670 by Sir John Yeamans, a plantation owner from Barbados.

Pennsylvania (1682)

As early as 1647, Swedish, Dutch, and English settlers tried to establish permanent settlements in Delaware. In 1681, a large territory, which included Pennsylvania, was granted to William Penn. Penn was a member of a religion persecuted in England, the Quakers. He made Pennsylvania a safe haven for Quakers, and a large number of German Quakers settled in the colony. In 1683, the first group of settlers arrived in Pennsylvania and formed Germantown near Philadelphia.

Georgia (1732)

This colony was founded with two main purposes: to establish a buffer zone from the Spanish settlement south of the colony and to provide a safe haven for poor people.

Table 3-4 summarizes the key historical characters and events of the colonies.

Indentured Servants

The indentured servant system was used to bring workers to the new world. In practice, the indentured servant would sell him- or herself to an agent or ship captain before leaving England. In turn, the contract would be sold to a buyer in the colonies to recover the cost of the passage. Criminals and people in debt could also be sold for life or until they paid their debts. In some cases, at the end of the service, servants remained as salaried workers, or in the best situations, the servants were given a piece of land for their services. This system of provisional servitude was not applied to Africans; instead, permanent slavery was instituted.

The Enlightenment—The Age of Reason

The **Enlightenment** refers to a period during the seventeenth and eighteenth centuries when people began questioning religious dogmas and emphasizing scientific reasoning and knowledge. The result of this quest for knowledge was the development of modern chemistry and biology. People also began questioning governments and started searching for individual freedom. The search for freedom led countries to seek independence and fight tyranny. For example, the quest for freedom led to the French Revolution and the American War of Independence. The American Revolution motivated the Spanish colonies to seek independence. Some of the leading thinkers of this period were Jean-Jacques Rousseau, John Locke, Charles Montesquieu, Voltaire, and Francis Bacon.

American Revolution

The main reasons for the War of Independence were economic in nature. England, as well as other European nations, had established the mercantilism system to exploit the colonies. This system had three main principles:

- The wealth of the nation is measured in terms of commodities accrued, especially gold and silver.

- Economic activities can increase the power and control of the national government.

- The colonies existed for the benefit of the mother country.

England used the system of mercantilism quite effectively in the thirteen colonies, but after more than a century of British rule, the colonies were primed for independence, and war with England became inevitable.

Another reason for the rebellion was the cost of the French and Indian War. This war, which was the North American portion of the Seven Years' War, emptied the

Table 3-4. The Thirteen American Colonies

Colony	Year Established	Colonizer	Historical Features/ Characters
Virginia	1607	London Company	Captain John Smith, John Rolfe, and Pocahontas
Massachusetts	1620	Puritans with a patent from the London Virginia Company	Puritans, Mayflower, Mayflower Compact, John Smith
New Hampshire	1623	Proprietary colony	Captain John Mason and John Wheelwright
New Jersey	1623	Dutch possession, then a proprietorship	Duke of York
New York	1624	Dutch possession, then a proprietorship	Purchase of the island of Manhattan, Duke of York
Maryland	1633	Proprietorship	George Calvert (Lord Baltimore), refuge for Catholics
Rhode Island	1636	Corporate colony	Roger Williams and Anne Hutchinson
Connecticut	1636	Corporate colony	Thomas Hooker and John Winthrop
Delaware	1638	Corporate colony	First under the Dutch, Swedish, and British control, William Penn
North Carolina	1653	Proprietorship	King Charles II
South Carolina	1663	Proprietorship, then a charter colony	King Charles II, Sir John Yeamans
Pennsylvania	1682	Proprietorship	William Penn and Quakers
Georgia	1732	Charter colony	James Edward Oglethorpe

British coffers, and the British Crown needed a quick way to recover financially. The taxation system that followed the French and Indian War was unbearable for the colonies. The colonies responded with civil disobedience and by boycotting the government of King George. In response to civil disobedience, the British sent troops to Boston, where the groups clashed and several colonists were killed. The event was called the Boston Massacre. One of the best-known boycotts was the Boston Tea Party, in which colonists dumped tea in the Boston harbor to protest against taxation. All these events and the repression that followed led to the American War of Independence.

Continental Congress

Following the events in Massachusetts, representatives of the colonies met in Philadelphia to discuss the political and economic situation in the colonies. No clear solutions were reached at this congress. Once the hostilities started, the Second Continental Congress met to discuss preparations for war. George Washington was elected commander of the American forces, and war was declared against the British. The congress named a committee, led by Thomas Jefferson, to prepare the Declaration of Independence, which was officially signed on July 4, 1776.

Revolution

The American Revolution began in Massachusetts in the outskirts of the towns of Concord and Lexington. In 1775, while the colonists were preparing for war, hundreds of British soldier marched against them. Paul Revere warned the colonists of British troop movements, and minutemen took up arms to face the enemy. At Concord, the British were repelled and forced back to Boston. On their way back, American sharpshooters ambushed and killed hundreds of British soldiers. Following this initial victory for the colonists, the battle of Bunker Hill was fought near Boston. In this battle, the British lost large numbers of soldiers but managed to defeat the colonial troops. Later, in Long Island, the British won another decisive victory over the Americans.

The French joined the war in support of the Americans, in retaliation for their defeat at the hands of the British in the Seven Years' War. Eventually, with the support of the French, the American troops defeated the British forces in Yorktown, Virginia, in 1781. The Treaty of Paris, officially signed in 1783, ended the war and gave independence to the new nation.

For additional details about the American Revolution, go to HistoryCentral.com at *www.multied.com/ Revolt/index.html*.

Articles of Confederation

During the Revolutionary War, the Second Continental Congress ran the government. After independence, the Articles of Confederation defined a new form of government. The new government was composed of representatives from thirteen independent states with limited power. The Congress could not declare war or raise an army. They could ask the states for money or for soldiers, but it was up to the states to agree to provide them. Under this type of government, each state printed its own money and imposed taxes on imports from the other states.

On the positive side, the new government provided for a common citizenship—citizens of the United States. It organized a uniform system of weights and measurements and the postal service. It also became responsible for issues related to Native Americans living within the borders of the new nation. The confederation served as the official government of the young republic until 1789, when the states ratified the Constitution.

U.S. Constitution

After six years under the Articles of Confederation, the leaders of the nation realized that the American government needed revision to bolster its strength. To accomplish this goal, a constitutional convention was held in Philadelphia in 1787. The leaders of this initiative were George Washington, James Madison, Benjamin Franklin, and Alexander Hamilton. From this convention, a new form of government emerged. The Constitution was officially ratified in 1788, and in 1789 George Washington was selected to be the first president of the United States. The republic defined by the Constitution was composed of three branches, the executive, judicial, and legislative, and a system of checks and balances to regulate each branch.

To learn more about historical American documents, go to "A Chronology of U.S. Historical Documents," a Web site created and maintained by the University of Oklahoma Law Center, at *www.law.ou.edu/hist*.

Policies of the New Nation

Monroe Doctrine

In 1823, President Monroe made clear to European countries that the United States was not going to permit the establishment of colonies in the Western Hemisphere. Monroe also banned European countries from attacking the new American republics that were just becoming established in the early nineteenth century. Nor was the U.S. to become involved in European affairs. This concept of "America for Americans" is known as the Monroe Doctrine.

Manifest Destiny

In 1844, President James K. Polk declared to the world that the United States will eventually become a world power and expand to its natural borders. Some of the borders mentioned were the Pacific to the west and Mexico to the south. Eventually, Polk's expectations became a reality as a result of the war between Mexico and the United States from 1846 to 1848.

Slavery in the United States

The Dutch brought the first African slaves to Virginia in 1619 to work on plantations. From 1640 to 1680, large numbers of slaves were brought to the Americas. With the invention of Eli Whitney's cotton gin, cotton became the economic mainstay of the South, and the demand for labor increased the slave trade. From 1798 to 1808, more than 200,000 African slaves were brought to America, mostly to the southern region.

Beginning in 1774, the North began regulating and eventually prohibiting slavery. By 1804, New York and New Jersey had passed gradual emancipation laws. Meanwhile, the slave trade in the South grew to meet the economic needs of the area. Eventually, the issue of slavery, along with other economic and ideological differences between the regions, resulted in the American Civil War. In 1862, Abraham Lincoln issued an emancipation proclamation, granting freedom to slaves in the South. After the war, slavery was officially abolished by the Thirteenth Amendment to the Constitution. Additionally, in 1866 the Fourteenth Amendment gave African Americans full citizenship, and the Fifteenth Amendment granted voting rights to black men.

Civil War

With the expansion of the United States came additional problems for the young nation. One problem that divided the nation was the issue of slavery. By the 1800s, slavery had been virtually abolished in the North. The northern states' reasons for turning against slavery were primarily economic: the North had become more urban and industrialized than the South, and northern states received large numbers of immigrants who provided the necessary labor.

Southern states remained mostly rural and received few immigrants, making slavery the foundation of their economy. With the nation's expansion westward and the addition of new states, the question of slavery became a contentious issue. Any new state would affect the balance between the free and slave states. The issue of slavery became the main topic of the presidential election

of 1860. The candidates were clearly aligned either in favor of or against slavery. The southern Democrats backed a strong proslavery candidate, John C. Breckinridge of Kentucky, while the new Republican party selected a strong antislavery candidate in the figure of Abraham Lincoln. The election of Abraham Lincoln resulted in the secession of the southern states from the union, the creation of the Confederacy, and the start of the American Civil War. The southern states created the Confederate States of America and selected Jefferson Davis as president.

Battle of Gettysburg

Several battles were fought in this war, but none was as memorable as the Battle of Gettysburg. Fought in 1863, this battle was the most disastrous event of the war and perhaps in the history of the United States. In this battle, more than 50,000 soldiers from the North and the South lost their lives. In a speech delivered on the battlefield in November 1863, President Lincoln eulogized the fallen Union soldiers in a speech known as the Gettysburg Address.

After five years of fighting and the loss of thousands of lives and millions of dollars in property, in 1865 the commander of the Confederate army, General Robert E. Lee, surrendered to General Ulysses S. Grant, commander of the Union forces.

Reconstruction Era (1865–1877)

Because the war was fought primarily in the South, that area was practically destroyed. Therefore, the physical reconstruction of the country focused on the South. However, the emotional reconstruction and the reconstruction of American unity had to be done nationwide, and admission of rebel states back into the Union was not automatically granted. The Reconstruction period was characterized by hatred and violence. Because Lincoln was assassinated in 1865, shortly after the end of the war, leadership of the reconstruction effort fell on the shoulders of Andrew Johnson, a southerner who was disliked by the North as well as the South. Eventually, he was impeached and almost removed from power.

A major obstacle to the reunification of the nation resulted from the black codes. These very restrictive laws were passed by southern legislatures to control former slaves. Some black codes restricted free assembly, while others restricted the types of jobs that they could do. In 1867, Congress, still composed entirely of northerners, passed legislation to eliminate the black codes. Additionally, Congress required southern states to ratify the Fourteenth Amendment to the Constitution prior to being allowed back into the Union. The Fourteenth Amendment gave citizenship to blacks. Finally, in 1870, the southern states were allowed back in the Union.

Ku Klux Klan

The Ku Klux Klan was one of various secret societies established during Reconstruction to continue the implementation of the black codes and to terrorize African Americans. Members of the group warned blacks not to vote or exercise individual freedoms. The Klan divided the South based on color lines. More subtle legislation was passed in the South to control the progress of African Americans. These new laws were known as Jim Crow laws. Racial separation characterized life in the South and other parts of the nation for most of the twentieth century.

Economic Development

After the reunification of the country, energy was redirected to the economic development and growth of the nation. New inventions, together with the development of the railroad, paved the way to economic recovery. The reconstruction that followed the war also played a vital role in the development of the United States as a solid economic and industrial nation.

Conflicts and Wars

Spanish American War of 1898

The war between Spain and the United States made the United States a world power. As a result of this war, the United States established its power and influence in the Caribbean Sea and Pacific Ocean. Cuba became an independent nation, and the United States gained control of the Philippines, Guam, and Puerto Rico. Eventually, the Philippines became an independent nation, while Puerto Rico and Guam remained U.S. territories.

Eventually, the people from Guam and Puerto Rico became American citizens.

World War I

The first global war began in Europe and involved two alliances: the Allies and the Central Powers. The Allies were England, France, Russia, and Italy. The Central Powers were Germany, the Austria-Hungary Empire, Turkey, and Bulgaria. Initially, the Americans remained neutral and benefited extensively from trading with the Allies. America's neutrality was challenged, however, when the Germans developed a new weapon, the submarine, and used it successfully to destroy Allied ships. In 1915, the Germans sank a British liner, the *Lusitania*, killing more than 1,100 passengers, including 128 Americans. Additionally, American cargo ships were sunk, which forced President Wilson to ask Congress to declare war against Germany and the Central Powers. The influx of fresh American forces fostered the Allies' victory in 1918.

With the Treaty of Versailles, the war officially ended. In this treaty, the Central Powers were severely punished and forced to pay for the war. Additionally, the Austria-Hungary Empire was dismembered and new countries created. The punitive conditions of the Treaty of Versailles created the resentment of the Germans that eventually led to the second global confrontation, World War II.

The Bolshevik Revolution in Russia

In 1917, the Communists, led by Vladimir Lenin, took over the government in Russia. As a result of this revolution, Russia underwent a period of governmental reconstruction to incorporate the communist philosophy in the nation. With a new government in power, Russia withdrew from World War I.

Great Depression

After World War I, the United States enjoyed a period of prosperity, the golden 1920s. However, on October 29, 1929, the stock market crashed, initiating a ten-year period of what we now call the Great Depression. During the Depression, millions of people lost their capital and jobs. Between 1933 and 1937, President Franklin D. Roosevelt implemented a series of government-sponsored programs, called the New Deal, designed to revitalize the economy and alleviate poverty and despair caused by the Depression.

World War II

The emergence of totalitarian countries like Russia, Germany, and Italy created instability in Europe and eventually led to war. Communist Russia, under the leadership of Stalin, became a threat to European countries. Italy was a fascist, belligerent state where individual liberties were ignored. Germany, under the leadership of Adolf Hitler, was ready to avenge the ignominious treatment it suffered as a result of World War I. In the Pacific, Japan was building an empire that had already conquered parts of China. All these conditions promoted the creation of military alliances that eventually led to World War II.

Germany, Italy, and Japan created the Axis powers, and Russia, France, and England became the Allies. The war started with the German invasion of Poland in 1939. Two days later, France and England declared war against Germany. Hitler conquered most of Europe in a relatively short time. France was occupied, and England was brought close to submission. The United States supported the Allies with supplies and weapons but did not send troops. Although it remained neutral for the first few years of the war, the United States joined the Allies when Japan attacked its naval base in Pear Harbor, Hawaii, in 1941.

D-Day

With Hitler in full control of Europe, the United States joined England and representatives of the French government to plan and execute the invasion of Europe in 1944. On June 6, General Dwight D. Eisenhower, together with a quarter of a million Allied soldiers, crossed the English Channel into France and launched one of the largest offensives against the German occupying forces. This large attack on Germany was known as D-day. As a result of the collective effort of the Allies, France was freed from German occupation. With the combined forces of England, Russia, Canada, and the United States, Hitler and the Axis forces were finally defeated.

Yalta Conference

The Allies met in Yalta, Russia, to discuss the terms of the treaty to end the war. In this meeting, the leaders

of the Allied forces—Winston Churchill, Joseph Stalin, and Franklin D. Roosevelt—met to discuss peace. Under the terms of peace agreed to at Yalta, Germany was to be divided into four sections, each controlled by an Allied country—Britain, France, Russia, and America. The Germans were to pay Russians for war reparations in money and labor. Poland was divided, and the Russians received control of one section (later they took full control of the nation). Finally, plans were set to organize the United Nations to prevent future conflicts in the world.

Hiroshima and Nagasaki

The United States was fighting the war on two fronts, and the Japanese appeared to be invincible. The best available option seemed to be the atomic bomb. By the order of President Harry Truman, the United States dropped two atomic bombs on the cities of Hiroshima and Nagasaki. The destruction caused by these two nuclear devices forced the Japanese government to surrender.

Marshall Plan

The Marshall Plan was a U.S.-supported program to rebuild the economic infrastructure in Europe. The United States provided money and machinery for the reconstruction of the continent.

Holocaust and Creation of Israel

During World War II, Hitler devised a "master plan" to exterminate the Jewish population. Germany placed European Jews in concentration camps and systematically killed millions. This act of genocide is known today as the Holocaust.

At the end of the war, under the leadership of the Great Britain, the United States, and the United Nations, the state of Israel was created in Palestine. On that same day, an Arab "liberation Army" was created to fight the Jewish state. This liberation movement has resulted in several wars between Israel and the Arabs. Today, this war has expanded to include Europe and America, with many terrorist attacks committed during the new century.

Truman Doctrine

In response to the threat of the Soviets, Harry Truman issued a proclamation warning communist countries that the United States will help any nation in danger of falling under communist control. This declaration was called the Truman Doctrine. As a result of this doctrine, the United States became involved in two major military conflicts: the Korean War and the Vietnam War.

Cold War

As a result of the Yalta agreement, Russia became the most powerful country in the region. After taking over Poland and building the Berlin Wall, a new war emerged between the Soviet Union and the United States—the Cold War. Although war was never formally declared between the two nations, confrontations occurred from 1945 to 1991. In 1963, the two nations were on a verge of nuclear war that was called the Cuban Missile Crisis. The Cold War finally ended with the fall of the Soviet Union under the leadership of Mikhail Gorbachev. The fall of the Soviet empire resulted in the reunification of Germany and the creation of multiple smaller countries in Russia that gained independence.

War on Terrorism

In 2001, terrorists attacked American soil. The attack on the Twin Towers in New York on September 11 killed more than 3,000 people. As a result of the attack, the United States declared war on terrorism and attacked the Taliban regime in Afghanistan. American forces succeeded in conquering the country but failed to capture Osama Bin Laden, the intellectual architect of the 9/11 attack. The search for weapons of mass destruction led the United States into war with Iraq. Currently, the United States is still fighting to stabilize the region.

History of Texas

Before European Colonization

The territory known today as Texas was inhabited by several Native American groups. The three groups living in the coastal plains—the Coauhilatecans, Kawakawas, and Caddos—were food gatherers, fishermen, and farmers. When the Spanish arrived in Texas, they made initial contact with these groups. The name

Texas came as a result of contact with the Caddos. Attempting to communicate to the Spaniards that they were not hostile, some Caddos identified themselves with the word *taysha*, which in their language meant "friend" or "ally" (Texas—History 2005). When the Spaniards heard the word *taysha*, they thought the Caddos were identifying the name of the region. From that exchange, the name Texas and the state motto, "Friendship," emerged.

A fourth group, the Jumanos, lived in the mountains and basins of West Texas. The information about this group is limited because they virtually disappeared before the Spaniards arrived in the area. The last two groups are the Comanches and the Apaches. These two groups coexisted with Europeans and offered resistance to the colonization efforts. After they domesticated horses, previously introduced by the Spanish, the Comanches and Apaches became fearless warriors and successful buffalo hunters. The domestication of the horse allowed the development of the culture of the buffalo. When buffalo were later annihilated in the area, these two groups became practically extinct. Table 3-5 presents a summary of Native American groups from Texas.

European Colonization

Cabeza de Vaca

The Spanish exploration of the territory today known as Texas began in 1528, when Cabeza de Vaca and three companions landed in the territory. The four Spaniards made contact with the Caddo in the southeastern part of the state, near modern-day Houston. In his account of the meeting, De Vaca described the Caddo as a very sophisticated Native American group. From there, De Vaca continued exploring the region of modern-day New Mexico and Arizona (Sheppard n.d.). No other significant event happened in the region until 1541, when Francisco Vázquez de Coronado explored Texas.

Francisco Vázquez de Coronado

In response to reports of the mythical Seven Cities of Cibola, Coronado led an expedition of almost a thousand men in search of the golden cities. The expedition left Mexico City and explored the southwestern United

Table 3-5. Native American Groups from Texas

Regions	Native Group
Coastal plains, flatland	**Coauhilatecan** (Rio Grande Valley) **Economic Activity:** Food gatherers and hunters—roots, beans of the mesquite tree, rabbit, birds, and deer **Features:** Lived in family groups **Karankawa** (Southeastern Texas) **Economic Activity:** Fishing and food gathering **Features:** Lived as nomads and used canoes for fishing **Caddo** (East Texas, Piney Woods) **Economic Activity:** Farming—squash, pumpkins, tobacco, and corn (good food supply) **Features:** Built villages and lived in groups
Central plains, flatland and hills	**Apache** (Central and western Texas) **Economic Activity:** Farming and hunting **Features:** Lived as nomads, built portable housing called tepees, domesticated horses, and hunted bison
Great Plains, flatland and hills	**Comanche** **Economic Activity:** Hunters **Features:** Lived as nomads and built portable housing; also domesticated the horse and hunted the buffalo
Mountains and basins	**Jumano** (West Texas) **Economic Activity:** Farming and hunting **Features:** Mostly sedentary and built homes of adobe

States and northern Texas. In 1542, Coronado returned to Mexico empty handed. For the next 140 years, the Texas region remained isolated, and no other attempts were made to colonize it.

Juán de Oñate

In 1595, Oñate received permission from King Philip II of Spain to colonize New Mexico. In 1598, he founded the first European settlement west of the Mississippi in New Mexico.

First Mission in Texas

In 1682, the Spanish established the first permanent settlement in Texas—the mission of Ysleta del Sur near the present-day city of El Paso. After this mission, no serious efforts were made to colonize the area until the

French began to threaten the Spanish hegemony in East Texas.

French Influence in Texas

In 1682, **Robert de la Salle** established a French settlement in Fort Saint Louis in East Texas. A few years later, the Spaniards expelled the French and established a series of missions in East Texas to control the French threat in the region.

San Antonio

In 1718, the Spanish established a mission and a fort—San Antonio de Valero and Fort San Antonio de Bexar—near what is now the city of San Antonio. These settlements were established to provide protection and support to the settlements in East Texas.

Mexican Independence

During the first part of the nineteenth century, the Spanish empire began crumbling. Mexico obtained its independence in 1821 and took control of the colony of Texas.

Anglo-American Presence in Texas

In 1820, Moses Austin received permission from the Spanish government to bring Anglo-American families to settle in Texas. This agreement was voided when Mexico took control of the territory. Later, Austin's son, Stephen, negotiated with the Mexican government and obtained a similar agreement to allow Anglo-Americans to settle in Texas. By 1835, the settlers were the majority in the region, which antagonized the Mexican government and resulted in war.

Texas War for Independence

Conflicts between Texans and the Mexican government started as early as 1830. The colonists felt that the government was not providing adequate support and protection to Texas. Initially, they wanted to negotiate with the new president, Santa Anna, and sent Stephen Austin to Mexico City to represent the colony. The Mexican government was not willing to negotiate and jailed Austin for a year.

First Battle in Gonzales

The town of Gonzales had cannon to protect the colonists from the Indians. By order of the government, Mexican soldiers came to take the cannon from the colonists in October 1835. The Texans refused to relinquish their weapon and fired the cannon against the Mexican soldiers. With this incident in Gonzales, the war for Texas independence began.

Sam Houston

A delegation of Texans traveled to Washington, D.C., to secure support from the U.S. government. Sam Houston, a former governor of Tennessee, volunteered to fight for Texas and eventually became the commander in chief of the Texas army.

The Alamo and Goliad

The first meaningful battle of the Texas war for independence took place near the present-day city of San Antonio in a small mission and fort known as the Alamo. When the war began, fewer than 200 men, led by Colonel William Travis, protected the Alamo. Eventually, additional historical characters like James Bowie and Davy Crockett joined Travis in defending the fort. In 1836, General Antonio López de Santa Anna and the Mexican army took the fort and killed all its defenders, including Texans of Mexican ancestry. Following this victory, Santa Anna continued marching against the rebels and took the city of Goliad, where more than 300 rebels were killed. These two battles provided the patriotic emotion that resulted in the creation of an army and eventually led to victory against Mexico.

Texas Declaration of Independence

A few days before the Battle of the Alamo, a group of Texans met at Washington-on-the-Brazos to issue a declaration of independence and to form the new government. An interim government for the republic of Texas was established, with David D. Burnet as president and Lorenzo de Zavala as vice president.

Battle of San Jacinto

While the colonists were fighting the Mexican army at the Alamo and in Goliad, General Sam Houston was strengthening the army of the new republic. The Texan army continued retreating ahead of the Mexican forces until they reached the San Jacinto River, near the city of Houston. In a battle that lasted less than twenty minutes, Houston's troops defeated the Mexican army and captured General Santa Anna. Texas President Burnet and Mexican President Santa Anna signed the Treaty of Velasco, with Santa Anna agreeing to withdraw his troops from Texas in exchange for safe conduct back to Mexico, where he would lobby for recognition of Texas independence. Santa Anna's commitment never materialized, and the Mexican government refused to recognize Texas as an independent republic. Nevertheless, Sam Houston became the president of the new republic, and from 1836 to 1845, Texas functioned as an independent nation. However, the Mexican government still considered it one of its rebellious provinces that it would one day reclaim (Texas State Library n.d.).

Republic Period

Despite the economic hardship typical of new nations, Texas managed to remain independent for ten years and was recognized by several nations in the world, including the United States. However, unable to secure its borders and reverse its financial situation, the new nation sought the support of the United States.

Texas Joins the United States

In 1845, Texas became the twenty-eighth state of the American union. Immediately, the U.S. government sent troops to the Rio Grande (which Mexicans considered their territory) to secure the Texas border. The ensuing clashes between Mexican and U.S. forces resulted in Congress declaring war in May 1846.

Mexican-American War

Between 1846 and 1848, Mexico and the United States waged a war that ended with a decisive victory and tremendous land acquisitions for the United States. As a result of the Treaty of Guadalupe Hidalgo, Mexico withdrew its claim over Texas and established the Rio Grande, or Rio Bravo as it is known in Mexico, as the official border between the two countries. Mexico also ceded to the United States California and the territory known today as the American Southwest.

Confederacy Period (1861–1865)

At the onset of the American Civil War, Texas left the union and joined the Confederacy as a proslavery state. For eight years, the Union forces led by General Ulysses S. Grant and the Confederate army led by General Robert E. Lee battled for control of the nation. Finally, in 1865 Lee surrendered and the American union was restored. As a result of the war, slavery was abolished in the United States.

Summary

Figure 3-9 presents a time line of important events in Texas from 1528 to 1861.

Reconstruction Period

During Reconstruction, Texas was briefly under occupation by U.S. troops. Texas was allowed to rejoin the union in 1870. The Ku Klux Klan became very active at this time, terrorizing African Americans in Texas and the southern states.

Economic Development after Reconstruction

After Reconstruction, the Texas economy flourished largely based on the growth of the cattle industry. Barbed wire was introduced in 1880, and ranchers began using

1528 Cabeza de Vaca lands in Texas	1541 Coronado explores Texas	1682 Mission founded in El Paso	1682 La Salle (French) lands in Texas	1690 First mission in East Texas San Francisco de los Tejas	1718 Mission and fort founded in San Antonio	1820 Austin arrives in San Antonio
1861 Texas secedes from the union	1848 Treaty of Guadalupe Hidalgo	1846 Mexican-American war begins	1845 Texas the 28th state in the union	1836 Battle of San Jacinto, Texas declares independence	1835 Battle of Gonzales marks beginning of Texas revolution	1833 Santa Anna president of Mexico

Figure 3-9. Texas Time Line from 1528 to 1861

scientific cattle breeding to increase production and improve the quality of meat.

Oil in Texas

In 1901, oil was discovered in the Spindletop Oil Field near Beaumont. The development of the oil industry made Texas the leading producer of oil in the United States. As a result of this boom, cities like Houston and Dallas became large urban and industrial centers.

World Wars and Beyond

As a result of World War I, Texas emerged as a leading military training center. Several military bases were established in the state, bringing economic growth. The rapid development of the aircraft industry and highly technological businesses led to rapid industrialization in the state. By World War II, Texas was a leading state in the defense industry. The modern economy of Texas still relies on agriculture, ranching, and oil production, but new high-technology industries are rapidly becoming the top economic activities in the state.

Six Flags over Texas

The reference made to six flags over Texas describes the different countries that have exerted control in Texas from 1519 to the present:

- Spain (1519–1821)
- France (1685–1690)
- Mexico (1821–1836)
- Republic of Texas (1836–1845)
- United States (1845–1861)
- Texas in the Confederacy (1861–1865)
- Back to the American union (1870–present)

State Facts and Symbols

State flower	Bluebonnet
State bird	Mockingbird
State tree	Pecan
State motto	Friendship
Border states	Oklahoma, Louisiana, Arkansas, and New Mexico
State song	"Texas, Our Texas," by William J. Marsh and Gladys Yoakum Wright

Texas, our Texas! All hail the mighty State! Texas, our Texas! So wonderful so great! Boldest and grandest, withstanding ev'ry test; O Empire wide and glorious, you stand supremely blest. [Refrain] God bless you Texas! And keep you brave and strong,That you may grow in power and worth, thro'out the ages long.

Key Principles of the Competency

- The Enlightenment period of European History (eighteenth century) helped to restore religious unity that had been disrupted by the Protestant Reformation.

- The American Revolution influenced political development in Latin America by demonstrating that it was possible to overthrow European colonial rule.

- The introduction of horses and firearms had a great impact on the colonization of the American plains and the West.

- Early civilizations in Asia and Africa were located near river valleys. Some of these civilizations were Egypt, Mesopotamia, and Persia (Iran). This location provided access to fresh water for crop growing and for human consumption.

- The civil rights movement of the 1960s addressed issues that were major topics during the Reconstruction era following the Civil War—individual and human rights.

- Louis Pasteur's germ theory of diseases was one of the most important breakthroughs of nineteenth-century Europe.

- Every culture has a way to explain the formation of the earth and develops a way to adapt to the physical environment.

- In 1492, Columbus claimed America for Spain. Following that, they established colonies in the Caribbean. In 1519, Spain initiated the colonization of Mexico. Presidios and missions were established to protect the colony and to convert the natives to Christianity.

- In 1598, Juan de Oñate founded the first European settlement west of the Mississippi in New Mexico.

- The first Spanish missions in Texas were established to strengthen the control of Spain in the area and to reduce the threat of the French: San Francisco de Tejas (1690) in East Texas and Fort San Antonio and the Alamo (1718).

Competency 018 (Geography and Culture)

The teacher demonstrates knowledge of geographic relationships among people, places, and environments in Texas, the United States, and the world; understands the concept of culture and how cultures develop and adapt; and applies social science skills to geographic and cultural information, ideas, and issues.

Geography

Geography is the study of the earth's surface, the organisms that populate it, and their interaction within the ecosystem. Geography can be divided into two main areas: physical geography and cultural geography. **Physical geography** refers to the physical characteristics of the surface of the earth and how those features affect life. **Cultural geography** deals with the interaction of humans with their environment and how that interaction produces changes. Humans can alter the physical environment of the earth, but the physical environment can also shape humans and their culture. For example, the Incas built the capital of their empire, Cuzco, in the Andes Mountains in what is now Peru. This city has an altitude of 11,152 feet above sea level, where oxygen is scarce and agriculture is a challenge. However, the Incas managed to live and flourish under these conditions. They carved the land for agriculture and built roads and cities. In turn, the environment changed the Incas, who had to evolve to tolerate the low levels of oxygen. Studies conducted on the Indians from Peru suggest that people of the Andes developed genetic adaptations for high-altitude living (Genes help high-altitude dwellers 2004). By adapting to the conditions of their environment, inhabitants of the area not only survived but flourished in less-than-ideal conditions.

Locating Places and Regions on a Map

Maps are symbolic representations of the earth's surface. Locating places on a map requires a grid system—a network of horizontal and vertical lines used to locate points on a map or a chart by means of **coordinates**. The vertical lines are called longitude and the horizontal lines are latitude.

Longitude and Time Zones

Time zones are established based on the lines of longitude, or meridians. These lines run from north to south. The **prime meridian**, or the meridian at 0 degrees, has been set in Greenwich, England. On the other side of the globe is the **international date line**. The prime meridian divides the earth into the Western and Eastern hemispheres. Following the sunlight as it travels along the rotating earth, the time decreases moving from east to west. When people travel from China (east) to the United States (west), they save a day; that is, they might spend a day traveling but still arrive on the same calendar day. The United States has six time zones of one hour difference each—Eastern, Central, Mountain, Pacific, Alaska, and Hawaii. Figure 3-10 represents the six time zones in the United States with a key city for each zone.

For more information about time zones, go to a Web site provided by the National Institute of Standards and Technology (an agency of the U.S. Department of Commerce) and the U.S. Naval Observatory, at *www.time.gov/about.html.*

Latitude

The lines of latitude, or parallels, run from west to east. The **equator** is the latitude at 0 degrees and divides the globe into the Northern and Southern hemispheres.

Regions of the United States

The concept of regions facilitates the examination of geography by providing a convenient and manageable unit for studying the earth's human and natural environ-

West ◀─── East					
Hawaii	Alaska	Pacific	Mountain	Central	Eastern
1:00 PM	2:00 PM	3:00 PM	4:00 PM	5:00 PM	6:00 PM
Honolulu	Anchorage	Los Angeles	Phoenix	Dallas	New York City

Figure 3-10. Time Zones in the United States

ment. The continental United States can be divided into eight broad geographic divisions:

- **Laurentian Highlands** are part of the Canadian shield that extends into the northern United States and the Great Lakes area. This area has a hard winter, and agriculture is very limited.

- **Atlantic–Gulf Coastal Plains** are the coastal regions of the eastern and southern states. It includes New York City in the North, the mid-Atlantic states to Florida in the South, and all the way west to Texas in the Gulf Coast.

- **Appalachian Highlands** covers the Appalachian Mountains, the Adirondack Mountains, and New England—the states of Connecticut, Maine, Massachusetts, New Hampshire, Rhode Island, and Vermont.

- **Interior Plains and the Great Plains** covers the interior part of the United States. Included in this area are the states west of the Appalachians, south of the Great Lakes, and as far west as Montana, Wyoming, Colorado, New Mexico, and northwestern Texas. Most of the nation's wheat, corn, and feed crops are grown in this area.

- **Interior Highlands** is also part of the interior continental United States. This area includes the Ozark Mountains and the states of Missouri, Arkansas, Kentucky, and part of Oklahoma and Kansas.

- **Rocky Mountain System** is in the western United States and Canada extending from British Colombia to Montana, Utah, Colorado and New Mexico. The mountain range is called the **Continental Divide**, because it separates the eastward-flowing rivers from the westward-flowing rivers. The waters that flow eastward empty into the Atlantic Ocean, and those that flow westward empty into the Pacific Ocean.

- **Intermontane Plateaus** is a large region that includes the Pacific Northwest, the Colorado Plateau, and the basins of the southwestern United States. This area covers the states of Washington, Oregon, Idaho, part of Utah, New Mexico, and Arizona. It also covers the areas of the Grand Canyon and Death Valley.

- **Pacific Mountain System** covers the West Coast of the United States. This area extends from the Cascade Mountains in the north down the entire West Coast through the states of Washington, Oregon, and California.

Texas Regions and Economic Activity

Texas is the second-largest state in the United States behind Alaska. Covering 268,601 square miles, the state contains five geographic regions within its boundaries. Table 3-6 lists the regions and the key cities and main economic activities of each.

Largest Rivers in the World

These are the three largest rivers in the world:

- The Nile (North and East Africa) is the longest river in the world. It originates in Lake Victoria in Uganda and ends in the Mediterranean Sea.

- The Amazon (South America) is the second-largest and the widest river in the world. It originates in Peru, and its mouth is at the Atlantic Ocean off the cost of Brazil.

- The Chang Jiang or Yangtze (China) is the third-largest river in the world. Its source is the Tibetan Plateau, and its mouth is the East China Sea.

Table 3-6. Regions and Economic Activity in Texas

Region	Key Cities	Main Economic Activities	Key Statistics
Coastal plains, flatland	Dallas, Houston, San Antonio, Austin, Corpus Christi, Laredo	Lumber—East Texas (Piney Woods) Oil—Refineries in Houston Farming—Rice, oranges, cotton, wheat, milo Ranching—Cattle in Kingsville Shipping—Houston	Population—High: 1 of 3 Texans Rainfall—High Distinguishing Mark—Hurricanes
Central plains, flatland and hills	Fort Worth, Arlington, San Angelo, Abilene	Ranching—Cattle, wool (mohair), sheep Farming—Grains	Population—High Rainfall—Medium Distinguishing Marks—Tornadoes, northerlies (cold winds), hailstorms; large ranches
Great Plains Flatland and hill country	Midland, Odessa, Lubbock, Amarillo, Texas Panhandle	Ranching—Cattle, sheep Minerals—Graphite Oil—Odessa and Midland Farming—Wheat	Population—Average Rainfall—Medium Distinguishing Marks—Snowstorms, dust storms, windmills, use of aquifers
Mountains and basins, Rocky Mountains, Davis, Chisos, and Guadalupe, Chihuahuan Desert	El Paso	Ranching—Limited large ranches Mexico-U.S. border economy based on trading of goods produced by the industries established in Mexico—Maquiladoras.	Population—Low Rainfall—Low; hard rain wears out the rocks and land Distinguishing Mark—Big Bend National Park

For information about the world's largest rivers, go to the Social Studies for Kids Web site at *www.socialstudiesforkids.com/articles/geography/longestriverstable.htm*.

Rivers in the United States

These are the largest and most important rivers in the United States:

- The **Mississippi** is the longest river in the United States and the fourteenth longest in the world. It begins in Minnesota and ends in the Gulf of Mexico.

- The **Ohio River** begins near Pittsburgh and runs southwest, ending in the Mississippi River on the Illinois and Missouri borders.

- The **Rio Grande** begins in the San Juan Mountains of southern Colorado and ends in the Gulf of Mexico. The river is the official border between the United States and Mexico, where it is known as the Rio Bravo.

- The **Colorado River** begins in the Rocky Mountains and ends in California.

- The **Missouri River** begins in the Rocky Mountains, flowing north first and then generally southeast across the central United States, ending at the Mississippi River, just to the north of St. Louis, Missouri.

For information about rivers in the United States, visit WorldAtlas.com. To view the most significant rivers of the continental United States, visit

www.worldatlas.com/webimage/countrys/namerica/
usstates/artwork/rivers/uslayout.htm.

Mountains in the World

With notable exception of the peak known as K2, which is part of the Karakoram Range, the tallest mountains in the world are located in the Himalayas, ranging across the countries of China, Pakistan, Nepal, and Tibet. Table 3-7 lists the top ten mountains.

Compared with the world's tallest peaks, the United States' mountains are small. The highest mountain is Mt. McKinley in Alaska. In fact, the state of Alaska has the sixteen highest peaks in the United States. A list of the mountains with 16,000 feet or above is presented in Table 3-8.

For additional information about the world's mountains, go to the Infoplease.com Web site at *www.infoplease.com/ipa/A0001771.html.*

Deforestation

Deforestation can increase soil erosion and in some instances can lead to tragedies like the mudslides that

Table 3-7. Tallest Mountains in the World

Mountain	Location	Height (in feet)
Everest	Nepal and Tibet	29,035
K2	Pakistan/China	28,250
Kanchenjunga	India and Nepal	28,169
Lhotse I	Nepal and Tibet	27,940
Makalu I	Nepal and Tibet	27,766
Cho Oyu	Nepal and Tibet	26,906
Dhaulagiri	Nepal	26,795
Manaslu I	Nepal	26,781
Nanga Parbat	Pakistan	26,660
Annapurna	Nepal	26,545

Table 3-8. Tallest Mountains in the United States

Mountain	Location	Height (in feet)
Mt. McKinley	Alaska	20,320
Mt. St. Elias	Alaska	18,008
Mt. Foraker	Alaska	17,400
Mt. Bona	Alaska	16,500
Mt. Blackburn	Alaska	16,390
Mt. Sandford	Alaska	16,237

occurred in 2006 in the Philippines, where thousands of people were buried alive. The rate of soil erosion is most likely to exceed the rate of soil formation in areas like Brazil, where people have cut forest to clear land for farming.

Deposition

Deposition is the process of carrying soil from one place to another, usually by means of water or wind. This process is responsible for the creation of beaches, sand dunes found in desert areas, and landforms created by glaciers.

Map Skills by Grade—Scope and Sequence

In addition to the basic knowledge required in the Texas Essential Knowledge and Skills (TEKS), each student in kindergarten through grade 4 is required to acquire the following specific geography skills and concepts.

Kindergarten

- Understands and uses terms related to location, direction and distance (up, down, left, right, here, near, far).
- Recognizes a globe as a model of the earth.
- Recognizes and uses terms that express relative size and shape (big, little, large, small, round, square).

- Identifies school and local community by name.

- Recognizes and uses models and symbols to represent real things.

- Identifies bodies of water—oceans, seas, lakes, rivers, ponds, bayous (TEKS).

- Identifies landforms—plains, mountains, deserts, hills, and canyons (TEKS).

- Identifies natural resources—water, soil, trees, metals, fish (TEKS).

Grade 1

- Makes and uses simple classroom maps to locate objects.

- Knows geographical location of home in relation to school and neighborhood.

- Knows the layout of the school campus.

- Identifies state and nation by name.

- Follows and gives verbal directions (here, there, left, right, below, above).

- Distinguishes between land and water symbols on globes and maps.

- Relates locations on maps and globes to locations on the earth.

- Observes, describes, and builds simple models and maps of the local environment.

- Knows the four cardinal points (TEKS).

- Identifies the physical characteristics of places—precipitation, body of water, landforms, types of vegetation, and climate (TEKS).

Grade 2

- Makes and uses simple maps of the school and neighborhood.

- Interprets map symbols using a legend.

- Knows and uses cardinal directions.

- Locates community, state, and nation on maps and globes.

- Identifies local landforms.

- Differentiates between maps and globes.

- Locates other neighborhoods studied on maps.

- Knows the continents of the world (TEKS).

- Identifies important landmarks—Statue of Liberty and others (TEKS).

- Identifies natural resources (TEKS).

- Identifies aspects of the physical environment, from organisms to communities (TEKS).

Grade 3

- Uses distance, directions, scale, and map symbols.

- Compares own community with other communities.

- Compares urban and rural environments.

- Uses charts to record and present information (TEKS).

- Understands climate and the elements that influence climate like wind velocity, precipitation, and proximity to bodies of water.

- Uses the compass rose as a means of orientation on a map on the earth (TEKS).

- Uses graphs (TEKS).

- Uses graphic organizers and diagrams to arrange items in meaningful way (TEKS).

- Understands that landforms change through the processes of erosion and deposition (TEKS).

- Understands that regions are areas of the earth's surface (TEKS).

- Uses scale to represent distances (TEKS).

- Uses time lines to chronologically list events.

Grade 4

- Interprets pictures, graphs, charts, and tables.

- Works with distance, directions, scale, and map symbols.

- Relates similarities and differences between maps and globes.

- Uses maps of different scales and themes.

- Recognizes the common characteristics of map grid system.

- Compares and contrasts regions on a state, national, or world basis.

- Understands the concepts of adaptation and modification, such as changing the landscape to meet survival needs and building to adjust to new environment (TEKS).

- Identifies elements that affect the climate (TEKS).

- Uses a compass rose to find true directions.

- Indentifies key explorers and their achievements (TEKS).

- Identifies geographic factors that affect the settlement and development of places.

- Understands the connection between climate and vegetation on earth.

- Identifies global divisions, like the meridian at 0 degrees, the equator, the Northern and Southern hemispheres, and the Eastern and Western hemispheres (TEKS).

Cultural Diffusion

The term *cultural diffusion* describes the exchange or transmission of cultural information and lifestyles from people around the world. For example, most people in the world use cotton, a fabric developed in India, and silk, developed in China. Chicken and pigs were originally domesticated in Asia, but by the process of cultural diffusion, these animals are common today in most countries in the world. Many countries are predominantly Christian today, but Christianity was born in the Middle East, a place where most people are Muslim. The Romans facilitated the cultural diffusion of Christianity around the ancient world. Travelers to Morocco, a Muslim country in North Africa, may be surprised to hear Puerto Rican salsa and Jamaican reggae music being played in local nightclubs. The popularity of Latin and Caribbean rhythms in a predominantly Muslim country is an example of the powerful effect of cultural diffusion.

Competency 019 (Government, Citizenship, and Economics)

The teacher understands the concepts and processes of government and the responsibilities of citizenship; knows how people organize economic systems to produce, distribute, and consume goods and services; and applies social science skills to information, ideas, and issues related to government and economics.

American Government

The governmental system of the United States is a constitutional representative democracy. The Constitution is the supreme law of the nation. It contains a description of the government and the rights and responsibilities of its citizens. The document can be amended with the approval of two-thirds of the House and the Senate and the ratification of individual state legislatures. Amendments to the U.S. Constitution have made it more democratic than the original document. The first ten amendments to the Constitution are known as the Bill of Rights.

Executive Branch

The executive branch of the U.S. government is composed of a president and a vice president elected every four years by electoral votes. The president is the commander-in-chief of the armed forces. He or she appoints cabinet members, nominates judges to the federal court system, grants pardons, recommends legislation, and has the power to veto legislation.

Judicial Branch

The judicial branch is composed of a federal court system that includes the Supreme Court and a system of lower courts—district courts, appeals courts, bankruptcy courts, and special federal courts. Federal judges are nominated by the president of the United States and confirmed by the Senate. All federal judges are appointed for life. The Supreme Court is composed of nine judges, and their ruling is considered final. Some of the major responsibilities of this body are to interpret the Constitution, resolve conflicts among states, and interpret laws and treaties.

Legislative Branch

The legislative branch is composed of the Congress, which is divided in two parts—the Senate and the House of Representatives. The Senate comprises two senators from each state, while the composition of the House is based on the population of each state. The Congress makes the laws of the nation, collects taxes, coins money and regulates its value, can declare war, controls appropriations, can impeach public officials, regulates the jurisdictions of federal courts, and can override presidential vetoes.

System of Checks and Balances

The U.S. Constitution provides for a system of checks and balances among the three branches of the government. In this type of system, individual branches check the others to be sure that no one assumes full control of the central government. The legislative branch can check the executive branch by passing laws over presidential veto (by a two-thirds majority in both houses). This branch exerts control over the judicial branch by refusing to confirm the president's judges. The executive can check the legislative branch by the use of the veto, and the judicial branch by appointing federal judges. The judicial branch can check the other two branches through the process of judicial review, which can declare legislation unconstitutional or illegal.

Judicial Review Process— *Marbury v. Madison*

A dispute that occurred as the Thomas Jefferson administration came into power fundamentally altered the role of the judicial branch and emphasized the system of checks and balances of the American government. In this case, the judicial branch confirmed its power to review and assess the constitutionality of the legislation passed by Congress and signed by the president. This process is now called the judicial review.

Bill of Rights

After the U.S. Constitution was enacted in 1783, the founders felt that additional measures were necessary to preserve basic human rights. The first ten amendments to the U.S. Constitution came to be the Bill of Rights. A summary of the first ten amendments follows:

- **First Amendment**—separation of church and state, freedom of religion, speech, press and the right to peaceful assembly

- **Second Amendment**—rights to keep and bear arms

- **Third Amendment**—made it illegal to force people to offer quarters to soldiers in time of peace

- **Fourth Amendment**—right to privacy and unreasonable searches or seizures

- **Fifth Amendment**—rights of due process, protection against self-incrimination, and protection from being indicted for the same crime twice (double jeopardy)

- **Sixth Amendment**—rights to speedy public trial by an impartial jury, and to counsel for ones defense

- **Seventh Amendment**—right to sue people

- **Eighth Amendment**—protection against cruel and unusual punishment

- **Ninth Amendment**—enumeration of specific rights in the Constitution cannot be taken as a way to deny other rights retained by the people

- **Tenth Amendment**—rights not delegated to the federal government by the Constitution are reserved to the states or to the people

Power Sharing Between State and Federal Governments

One of the most significant principles of the U.S. Constitution is the concept of power sharing between the federal and state governments. Some of the powers reserved to the federal and state governments follow.

Powers Reserved for the Federal Government

- Regulate interstate and foreign commerce

- Print money and regulate its value

- Establish the laws for regulation of immigration and naturalization

- Regulate admission of new states

- Declare war and ratify peace treaties

- Establish a system of weights and measures

- Raise and maintain armed forces

- Conduct relations with foreign nations

Powers Reserved for State Governments

- Conduct and monitor local, state, and federal elections

- Provide for local governments

- Ratify proposed amendments to the Constitution

- Regulate intrastate commerce

- Provide education for its citizens

- Establish direct taxes like sales and state taxes

- Regulate and maintain police power over public health and safety

- Maintain control of state borders

In addition to the powers reserved to the states, the Tenth Amendment of the U.S. Constitution provides additional powers to the state. In this amendment, the powers not specifically delegated to the federal government are reserved for the states.

Local and State Governments

Most states in the United States follow the type of government established in the U.S. Constitution. State governments generally have three branches—executive, legislative and judicial. The main difference is that the executive branch is led by a governor and the judicial branch is composed of a state court system subordinate to the federal court system. The city government is generally headed by a mayor or city manager with the support of a city council.

Citizenship

The development of civic ideas and practices is a lifelong process that begins in school by observing patriotic holidays, learning about the contribution of historical characters, and pledging allegiance to the American and Texas flags each day. In first grade, encouraging good citizenship continues with the introduction of the American anthem and the mottoes of Texas and the United States. Civic education and the principles of democracy are infused through active participation in community activities. To promote civic responsibility, students can get involved in discussions about issues that affect the community. Teachers guide students to suggest possible solutions to community problems, while students are guided to listen and analyze contributions. Through this exchange, students are guided to practice principles of democracy and to value individual contributions to solve community problems.

Children as early as prekindergarten can be guided to develop civic responsibility. Teachers can promote this sense of responsibility by involving students in real-life situations in which they take civic responsibility. For example, teachers can make children aware of how producing trash can affect the environment. As part of this process, students can be guided to examine the amount of trash that they produce daily and explore ways to reduce it. Promoting a sense of responsibility to the well-being of everyone constitutes the main principle for developing responsible citizenship.

Basic Principles of Economy

Economics is a social science that analyzes the principles that regulate the production, distribution, and consumption of resources in society. It emphasizes how these principles operate within the economic choices of individuals, households, businesses, and governments. Economics can be divided into two main areas: macroeconomics and microeconomics. **Macroeconomics** is the study of the economy at the world, regional, state, and local levels. Some of the topics include reasons and ways to control inflation, causes of unemployment, and economic growth in general. **Microeconomics** deals with specific issues related to the decision-making process at the household, firm, or industry levels.

Theory of Supply and Demand

This theory states that prices vary based on balance between the availability of a product or service at a certain price (supply) and the desire of potential purchasers to pay that price (demand). This balance of supply and demand can occur naturally or created artificially. An example of an artificially created balance is the intentional destruction of a surplus of a given product on the world market to maintain the price level. Another example increasing prices by creating an artificial scarcity of a product. For instance, the Organization of Petroleum Exporting Countries (OPEC) often reduces its production of oil to cause an increase in price.

Goods and Services

The use of machines increases the availability of goods and services to the population. This kind of production can decrease the cost of producing the goods and consequently its price. For example, as a result of the division of labor and the use of assembly lines developed by Eli Whitney in 1799, production costs of manufactured goods decreased and productivity increased. Mass production that came as a result of the Industrial Revolution made contemporary families and children more likely to become consumers rather than producers. However, before the Industrial Revolution, especially in colonial America, children were used to produce goods and contribute to the group.

Free Enterprise

Free enterprise is an economic and political doctrine of the capitalist system. The concept is based on the premise that the economy can regulate itself in a freely competitive market through the relationship of supply and demand, and with minimum governmental intervention. One of the main benefits of the system of free enterprise is the competition among businesses that results in a greater choice and better prices for consumers.

The system of free enterprise has led to globalization. **Globalization** can be defined as a continuous increase of cross-border financial, economic, and social activities. It implies some level of economic interdependence among individuals, financial entities, and nations. As a result of globalization, trade barriers have been eliminated and tariffs imposed on imported products have been largely discontinued. In a global market, it is difficult to determine the origins of products. For example, Toyota from Japan and Ford from the United States joined forces to build cars using parts and labor from Mexico.

The concept of **economic interdependence** describes a positive, close connection between producers and consumers of goods and services within a nation or across nations. This economic interdependence has guided nations to establish large markets of free trade zones like the North American Free Trade Agreement (NAFTA) and the European Union (EU) trade agreement.

Money and Banking

Under the presidency of Woodrow Wilson, the **Federal Reserve System** was established. The main purpose of this institution is to keep the banking industry strong to ensure a supply of currency. The Federal Reserve is administered by the Board of Governors, a seven-member body appointed for fourteen-year terms. Alan Greenspan served as Chairman of the Federal Reserve Board from 1987 to 2006. The current chair is Ben S. Bernanke.

The main function of the Federal Reserve Bank is to promote fiscal stability and economic growth in the nation and to regulate inflation and deflation. The Board of Governors controls the flow of money and sets the interest rate that banks use to lend money. They increase the interest rate to control inflation and lower the interest rate when business slows down.

Inflation and Deflation

Inflation is the fall of purchasing power of money within an economic structure. Inflation reduces the purchasing power of money, which technically affects the value of the currency. Countries generally devalue their currency to keep up with inflation. **Deflation** is the opposite of inflation: the purchasing power of money increases, thereby lowering the prices of goods and services. In a period of deflation, consumers benefit but industry suffers. The Federal Reserve controls the flow of money and keeps a healthy balance between inflation and deflation.

American Federal Income Tax System

In 1913, the Sixteenth Amendment of the U.S. Constitution allowed the imposition of direct taxation of citizens. This direct taxation is known as the federal income tax.

Interdependence of State, National, and World Economies

The economy of Texas is based primarily on telecommunications, software, financial services, business products and services, semiconductors, biotechnology, and oil and coal. Agriculture and ranching are still viable economic activities, but they are no longer carrying the economy. A large percentage of these products are exported to members of NAFTA—Mexico and Canada—and to the world markets. According to the Texas Economic Update, if Texas were a nation, it would rank as the eighth-largest economy in the world (Strayhorn 2004).

The Texas economy relies heavily on exports of goods and services. From 2002 through 2005, Texas was ranked as the number one state in terms of export revenues (BIDC 2006). Without its exports, the Texas economic could not sust in its growth. Because of the interdependence of state and global economies, political turmoil and economic problems in the world can have a direct impact on the Texas economy. For example, because part of the economy of Texas is based on petroleum, the decisions of OPEC have a direct impact on the state's economy.

References

Arends, R. 1998. *Learning to teach*. 4th ed. Boston: McGraw-Hill.

Business and Industry Data Center (BIDC). Office of the Governor, Economic Development and Tourism. 2006. Overview of the Texas economy. http://www.bidc.state.tx.us/overview/2-2te.htm.

Echevarria, J., M. Vogt, and D. Short. 2000. *Making content comprehensible for English language learners*: *The SIOP model*. Needham Heights, MA: Allyn and Bacon.

Ganeri, A., H. M. Martell, and B. Williams. 1999. *The world history encyclopedia*. Bath, UK: Parragon.

Genes help high-altitude dwellers. 2004. *Discovery*, March 10.

Kagan, S. 1985. *Cooperative learning resources for teachers*. Riverside, CA: Spencer Kagan.

Library of Congress. n.d. Hispanic reading room. http://www.loc.gov/rr/hispanic/.

Lyman, F. T. (1981). The responsive classroom discussion: The inclusion of all students. In A. S. Anderson (Ed.), Mainstreaming Digest (pp. 109–113). College Park: University of Maryland Press.

National Council for the Teaching of Social Studies (NCTSS). 2006. *National standards for social studies teachers: Volume 1*. http://www.socialstudies.org/standards/teachers/vol1/.

Parker, W. C. 2001. *Social studies in elementary education*. 11th ed. Columbus, OH: Merrill Prentice-Hall.

Potts, J. 1994. *Adventure tales of America*. Dallas, TX: Signal Media.

Rosado, L., and D. Salazar. 2002–2003. La conexión: The English/Spanish connection. *National Forum of Applied Educational Research Journal* 15(4): 51–66.

Rowe, M.B. 1986. *Wait times: Slowing down may be a way of speeding up*. Journal of Teacher Education, 37, 43-50.

Schifini, A. 1985. *Sheltered English: Content area instruction for limited English proficiency students*. Los Angeles County Office of Education.

Schifini, A., H. García, D. J. Short, E. E. García, J. Villamil Tinajero, E. Hamayan, and L. Kratky. 2004. *Avenues: Success in language, literacy and content*. Carmel, CA: Hampton-Brown.

Sheppard, D. E. n.d. *Cabeza de Vaca in North America*. http://www.floridahistory.com/cabeza.html.

Slavin, R. 1986. *Student learning: An overview and practical guide*. Washington, DC: Professional Library National Education Association.

Strayhorn, C. K. 2004. The rebound is here. *Texas economic update*, Fall. http://www.window.state.tx.us/ecodata/teufall04/.

Texas—*History*. 2005. Thomson Gale. http://www.city-data.com/states/Texas-History.html.

Texas State Library and Archives Commission. *The republic of Texas*. http://www.tsl.state.tx.us/treasures/republic/.

Thelen, H. 1981. *The classroom society*. New York: Wiley.

Domain IV: Science

Competency 020 (Science Instruction)

The teacher uses knowledge of science content and methods to plan effective, engaging, and safe instruction and to assess learning.

Science Curriculum

The National Science Teachers Association (NSTA) supports the idea that scientific inquiry should be a basic component of the curriculum in every grade in American schools (2002). A position paper of the organization published in 2002 emphasizes the importance of offering students early experience in problem solving and scientific thinking. The report suggests that children learn science best under the following conditions:

- Students are actively involved in firsthand exploration of scientific concepts.
- Instruction is related and built on the abilities and experiences of the learners.
- Instruction is organized thematically.
- Mathematics and communication skills are integrated with science instruction.

The report also indicates that curriculum should emphasize the contributions of people from a variety of cultures. Finally, the NSTA (2002) states that science education can be successful if teachers receive adequate professional development and school administrators show a genuine interest in science education.

Scientific Inquiry

Scientific inquiry is promoted through hands-on activities and experimentation. From their experiences conducting scientific experiments, students acquire information firsthand and develop problem-solving skills. Children in the early grades are inquisitive and want to understand the environment around them. Teachers can use this interest to provide young students with opportunities to use electronic and printed sources to find answers to their questions and to expand their knowledge about the topic. Once students have developed a working knowledge of a topic, they can develop testable hypotheses. With the formulation of hypotheses, students begin the process of scientific inquiry and scientific experimentation.

Data Gathering

In planning and conducting experiments, teachers should guide children to develop an appropriate procedure for testing hypotheses, including the use of instruments that can yield measurable data. Even at the early stages of scientific experimentation, the procedure must be clear and tangible enough to allow replication by other students or scientists.

Scientific Vocabulary

Teachers need to be sure that students begin using scientific vocabulary to add precision to scientific inquiry and to avoid miscommunications. Generally, the appropriate scientific vocabulary should be introduced in class before students begin studying a topic and indirectly while they perform experiments. Making a connection between the hands-on activities and scientific vocabulary is beneficial to all students but especially to English language learners (ELLs), who can link the actions with the appropriate concept and vocabulary words without engaging in translations.

Data Analysis

When students complete their experiments, teachers have to be sure to analyze the data and link the findings to the research questions or hypotheses they posed before experimentation began. Students should be able to present pertinent data using graphic representations, like charts or graphs.

Interpreting and Communicating Results

Interpreting results is one of the most challenging phases of scientific inquiry for children in elementary school. Students can easily discuss the observable results but might have difficulty interpreting their meaning. Teachers have to use developmentally appropriate practices to guide students to make extrapolations and infer information from the data.

Communicating results in the elementary classroom can be tailored to the age and level of understanding of students in the EC-4 classroom. However, the report should include the following basic components, which can be simplified by developing questions to guide children to address each basic component.

- **Purpose of the Study**—What do you want to study?
- **Hypothesis**—What results are you expecting?
- **Methodology**—How do you plan to carry out the experiment?

- **Results**—What did you discover?
- **Interpretation**—What is the meaning of the results?

Science in Daily Life

Parents can promote scientific inquiry at home, using observation of daily activities to demonstrate scientific principles. With parental guidance, children can observe events and explain the scientific principles behind them. For example, children can watch the sunrise and sunset and then discuss the causes and implications of the two events. Do we see the sun rise and set because of the movement of the earth or the sun? Does everyone on the earth see these events at the same time? Other consistently occurring events, like the phases of the moon, the formation of clouds, and types of precipitation, can also be easily analyzed and discussed with young learners.

Scientific experimentation using common household items and food can also help parents introduce their children to the role of science in daily life. However, parents have to be sure that children know the types of experiments that they can do on their own and those that should be done only with adult supervision. A simple experiment to discover how soap works can motivate children to discover science in daily routine activities. For an explanation of this and other experiments using household items, go to "Kitchen Chemistry: Fun Food Activities and Experiments," a Web site from the Pittsburgh Teachers Institute of Chatham College, at *www. chatham.edu/PTI/Kitchen_Chem/BCleveland_01.htm*.

Health and Safety

Teachers have to create a safe environment for children involved in scientific inquiry. Here are some of the principles and practices that teachers can follow to reduce risks and protect children:

- Require students to use appropriate personal protective gear, like goggles, laboratory coats, and gloves.
- Use appropriate procedures for cleaning and disposing of materials.
- Adhere to appropriate disciplinary procedures to avoid accidents; for example, do not allow horseplay or teasing.
- Substitute less hazardous equivalent materials when possible; for example, use cleaning products instead of chemicals in their pure form.

- Use polyethylene or metal containers in place of glass.
- Advise children to avoid tasting or ingesting substances or materials.
- Label containers appropriately to avoid confusion.
- Control the use of sharp objects that can puncture the skin.
- Supervise the use of living organisms and the cleaning of instruments.
- Avoid experimenting with human cells and bodily fluids.
- Share the responsibility for the safety of the students with the whole group; that is, students should motivate each other to follow safety procedures.
- Make provision for the movement and handling of equipment and materials for students with special needs.

Assessing the Science Curriculum

As part of the accountability system, the state of Texas has a very comprehensive assessment system to measure the state uniform curriculum—the Texas Essential Knowledge and Skills (TEKS). In this system, students take the Texas Assessment of Knowledge and Skills (TAKS) test in grades 3 through 12. However, the science component of TEKS is assessed only in grades 5, 8, and 10. The fifth-grade science test is available in Spanish; thus, Spanish-speaking ELLs can take the test in Spanish. In addition to the required science TAKS examinations, students are assessed through teacher- and district-developed tests in kindergarten through grade 12.

Developmentally Appropriate Practices

Children's processing of scientific inquiry can begin as early as age 3 or 4. However, teachers must be aware of the stages of cognitive, social, and emotional development of children to appropriately introduce children to science concepts. For example, observing and experimenting with water and colors can easily be done by 3- or 4-year-olds, but using microscopes to observe and analyze animal or vegetable cells might be more appropriate for children in third and fourth grade.

Teachers can guide students at various levels of development to observe events, and through questioning, teachers can help students develop high-order thinking skills. For example, a teacher can lead children to make predictions while conducting experiments with objects that float or sink in water. By asking students to predict and explain why an object might sink or float, the teacher is leading students to analyze the properties of the object and the water to make an evaluative decision; that is, the children are using analysis and evaluation to complete that simple task.

Key Principles of the Competency

- Give students opportunities to develop and test hypotheses.
- Examine the terminology used in research. For example, *reliability* is based on similar results being obtained each time an experiment is conducted. To increase reliability, conduct the experiment or activity several times and calculate the average.
- Make students aware of common safety practices. For example, the safest way to heat up a test tube containing liquid is by using a test tube holder, positioning it at a 45-degree angle with its mouth pointing away from people and moving the tube back and forth through the flame.

Competency 021 (Physical Science)

The teacher understands the fundamental concepts, principles, and processes of physical science.

Matter

Matter is anything that takes up space and has mass. The **mass** of a body is the amount of matter in an object or thing, and **volume** describes the amount of space that matter takes up. Mass is also the property of a body that causes it to have weight. **Weight** is the amount of gravitational force exerted over an object.

There are 112 basic kinds of matter, called **elements**, which are organized into the **periodic table**. An element is composed of microscopic components called **atoms**. Atoms are made up of particles called **electrons**, **neutrons**, and **protons**. The mass of the atom is located mostly in the nucleus, which is made up of protons and neutrons. The electron contains little mass and follows an orbit around the nucleus.

States of Matter

Matter can exist in four distinct states: solid, liquid, gas, and plasma. Most people are familiar with the basic states of matter, but they might not be familiar with the fourth one, plasma. Plasmas are formed at extremely high temperatures when electrons are stripped from neutral atoms (University of California 2006). Stars are predominantly composed of plasmas.

Compounds consist of matter composed of atoms that are chemically combined with one another in definite weight proportions. An example of a compound is water; water is oxygen and hydrogen combined in the ratio of two hydrogen molecules to one molecule of oxygen—H_2O.

Mixtures are matter that is made up of two or more types of molecules, not chemically combined and without any definite weight proportions. For example milk is a mixture of water and butterfat particles. The components of a mixture can be separated physically. For example, milk producers and manufacturers remove the butterfat from whole milk to make skim milk.

Solutions are mixtures that are homogeneous, which means that the components are distributed evenly. Examples of solutions are seawater and ammonia. Seawater is made up of water and salt, and ammonia is made up of ammonia gas and water.

Properties of Matter

Matter has physical, thermal, electrical, and chemical properties.

Physical Properties

The physical properties of matter are the way matter looks and feels. It includes qualities like color, density, hardness, and conductivity. **Color** represents how matter is reflected or perceived by the human eye. **Density** is the mass that is contained in a unit of volume of a given substance. **Hardness** represents the resistance to penetration offered by a given substance. **Conductivity** is the ability of substances to transmit thermal or electric current.

Thermal Properties

Matter is sensitive to temperature changes. Heat and cold produce changes in the physical properties of matter; however, the chemical properties remain unchanged. For example, when water is exposed to cold temperature (release of heat), it changes from liquid to solid, and when exposed to heat, it changes from solid to liquid. With continued heat, the water changes from liquid to gas (water vapor). Water vapor can be cooled again and turned back into liquid. However, through all these states, water retains its chemical properties—two molecules of hydrogen and one molecule of oxygen.

Electrical Properties

Matter can be classified as a conductor or nonconductor of electricity. Conductive matter allows the transfer of electric current or heat from one point to another. Metals are usually good conductors, while wood and rocks are examples of nonconductive matter.

Chemical Properties

The chemical properties of one type of matter (element) can react with the chemical properties other types of matter. In general, elements from the same groups will not react with each other, while elements from different groups may. The more separated the groups, the more likely they will cause a chemical reaction when brought together. A type of matter can be chemically altered to become a different type of matter; for example, a metal trash can will rust if it is left out in the rain.

Scientific Tools and Their Use

Various tools or instruments are used in scientific experimentation in kindergarten through grade 4. The elementary classroom can be equipped with measuring devices like graduated cylinders, beakers, scales, dishes, thermometers, meter sticks, and micrometers. They might also have anatomical models showing the body systems.

The TEKS requires students to gather information using specific equipment and tools. Examples of the tools required in kindergarten through grade 4 are presented in Table 4-1 (TEA 2006).

In addition to the TEKS requirements for grades K–12, the Texas Education Agency has established the guidelines to provide a means to align the prekindergarten programs with the state curriculum. The state **Prekindergarten Curriculum Guidelines** are available at *www.tea.state.tx.us/curriculum/early/prekguide. html#1*.

Table 4-1. Tools and Equipment Required in the TEKS

Tools and Equipment	Kindergarten	1st	2nd	3rd	4th
Non-standard measurements	√	√	√		
Hand lenses	√	√	√	√	√
Computers	√	√	√	√	√
Balances	√	√	√	√	√
Cups and bowls	√	√	√	√	√
Thermometers		√	√	√	√
Clocks			√	√	√
Meter sticks			√	√	√
Microscopes				√	√
Safety goggles				√	√
Magnets				√	√
Compasses				√	√
Timing devices					√
Calculators					√
Sound recorders					√

Force, Work, and Energy

Force is defined as the action of moving an object by pulling or pushing it. Force can cause an object to move at a constant speed or to accelerate. When force is applied over a distance, work is done. **Work** is the product of the force acting in the direction of movement and causing displacement. **Energy** is defined as the ability to do work; when a tow truck uses force to pull a car and move it to a different location, energy was used and work was accomplished.

Heat and Light

The most common form of energy comes from the sun. Solar energy provides heat and light for animals and plants. Through **photosynthesis**, plants capture radiant energy from the sun and transform it into **chemical energy** in the form of glucose. This chemical energy is stored in the leaves, stems, and the fruits of plants. Humans and animals consume the plants or fruits and get the energy they need for survival. This energy source is transformed again to create kinetic energy and bodily heat. **Kinetic energy** is used for movement and to do work, while **heat** is a required element for all warm-blooded animals, like humans. Cold-blooded animals also require heat, but rather than making it themselves through the transformation of plant sugar, they use solar energy to heat their body. Energy transformation constitutes the foundation and the driving force of an ecosystem.

In addition to heat and solar radiation, energy is available in the forms of electricity and magnetism.

Electricity

Electricity is the flow of electrons or electric power or charge. The basic unit of charge is based on the positive charge of the proton and the negative charge of the electron. Energy occurs naturally in the atmosphere through light. However, it is not feasible to capture that type of energy. The electricity that we use comes from secondary sources because it is produced from the conversion of primary (natural) sources of energy like **fossil fuels** (natural gas, coal, and oil) and **nuclear**, **wind**, and **solar** energy. Electricity is used as a source of light, heat, and force.

Magnetism

Magnetism is the force of attraction or repulsion between objects that results from the positive and negative ionic charges of the objects. Usually, the objects are metals, such as iron, nickel, and cobalt. Magnets have two poles: north (+) and south (−). When the north pole of a magnet is placed close to the north pole of a second magnet, repulsion occurs. When poles of different kinds (north and south) are place closed, they attract one another. The strength of the forces depends on the size and the proximity of the magnets. The charged area around a magnet is called a magnetic field.

Principles of Energy

Energy is available in many forms, including heat, light, solar radiation, chemical, electrical, magnetic, and sound. It exists in three states: potential, kinetic, and activation energies. An object possessing energy because of its ability to move has **kinetic energy**. The energy that an object has as the result of its position or condition is called **potential energy**. The energy necessary to transfer or convert potential energy into kinetic energy is called **activation energy**. All three states of energy can be transformed from one to the other. A vehicle parked in a garage has potential energy. When the driver starts the engine using the chemical energy stored in the battery and the fuel, potential energy becomes activation energy. Once the vehicle is moving, the energy changes to kinetic energy.

Conservation of Energy

The main principle of energy conservation states that energy can change form but cannot totally disappear. For example, the chemical energy stored in a car battery is used to turn on the engine, which in turn is used to recharge the battery. Another example of energy conservation is when a storeowner stocks merchandise on shelves. Energy was used to do the work (placing merchandise on a shelf) and it was stored as potential energy. Potential energy in turn can be converted to kinetic energy when the merchandise is pushed back to the floor. In this case, work was recovered completely, but often the recovered energy is less than the energy used to do the work. This loss of energy can be caused by friction or any kind of resistance encountered in the process of doing the work. For example, as a vehicle's tires roll across the pavement, doing the work of moving forward, they encounter friction. This friction causes heat energy to be released, as well as kinetic energy.

Heat and Temperature

Heat is a form of energy. Temperature is the measure of heat. The most common device used to measure temperature is the thermometer. Thermometers are made of heat-sensitive substances— mercury and alcohol —that expand when heated.

Heat Transfer

The transfer of heat is accomplished in three ways: conduction, convection, and radiation. **Conduction** is the process of transferring heat or electricity through a substance. It occurs when two objects of differing temperatures are placed in contact with each other and heat flows from the hotter object to the cooler object. For example, in the cooling system of a car, heat from the engine is transferred to the liquid coolant. When the coolant passes through the radiator, the heat transfers from the coolant to the radiator and eventually out of the car. This heat transfer system preserves the engine and allows it to continue working.

Radiation describes the energy that travels at high speed in space in the form of light or through the decay of radioactive elements. Radiation is part of our modern life. It exists in simple states as the energy emitted by microwaves, cellular phones, and sunshine or as potentially dangerous as X-ray machines and nuclear weapons. The radiation used in medicine, nuclear power, and nuclear weapons has enough energy to cause permanent damage and death.

Convection describes the flow of heat through the movement of matter from a hot region to a cool region. It occurs when the heating and circulation of a substance change the density of the substance. A good example is the heating of air over lands near coastal areas that leads to the influx of cooler sea breezes offshore. The heated air inland expands and thus decreases in density, causing the cooler, more dense air to rush in to achieve equilibrium. A more common example of convection is the process of heating water on a stove. In this case, heat is transferred from the stove element to the bottom of the pot to the water. Heat is transferred from the hot water at the bottom to the cooler water at the top by convection. At the same time, the cooler, denser water at the top sinks to the bottom, where it is subsequently heated. This circulation creates the movement typical of boiling water.

Machines

A machine is something that makes work easier. Machines can be as simple as a wedge or a screw or as sophisticated as a computer or gas engine. A **simple machine** has few or no moving parts and can change the size and direction of a force. A screw, hammer, wedge, and incline plane are examples of simple machines. Simple machines are part of our daily activities. For example, children playing on a seesaw are using a simple machine called a **lever**.

A complex machine is two or more simple machines working together to facilitate work. Some of the complex machines used in daily activities are a wheelbarrow, a can opener, and a bicycle.

Precision and Accuracy in Investigation

Scientific experimentation cannot always rely on our senses to record information. Instead, science requires the use of standard measuring devices to be sure that the information is clearly presented. The United States uses a combination of the English system of measurement (standard), and the metric system. In fact, the United States is the only technologically developed country in the world that uses the English system for business transactions and for day-to-day activities. However, for international business, engineering, and natural sciences, all countries use a more precise system of weights and measurement, the metric system. The English system uses pounds, gallons, and inches for measurement, while the metric system uses kilos, liters, and meters. The metric system uses a system of fractions and multiples of units that are related to each other by powers of 10, allowing conversion and comparison of measures simply by shifting a decimal point, and avoiding the lengthy arithmetical operations required by the English system. The TEKS requires the teaching of both the metric and the English systems.

Safety Management

The use of dangerous chemical substances in the elementary classroom is limited in scope; however, even household products contain chemicals that must be handled properly. Safety management of chemicals in the classroom requires teachers to have knowledge of those chemicals and their properties. For example, teachers need to be aware that a simple tool like a mercury thermometer can break and pose a danger to children. In general, maintaining safety requires teachers to take the following steps:

- Assess the relative danger of each chemical used in the classroom.
- Label and store chemicals appropriately.
- Implement safety procedures for the use and handling of materials and equipment.
- Follow appropriate procedures for cleaning containers and disposing of chemicals.

Key Principles of the Competency

- To help students develop higher-order thinking skills, teachers need to guide students to analyze research data and make extrapolations or inferences based on data analysis.
- Matter is anything that has mass and takes up space.
- Mass is the amount of matter something contains.
- Volume refers to the amount of space taken up by an object.
- The states of matter are solid, gas, and liquid.
- There are 112 basic kinds of matter called elements. Elements are made up of atoms. An atom is the smallest part of matter.
- A compound is a kind of matter made up of two or more elements. A chemical formula describes the kinds of elements present in a compound. The chemical formula of water is H_2O because it has two molecules of hydrogen and one molecule of oxygen.
- Physical properties of matter are the characteristics that can be seen or measured without changing the material.
- Chemical properties of matter are the characteristics that can only be seen when the material changes and new materials are formed; for example, wood burns and turns into ashes. A chemical property of wood is its ability to burn.
- Water boils at 212 degrees Fahrenheit or 100 degrees Celsius, and it freezes at 32 degrees Fahrenheit or 0 degrees Celsius.
- Weight is the amount of gravitational force exerted over an object.
- When measuring dry chemicals on a balance scale, teachers should follow these steps: (1) Place and weigh a watch glass or dish, (2) place the dry chemical inside the watch glass or dish, and (3) subtract the weight of the glass or dish from the total to obtain the real weight of the chemical.

Competency 022 (Life Science)

The teacher understands the fundamental concepts, principles, and processes of life science.

Cell System

The cell is the basic unit of living organisms and the simplest living unit of life. Living organisms are composed of cells that have the following common characteristics:

- Have a membrane that regulates the flow of nutrients and water that enter and exit the cell
- Contain the genetic material (DNA) that allows for reproduction
- Require a supply of energy
- Contain basic chemicals to make metabolic decisions for survival
- Reproduce and are the result of reproduction

Eukaryotic and Prokaryotic Cells

There are two kinds of cells—prokaryotic and eukaryotic. **Prokaryotic** cells are the simplest and most primitive type of cells. They do not contain the structures typical of eukaryotic cells. Some prokaryotic cells have external whiplike flagella for locomotion or a hairlike system for adhesion. Prokaryotic cells come in three shapes: cocci (round), bacilli (rods), and spirilla or spirochetes (helical cells).

Eukaryotic cells evolved from prokaryotic cells and in the process became structurally and biochemically more complex. The key distinction between the two cell types is that only eukaryotic cells contain many structures, or organelles, separated from other cytoplasm components by a membrane. The organelles within eukaryotic cells are the nucleus, mitochondria, chloroplasts, and Golgi apparatus. The nucleus contains the deoxyribonucleic acid (DNA) information. The mitochondria have their own membrane and contain some DNA information and proteins. They generate the energy for the cell. The chloroplast is a component that exists in plants only, allowing them to trap sunlight as energy for the process of photosynthesis. The Golgi apparatus secretes substances needed for the cell's survival.

Reproduction

An organism may consist of only one cell, or it may comprise many billions of cells of various dimensions. Cells are composed primarily of water and the elements oxygen, hydrogen, carbon, and nitrogen. Growth in most organisms is caused by nuclear cell division (**mitosis**) and replication (**meiosis**), in addition to enlargement of the cells themselves. Some cells are complete organisms, such as the unicellular bacteria; others, such as muscle cells, are parts of multicellular organisms. All cells have an internal substance called cytoplasm—a clear gelatinous fluid—enclosed within a membrane. Each cell contains the genetic material containing the information for the formation of organisms.

Classifications of Living Things

Living things are divided into five groups, or **kingdoms**: Monera (bacteria), Protista (protozoans), Fungi, Plantae (plants), and Animalia (animals). **Monera** consists of unicellular organisms. It is the only group of living organisms made of prokaryotic cells—the cells with a primitive organization system. Some examples of this organism are bacteria, blue-green algae, and spirochetes.

Protista contains a type of eukaryotic cell with a more complex organization system. This kingdom includes diverse, mostly unicellular organisms that live in aquatic habitats, in both freshwater and saltwater. They are not animals or plants but a unique organism. Some examples of Protista are protozoans and algae of various types.

Fungi are made of multicellular organisms with a sophisticated organization system—that is, containing eukaryotic cells. They exist in a variety of forms and shapes. Because they do not have chlorophyll, they cannot produce food through photosynthesis. Fungi obtain energy, carbon, and water from dead materials. Some examples of these types of organisms are mushrooms, mold, mildews, and yeast.

Plants are multicellular organisms with a sophisticated organization system. In addition to more familiar plants, moss and ferns also fall under this category. Plant cells have chloroplasts, a component that allows them to trap sunlight as energy for the process of photosynthesis. Photosynthesis eliminates carbon dioxide from the environment and produces the oxygen needed for the survival of animals.

Animals are also multicellular with multiple forms and shapes, and with specialized senses and organs. The Animalia kingdom is composed of organisms like sponges, worms, insects, fish, amphibians, reptiles, birds, and mammals. Animals are the most sophisticated type of living organisms and represent the highest levels of evolution. Animals live in all kinds of habitats, and they are as simple as flies or as sophisticated as humans.

For additional information about living things, go to the Web site of the Behavioral Sciences Department of Palomar College, San Marcos, California, at *http://anthro.palomar.edu/animal/default.htm*.

Animal and Plant Cells

Animal and plant cells are similar in appearance. Animal cells contain mitochondria, small round or rod-shaped bodies found in the cytoplasm of most cells. The main function of mitochondria is to produce the enzymes for the metabolic conversion of food to energy. This process consumes oxygen and is termed **aerobic respiration**.

Plants cells also contain mitochondria and similar organelles called chloroplasts. Chloroplasts contain chlorophyll, used in converting light into chemical energy. This process is called **photosynthesis**. Photosynthesis is the process by which chlorophyll-containing organisms convert light energy to chemical energy.

Systems of the Human Body

Musculoskeletal System

The human skeleton consists of more than 200 bones held together by connective tissues called ligaments. Movements are effected by contractions of the skeletal muscles, to which the bones are attached by tendons. Muscular contractions are controlled by the nervous system.

Nervous System

The nervous system has two main divisions: the somatic and automatic. The somatic allows the voluntary control of skeletal muscles, and the automatic, or involuntary, controls cardiac and glandular functions. **Voluntary movement** is caused by nerve impulses sent from the brain through the spinal cord to nerves to connecting skeletal muscles. **Involuntary movement** occurs in direct response to outside stimulus. Involuntary responses are called reflexes. For example, when an object presents danger to the eye, the body responds automatically by blinking or retracting away from the object.

Circulatory System

The circulatory system follows a cyclical process in which the heart pumps blood through the right chambers of the heart and through the lungs, where it acquires oxygen. From there it is pumped back into the left chambers of the heart, where it is pumped into the main artery (aorta), which then sends the oxygenated blood to the rest of the body using a system of veins and capillaries. Through the capillaries, the blood distributes the oxygen and nutrients to tissues, absorbing from them carbon dioxide, a metabolic waste product. Finally, the blood completes the circuit by passing through small veins, which join to form increasingly larger vessels. Eventually, the blood reaches the largest veins, which return it to the right side of the heart to complete and restart the process.

Immune System

The main function of the body's immune system is to defend itself against foreign proteins and infectious organisms. The system recognizes organisms that are not normally in the body and develops the antibodies needed to control and destroy the invaders. When the body is attacked by infectious organisms, it develops what we know as a fever. Fever is caused by the body's way of fighting invading molecules. The raised temperature of a fever will kill some bacteria. The major components of the immune system are the thymus, lymph system, bone marrow, white blood cells, antibodies, and hormones.

Respiratory System

Respiration is carried out by the expansion and contraction of the lungs. In the lungs, oxygen enters tiny capillaries, where it combines with **hemoglobin** in the red blood cells and is carried to the tissues through the circulatory system. At the same time, carbon dioxide passes through capillaries into the air contained within the lungs.

Animals inhale oxygen from the environment and exhale carbon dioxide. Carbon dioxide is used by plants in the process of photosynthesis, which produces the oxygen that animals use again for survival.

Digestive and Excretory Systems

The energy required for sustenance of the human body is supplied through the chemical energy stored in food. To obtain the energy from food, it has to be fragmented and digested. Digestion begins at the moment that food is placed in the mouth and makes contact with saliva. Fragmented and partially digested food passes down the esophagus to the stomach, where the process is continued by the gastric and intestinal juices. Thereafter, the mixture of food and secretions makes its way down the small intestine, where the nutrients are extracted and absorbed into the bloodstream. The unused portion of the food goes to the large intestine and eventually is excreted from the body through defecation.

For a detailed analysis of each component of the body system go to the Human Anatomy Online Web site at *www.innerbody.com/htm/body.html*.

Ecology

Ecology studies the relationship of organisms with their physical environment. The physical environment includes light, heat, solar radiation, moisture, wind, oxygen, carbon dioxide, nutrients, water, and the atmosphere. The biological environment describes living and nonliving organisms in the ecosystem. There are three main components of an ecosystem:

- **Producers** are green plants that produce oxygen and store chemical energy for consumers.
- **Consumers** are animals, both herbivores and carnivores. The herbivores take the chemical energy from plants and carnivores take the energy from other animals or directly from plants.
- **Decomposers,** like fungi and bacteria, are in charge of cleaning up the environment by decomposing and freeing dead matter for recycling back into the ecosystem.

Maintaining a Healthy Balance

A successful ecosystem requires a healthy balance among producers, consumers, and decomposers. This balance relies on natural ways to control populations of living organisms and is maintained mostly through competition and predation.

Competition

When a shared resource is scarce, organisms must compete to survive. The competition, which occurs between animals as well as between plants, ensures the survival of the fittest and the preservation of the system.

Predation

Predation is the consumption of one living organism, plant or animal, by another. It is a direct way to control population and promote natural selection by eliminating weak organisms from the population. As a consequence of predation, predators and prey evolve to survive. If an organism cannot evolve to meet challenges from the environment, it perishes.

Life Cycles

Life traditionally begins with a seed or a fertilized egg, which goes through metamorphosis until the organism is fully formed. The development and growth of organisms can take days, months, or years, but eventually they all go through similar stages: creation, maturation, reproduction, and death. Some organisms, like insects, go through a short cycle, reproducing once and then dying. Others, like vertebrates, spend more time in the reproductive stage. Some examples of living organisms and the changes that they go through are presented in Table 4-2.

Table 4-2. Life Cycles of Common Organisms

Organism	Stage 1	Stage 2	Stage 3	Stage 4	Stage 5
Fruit fly and butterfly	Egg	Larva/ caterpillar	Pupa (organism forms a cocoon or chrysalis)	Fully formed	Reproduction, death
Frog	Egg	Embryo	Tadpole	Frog	Reproduction (multiple), death
Human	Egg, sperm	Fetus	Child	Adolescent	Reproduction (multiple), death
Trees	Seed	Sprout	Growing plant	Mature plant	Reproduction (multiple), death

Some of the most spectacular metamorphoses are experienced by insects, amphibians, and humans. Insects, like the fruit fly and the butterfly, go through drastic changes in a period of weeks. Frogs go through similar transmutation that allows them to move from an aquatic environment to land. Humans, on the other hand, begin life as microscopic beings and after nine months develop into a six- to nine-pound physically functional individual.

The National Science Education Standards (NSES) and the TEKS emphasize that during the primary grades, students should be exposed to the concept of life cycles for plants and animals, including humans.

Life Cycle of Plants

The life cycle of plants generally begins with seeds. Mature plants produce the seeds, which are transported through various means: wind, water, hitchhiking on animals, or ingested as food and released as droppings or waste. For the seeds to germinate, grow, and mature, they must have the right kind of soil, sufficient water, and heat from the sun. As part of the growth process, plants develop a root system for support and to extract the water and minerals they need from the soil.

Through the process of **photosynthesis**, a plant containing chlorophyll captures energy from the sun and converts it into chemical energy. Part of the chemical energy is used for the plant's own survival, and the rest is stored in the stem and leaves. As part of the growth process, some plants produce flowers, which are pollinated by insects or through the wind. Once pollination occurs, fruits that contain the seeds are produced, and the cycle of the plant continues.

For information on how this process can be presented to children in the primary grades, visit the following site: "The Life Cycle of Plants," at *www.cast. org/teachingeverystudent*. For additional information about photosynthesis visit the following site: "Exploring Photosynthesis," at *www.botany.uwc.ac.za/ecotree/ photosynthesis/photosynthesis1.htm*.

Life Cycle of Animals

Many animals come from eggs. For some animals, the egg grows inside the female animal and is fertilized by the male. The egg has an outer lining to protect the animal growing inside. Bird eggs have hard shells, while the eggs of amphibians, like the turtle, have hard but flexible coverings. With the appropriate care and heat, an egg will hatch. After hatching, the parents protect and feed the newborn until it can survive on its own. On reaching adulthood, females begin laying eggs, and the cycle of life continues. Mammals are also conceived through egg fertilization, but the resulting embryo is kept inside the mother until it is mature enough for life outside the womb.

Needs of Living Organisms

Living organisms like plants and animals need to have ideal conditions for their survival. They need nutrients, the appropriate temperature, and a balanced ecosystem to survive and reproduce. A healthy ecosystem must contain an appropriate system for energy exchange, or a food chain. The right combination of herbivorous and carnivorous animals is necessary for a healthy ecosystem. The food chain generally begins with the primary source of energy, the sun. The sun provides the energy for plants, plants in turn are consumed by animals, and animals are consumed by other animals. These animals die and serve as food sources for fungi and plants. When this balance is disrupted either by the removal of organisms or the introduction of nonnative species, the ecosystem is affected, forcing animals and plants to adapt.

Adaptation for Survival

Changes in the environment force living organisms to modify their ways and even develop new physical features for survival. For example, the anteater developed a long snout to be able to reach for ants, and frogs developed a long, sticky tongue to catch flies. Adaptation for animals, plants, and even humans is a matter of life and death. Changes in the food chain of animals often force them to change their behaviors and adapt to new conditions.

For example, because their habitats are destroyed when land is developed by humans, raccoons and opossums have learned to coexist with humans and to get new sources of food. Bears have managed to successfully adapt to colder climates by hibernating during the winter and living on the fat they accumulate during the rest of they year. Other animals, like the chameleon or the fox, have developed camouflage to hide from predators. Humans are not exempt from the need to adapt to new situations. For example, humans have had to adapt and use tools to produce, preserve, and trade the food supplies they needed to sustain them. All these examples represent ways in which organisms adapt to deal with challenges in their ecosystem.

Animal Reproduction

As part of the cycle of life, organisms go through a cycle of reproduction in which they have offspring. Reproduction in animals can be subdivided into asexual and sexual. In the animal kingdom, **asexual** reproduction is basically restricted to unicellular organisms, with the parent cell splitting to create a new identical organism. **Sexual** reproduction, on the other hand, requires the insemination of an egg (ova) with sperm. Insemination for vertebrates occurs through copulation, and for fish and some amphibians it occurs through cross-fertilization. Cross-fertilization occurs outside the body; the female lays the eggs (ovum), and the males spray them with sperm to fertilize them.

Plant Reproduction

The reproduction of plants can also be divided into asexual and sexual. Asexual reproduction of plants takes place by cutting portions of the plant and replanting them. Sexual reproduction involves seeds produced by female and male plants, which are then cross-pollinated with help from insects or other animals. Seed germination requires the appropriate quantity of water and heat for the seed to sprout.

Key Principles of the Competency

- When working with animals, teachers are ethically responsible for their well-being. Teachers need to provide an adequate environment for the survival and development of animals under their care.
- By observing the development of frogs and butterflies, students directly acquire information on the life cycles. Students can also observe how organisms adapt to their environment.
- Fungi obtain energy, carbon, and water from dead material. Fungi do not have chlorophyll, so they cannot produce food through photosynthesis.
- Chromosomes contain the genetic code, or DNA.
- Mitosis describes the process of a cell splitting to create two identical cells.
- Photosynthesis is the process of capturing, storing and converting solar energy. It is also the source of oxygen in the atmosphere.
- Insects have three main parts: head, thorax, and abdomen.
- Humans have several body systems, including the musculoskeletal, nervous, circulatory, immune, respiratory, and digestive/excretory systems.

Competency 023 (Earth and Space Science)

The teacher understands the fundamental concepts, principles, and processes of earth and space science.

Structure and Composition of the Earth (Geology)

Minerals

Minerals are the most common form of solid material found in the earth's crust. Even soil contains bits of minerals that have broken away from rock. To be considered a mineral, a substance must be found in nature and must never have been a part of any living organism. Minerals can be as soft as talc or as hard as emeralds and diamonds. Dug from the earth, minerals are used to make various products:

- **Jewelry**—Gemstones such as amethysts, opals, diamonds, emeralds, topazes, and garnets are examples of minerals commonly used to create jewelry. Gold and silver are another type of mineral that can be used to create jewelry.

- **Construction**—Gypsum boards (drywall) are made of a mineral of the same name—gypsum. The windows in homes are made from another mineral, quartz.
- **Personal Use**—Talc is the softest mineral and it is commonly applied to the body in powder form.

Rock Types

The hard, solid part of the earth's surface is called rock. Rocks are made of one or more minerals. Rocks like granite, marble, and limestone are extensively used in the construction industry. They can be used in floors, buildings, dams, highways, or the making of cement. Rocks are classified by the way they are formed. Here are descriptions of the three types of rock:

- **Igneous** rocks are crystalline solids that form directly from the cooling of magma or lava. The composition of the magma determines the composition of the rock. **Granite** is one of the most common types of igneous rocks and is created from magma (inside the earth). Once magma reaches the earth surface, it is called lava. Lava that has cooled forms a rock with a glassy look, called **obsidian**.
- **Sedimentary** rocks are called secondary rocks because they are often the result of the accumulation of small pieces broken off from preexisting rocks and then pressed into a new form. There are three types of sedimentary rocks:

  - **Clastic** sedimentary rocks are made when pieces of rock, mineral, and organic material fuse together. These are classified as conglomerates, sandstone, and shale.
  - **Chemical** sedimentary rocks are formed when water rich in minerals evaporates, leaving the minerals behind. Some common examples are gypsum, rock salt and some limestone.
  - **Organic** sedimentary rocks are made from the remains of plants and animals. For example, coal is formed when dead plants are squeezed together. Another example is a form of limestone rock composed of the remains of organisms that lived in the ocean.

- **Metamorphic** rocks are also secondary rocks formed from igneous, sedimentary, or other types of metamorphic rock. When hot magma or lava comes in contact with rocks or when buried rocks are exposed to pressure and high temperatures, the result is metamorphic rocks. For example, exposing limestone to high temperatures creates marble. The most common metamorphic rocks are slate, gneiss, and marble.

For more information, go to *http://jersey.uoregon.edu/~mstrick/AskGeoMan/geoQuerry13.html*.

Rock Cycle

The formation of rock follows a cyclical process. For instance, rocks can be formed when magma or lava cools down, creating igneous rocks. Igneous rocks exposed to weathering can break into sediment, which can be compacted and cemented to form sedimentary rocks. Sedimentary rocks are exposed to heat and pressure to create metamorphic rocks. Finally, metamorphic rocks can melt and become magma and lava again (Badder et al. 2000).

Landform Characteristics

The formation of deserts, mountains, rivers, oceans, and other landforms can be described in terms of geological processes. Mountains are formed by colliding plates. For example, the Appalachian Mountains in the United States were formed when the tectonic plate carrying the continent of Africa collided with the plate carrying the North American continent 250 million years ago (Badder et. al. 2000). Rivers and natural lakes form at low elevations where rainfall collects and eventually runs down to the sea. The sediment gathered by the rivers in turn accumulates at river mouths to create deltas.

Layers of the Earth

The average circumference of the earth at the equator is 25,902 miles, and its radius is about 3,959 miles. The earth is divided into three main parts:

- The **crust** is the outer portion of the earth where we live. The thickness of the crust varies from about 3 miles to 40 miles, depending on the location. It contains various types of soil, metals, and rocks. The crust is broken down into several floating tectonic plates. Movements of these plates cause earthquakes and changes in landforms.
- The **mantle** is the thickest layer of the earth located right below the crust. It is composed mostly of rocks

and metals. The heat in the mantle is so intense that rocks and metals melt, creating magma and the resulting lava that reaches the surface.

- The **core** is the inner part of the earth. It is composed of a solid inner core and an outer core that is mostly liquid. The inner core is made of solid iron and nickel. Despite temperatures in the inner core that resemble the heat on the surface of the sun, this portion of the earth remains solid because of the intense pressure there.

For more information about the layers of the earth, go to *http://jersey.uoregon.edu/~mstrick/AskGeoMan/geoQuerry8.html*.

Continental Drift

In 1915, the German scientist Alfred Weneger proposed that all the continents were previously one large continent but then broke apart and drifted through the ocean floor to their present locations. This theory was called the Continental Drift, and it was the origin of today's concept of plate tectonics.

Tectonic Plates

Based on the theory of plate tectonics, the surface of the earth is fragmented into large plates. These plates are in continuous motion, floating on the liquid mantle and always changing in size and position. The edges of these plates, where they move against each other, are sites of intense geologic activity, which results in earthquakes, volcanoes, and the creation of mountains.

The Earth's Atmosphere

The earth is surrounded by a large mass of gas called the atmosphere. Roughly 348 miles thick, this gas mass supports life on the earth and separates it from space. Among the many functions of the atmosphere are these:

- Absorbing energy from the sun to sustain life
- Recycling water and other chemicals needed for life
- Maintaining the climate, working with electric and magnetic forces
- Serving as a vacuum that protects life

The atmosphere is composed of 78 percent nitrogen, 21 percent oxygen, and 1 percent argon. In addition to these gases, the atmosphere contains water and greenhouse gases like ozone, and carbon dioxide.

Gravity

Gravity is the force of attraction that exits between objects. Gravity keeps the earth in its orbit by establishing a balance between the attraction of the sun and the speed at which the earth travels around it. Some of the main functions of gravity are listed here:

- Keeping the earth's atmosphere, oceans, and inhabitants from drifting into space
- Pulling the rain to the rivers and eventually to the sea
- Guiding the development and growth of plants
- Affecting the way that our bones and muscles function

For information about the earth and space, go to the official Web site of the National Aeronautics and Space Administration (NASA) at *www.nasa.gov/home/index.html?skipIntro=1*. This site includes special sections for children, students from kindergarten through grade 12, and teachers.

Water Cycle

The hydrologic cycle describes a series of movements of water above, on, and below the surface of the earth. This cycle consists of four distinct stages: storage, evaporation, precipitation, and runoff. It is the means by which the sun's energy is used to transport, through the atmosphere, stored water from the rivers and oceans to land masses. The heat of the sun evaporates the water and takes it to the atmosphere from which, through condensation, it falls as precipitation. As precipitation falls, water is filtrated back to underground water deposits called aquifers, or it runs off into storage in lakes, ponds, and oceans.

Tides

The word *tides* is used to describe the alternating rise and fall in sea level with respect to the land, produced by the gravitational attraction of the moon and the sun. Additional factors such as the configuration of the coastline, depth of the water, the topography of the ocean floor, and other hydrographic and meteorological influences may play an important role in altering the range, interval, and times of arrival of the tides.

Forces That Change the Surface of the Earth

Three main forces and processes change the surface of the earth: weathering, geological movements, and the creation of glaciers.

Weathering

Weathering is the process of breaking down rock, soils, and minerals through natural, chemical, and biological processes. Two of the most common examples of physical weathering are exfoliation and freeze-thaw.

- **Exfoliation** occurs in places like the desert when the soil is exposed first to high temperatures, which cause it to expand, and then to cold temperatures, which make the soil contract. The stress of these changes causes the outer layers of rock to peel off.

- **Freeze-thaw** breaks down rock when water gets into rock joints or cracks and then freezes and expands, breaking the rock. A similar process occurs when water containing salt crystals gets into the rock. Once the water evaporates, the crystals expand and break the rock. This process is called salt-crystal growth.

Weathering can be caused by chemical reactions. Two of the most common examples of chemical weathering are acid formation and hydration. Acid is formed under various conditions. For example, sulfur and rain are combined to create acid rain, which can weather and change the chemical composition of rock. Hydration occurs when the minerals in rock absorb water and expand, sometimes changing the chemical composition of the rock. For example, through the process of hydration, a mineral like anhydrite can be changed into a different mineral, gypsum.

Erosion

After weathering, a second process called erosion can take place. **Erosion** is the movement of sediment from one location to the other through the use of water, wind, ice, or gravity. The Grand Canyon was created by the processes of weathering and erosion. The water movement (erosion) is responsible for the canyon being so deep, and the weathering process is responsible for its width (Badder et al. 2000).

Geologic Activity

Earthquakes and Geologic Faults

The movement of the earth's plates has forced rock layers to fold, creating mountains, hills, and valleys. This movement causes **faults** in the earth's crust, breaking rocks and reshaping the environment. When forces within the earth cause rocks to break and move around geologic faults, earthquakes occur. A fault is a deep crack that marks the boundary between two plates. The San Andreas fault in central California is a well-known origin of earthquakes in the area. The epicenter of an earthquake is the point on the surface where the quake is the strongest. The **Richter scale** is used to measure the amount of energy released by the earthquake. The severity of an earthquake runs from 0 to 9 on the Richter scale. Small tremors occur constantly, but every few months, a major earthquake occurs somewhere in the world. Scientists are researching ways to predict earthquakes, but their predictions are not always accurate.

Volcanoes

Volcanoes are formed by the constant motion of tectonic plates. This movement creates pressure that forces magma from the mantel to escape to the surface, creating an explosion of lava, fire, and ash. The pressure of the magma and gases creates a monticule, or a small cone, that eventually grows to form a mountain-like volcano. Volcanic activity can create earthquakes, and the fiery lava can cause destruction.

Space Science

Galaxies

Galaxies are large collections of stars, hydrogen, dust particles, and other gases. The universe is made of countless galaxies. The solar system that includes Earth is part of a galaxy called the Milky Way.

Stars

Stars like the sun are composed of large masses of hydrogen pulled together by gravity. The hydrogen, with strong gravitational pressure, creates fusion inside the star, turning the hydrogen into helium. The liberation of energy created by this process causes solar radiation, which makes the sun glow with visible light, as well as forms of radiation not visible to the human eye.

Solar System

The sun is the center of our solar system, which is composed of nine planets, many satellites that orbit the planets, and a large number of smaller bodies like comets and asteroids. Short definitions of these terms follows:

- Planets are large bodies orbiting the sun.
- Satellites are moons orbiting the planets.
- Asteroids are small dense objects orbiting the sun.
- Comets are small icy objects traveling through space in an elliptical orbit around the sun.

Planets

The **inner** solar system contains the sun, Mercury, Venus, Earth, and Mars, and the outer solar system comprises Jupiter, Saturn, Uranus, Neptune, and Pluto. The following mnemonic device can be used to guide children to remember the locations of the planets with respect to the sun:

For more details about the solar system, go to the Zoom Astrology Web site at *www.enchantedlearning.com/subjects/astronomy*.

Movements of Planet Earth

Earth performs two kinds of movement: rotation and revolution. **Rotation** describes the spinning of Earth on its axis. Earth takes approximately 24 hours to make a complete (360-degree) rotation, which creates the day and night.

While Earth is rotating rotates on its axis, it is also following an orbit around the sun. This movement is called **revolution**. It takes a year, or 365¼ days for Earth to complete one revolution. The tilt of Earth as it moves around the sun and its curvature create **climate zones** and seasons. The zones immediately north and south of the equator are called the tropics—Cancer (north) and Capricorn (south). The Arctic Circle (North Pole) and Antarctic Circle (South Pole) are the area surrounding Earth's axis points.

Phases of the Moon

During each lunar orbit around Earth (about 28 days), the moon appears to go through several stages based on the portion of the moon visible from Earth. The moon does not have its own source of light but reflects the light from the sun. The shape of the moon varies from a full moon, when Earth is between the sun and the moon, to a new moon, when the moon is located between the sun and Earth. A description of the major stages of the moon follows:

- **New Moon**—The moon is not visible to Earth because the side of the moon facing Earth is not being lit by the sun.
- **Crescent Moon**—At this stage between the half moon and the new moon, the shape of the moon is often compared to a banana.
- **Half Moon, or First Quarter**—During this stage, half of the moon is visible.

My	Very	Elegant	Mother	Just	Served	Us	Nutritious	Pizzas
Mercury	Venus	Earth	Mars	Jupiter	Saturn	Uranus	Neptune	Pluto*

*In August 2006, the International Astronomical Union (IAU) adopted a new definition for the concept of planet. As a result, Pluto is no longer considered a planet. The new classification for Pluto is "dwarf planet."

- **Gibbous Moon**—In this stage, about three quarters of the moon is visible.
- **Full Moon**—The whole moon is visible from Earth.

The term **blue moon** describes the appearance of two full moons in a single calendar month. The expression "once in a blue moon" represents an event that is not very frequent.

Key Principles of the Competency

- Our solar system is part of the Milky Way, one of many galaxies in the universe.
- Minerals and rocks are commonly used in our daily life.
- The movement of tectonic plates creates intense geologic activity that results in earthquakes and volcanic activity.
- The earth's atmosphere protects and preserves life.

- The water cycles are the movement and distribution of water within the earth's atmosphere.

References

Badder, W., D. Peck, L. J. Bethel, C. Sumner, V. Fu, and C. Valentino. 2000. *Discovery works*. Texas ed. Boston: Houghton Mifflin.

National Science Teacher Association (NSTA). 2002. *Elementary school science*. Position paper. *http://www.nsta.org/position statement&psid=8/.*

Texas Education Agency (TEA). 2006. *Prekinder curriculum guidelines.* *http://www.tea.state.tx.us/curriculum/early/prekguide.html#4.*

———. 2006. Texas Essential Knowledge and Skills. *http://www.tea.state.tx.us/teks/.*

University of California, Lawrence Livermore National Laboratory. 2006. *Plasma: The fourth state of matter.* *http://FusEdWeb.llnl.gov/CPEP/.*

Domain V: Fine Arts, Health, and Physical Education

Competency 024 (Visual Arts)

The teacher understands concepts, processes, and skills involved in the creation, appreciation, and evaluation of art and uses this knowledge to plan and implement effective art instruction.

Fine Arts or Visual Arts?

The term **fine arts** is an umbrella term used to describe artworks that appeal to people's aesthetics. Fine arts includes music, theater, sculpture, painting, print making, and other traditional forms of art. However, fine arts excludes applied arts or craftwork like basket weaving, ceramics, and textiles. To include more forms of artistic expression and to encompass these other forms of aesthetic expression, the term **visual arts** was coined. The term visual arts refers to "fine arts" such as sculpture, painting, and print making, but it also includes lesser known forms of art like textiles, basket weaving, ceramic making, metalworking—blacksmithing and jewelry, and more modern art forms like photography and film making. The term visual arts is a more inclusive term and a better descriptor for the type of arts produced in modern society.

Main Goal of Art Education

The overall goals of art education include developing aesthetic perception, examining many art forms, and providing opportunities to reflect on and discuss observations and reactions. Art education provides opportunities for children to develop and extend their own art abilities, and exposes children to characteristics of art and objects of arts. Art education empowers children to analyze diverse forms of visual arts using informed judgments. Due to these important benefits and life skills, art education is an important component of the Texas Essential Knowledge and Skills through from grades K through 12.

Texas Essential Knowledge and Skills (TEKS)

The state curriculum for fine arts and for visual arts is organized around four main strands—perception, creative expression, historical/cultural heritage, and critical evaluation. A summary of the key elements required from children in grades K–4 is presented in Table 5-1 (TEA, 2006).

Traditionally, these curriculum components are delivered by an art teacher in collaboration with EC–4 teachers. In the absence of specialized art teachers, the EC–4 teacher might be required to deliver the visual arts curriculum components.

The Art Classroom

Traditionally, elementary schools have at least one art room for the school. The room should allow for individual seating arrangements as well as small-group and large-group arrangements. There should be areas for the teacher to lecture and display students' work; space for learning centers; and areas for drawing, painting, printmaking, creating computer graphics, working with ceramics, modeling, and assembling crafts. There should be both natural and artificial lighting in the room. Materials should be stored in cabinets, with access controlled by the teachers. Safety guidelines are critical, and following them is mandatory. Ease of cleanup is a requirement; therefore, sinks and surfaces must have durable, cleanable finishes.

Table 5-1. Visual Arts Strands for K–4

Grade	Perceptions	Creative Expressions	Historical/Cultural	Critical Evaluation
Kindergarten	Identify colors, textures, forms in the environment.	Create art work using a variety of colors, forms and line.	Share ideas about personal artworks and show respect for different opinions.	Express ideas about personal artworks, and the artworks of peers or professional artists.
First Grade	Identify **art elements** such as color, texture, form, line with emphasis on nature and human-made environment.	Invent images that combine color, form and line, and organize forms to create designs.	Demonstrate a basic understanding of art history. Select artwork that show families and groups.	Make informed judgment about their personal artworks, and the work of peers.
Second Grade	Continue using color, texture, form, line, space, and art principles, like emphasis, patterns and rhythm to create artworks.	Produce drawings, paintings, prints, constructions, and modeled forms using a variety of art materials.	Develop respect for the tradition and contributions in arts of diverse groups.	Define reasons for preferences in artworks.
Third Grade	Continue emphasizing **art principles** such as emphasis, patterns, rhythm, balance, proportion, and unity in artworks.	Express ideas through original artworks using a variety of media. Develop compositions using design skills; and produce. drawings, print constructions, and ceramics.	Compare artworks from different cultures, and link it to different kinds of jobs in everyday life.	Apply simple criteria to identify main ideas in original artworks.
Fourth Grade	Communicate ideas about self, family, school and community using sensory knowledge and experiences.	Invent ways to produce artworks and to explore photographic imagery using a variety of media and materials.	Compare artworks from various groups; identify the role of art in American society.	Interpret ideas and moods in original artworks.

Visual Arts Activities for Grades K–4

Throughout the lower elementary grades, students engage in a variety of art activities such as drawing, painting, designing, constructing, crafts, sculpting, weaving, finger painting, and Styrofoam carving. In grades 3 and 4, students continue perfecting the skills from K through 2 and start working with new techniques like printmaking, sponge painting, graphics, film animation, and environmental design. Art materials for the elementary art program include scissors, wet and dry brushes, fabrics, wrapping papers, film, computers, clay, glue, Styrofoam, construction paper, crayons, beads, and multiple household items that can be used to create art. Through these activities, children are introduced to art appreciation and the basic elements and principles of art.

Elements and Principles of Art

Ideas, meanings, and human emotions are varied and numerous. To respond to these many stimulations, students must have knowledge of, and be able to use, many of the elements of art. These elements are the things that make up a painting, drawing, or design, and the basic principles of design.

The Elements of Art

The elements of art are the individual components that are combined to create artwork—line, shape, space, value, color, and texture (Wallace, 2006). Most works of art have some small aspect of each element. A description of each element follows.

- **Line** refers to marks from a pen or brush used to highlight specific part of a painting or a structure. More subtle lines can also be used to accomplish the opposite effect.
- **Shape** represents a self-contained, defined area of a two- or three-dimensional area creating a form. There are two basic types of shapes: geometric and organic. Geometric shapes refers to squares, triangles, circles and rectangles. Organic shapes describes more natural-looking shapes like leaves, animals, and clouds.
- **Space** describes the emptiness around or within objects. Space can be used to create perspective, to create objects or people in different planes, and to create a sense of depth. Positive space is the main

area or object of focus in an artwork. Smaller objects in a painting seem farther away, while larger objects will appear to be closer.
- **Value** refers to the darkness or lightness of an artwork. Values are commonly used to create the two-dimensional quality of artwork. Values also indicate the source of light in a work, and provide a three-dimensional view of figures by suggesting shadows. Values can also represent the mood of the artist and the artwork. Darker values are used to represent sadness, mystery or formality, while lighter values usually represent contentment and relaxation.
- **Color** represents reflected light and the way it bounces off objects. There are three primary colors (red, yellow, blue); three secondary colors (green, orange, violet); and an unlimited amount of tertiary colors, which are colors that fall between primary and secondary colors, and compound colors. Compound colors are colors containing a mixture of the three primary colors. There also warm colors (such as yellow, orange, and red) and cool colors (such as blue, green, and purple.) Artists use all these color combinations to create the environment of the painting.
- **Texture** describes the surface quality of a figure or shape. A shape can appear to be rough, smooth, soft, hard, or glossy. Texture can be physical (felt with the hand; e.g., a buildup of paint) or visual (giving the illusion of texture; e.g., the paint gives the impression of texture, but the surface remains smooth and flat).

Principles of Art

The principles of art describe the guidelines that artists follow to create art and to deliver their intended message. Artists use the elements of art to communicate the principles in their creations. The principles of art include emphasis, balance, rhythm, contrast, movement, and harmony (Wallace, 2006). A description of these components follows.

- **Emphasis** is the technique of making one part of a work stand out from the rest of the artwork. It guides viewers to pay attention to specific details or components of the artwork. Often the lines and texture lead viewers to the target feature. Lines in paintings and sculpture can point or lead to the focus of attention. By making texture different in one area from the rest of the artwork, the artist can also make the target area stand out.

- **Balance** refers to the positioning of objects in such a way that none of them overpower the other components of the artwork. Size, space, color, shape, and lighting can be used to create balance. A large shape, for example, that is close to the center can be balanced by a smaller shape that is close to the edge. A large light-toned shape can be balanced by a small dark-toned shape. There are two main kinds of balance: symmetrical and asymmetrical. Symmetrical balance describes balance between a figure that when the figure is folded in half both components appear identical. For example, the figure of a circle is symmetrical because when it is folded, both sides are identical. Asymmetrical balance occurs when two sides of an artwork are different. For example, the American Flag is asymmetrical.
- **Rhythm** describes the type of patterns used in the artwork. For example, placing a repetition of objects evenly spaced presents a regular type of rhythm. Elements increasing or decreasing in size in an artwork presents a progressive rhythm.
- **Contrast** is used to create interest through the combination of elements. Contrast is used to break the monotony or repetitious pattern in a work of art. Rembrandt paintings are well known for using value (lightness and darkness) to create contrast. He used lighter values to highlight portions of the paintings.
- **Movement** refers to the way that artists produce the appearance of motion. In painting, artists use the element of line to simulate the movement of wind or water. This technique leads viewers to perceive the effects of motion and action through the artwork.
- **Harmony** is used to represent a sense of completeness in the artwork. It shows the unity of the artwork. For example, texture and color can be combined to provide a sense of balance and harmony.

Identifying Characteristics of Style in Works of Art

A style is an artist's manner of expression. When a group of artists during a specific period (which can last a few months, years, or decades) have a common style, it is called an art movement. Art movements seem to occur mostly in the West and occur in both visual art and architecture.

There are eight main historical periods, with various styles and movements within each. Although some periods have only one or two unique art styles, the twentieth century has 36 unique styles. Descriptions of some of the best-known styles throughout history follow (Witcombe, 1995).

- The **Prehistoric** period is characterized through cave paintings that represent daily activities of a group. The best-known representation of this type of art is the Caves of Altamira, in modern Spain. The Paleolithic peoples of Europe produced small, stylized stone carvings of women as symbols of fertility. These small statues have been found most often in modern France, Italy, and Austria.
- The **Ancient** period produced a large number of masterpieces from varied civilizations, such as the Sumerians, Babylonians, Assyrians, Egyptians, Greeks, and Romans. These civilizations skillfully carved even the hardest rocks, such as granite and basalt, into narratives of battles and historical records. Egyptian statues, like their architectural monuments the pyramids, were often of colossal size in order to exalt the power of the society's leaders and gods. The art of ancient Greece has its roots in the Minoan civilization on the island of Crete, which flourished from about 2500 to 1400 BC. The palace at Knossos held characteristic wall paintings revealing a people enamored of games, leisure, and the beauty of the sea.
- The mainland Greeks of the classical period, about 1,000 years later than the ancient period, were fascinated by physical beauty. Fashioned in the human image, with a universal ideal of perfection and guided by a master plan, the Greeks recreated their Olympian gods in their idealized and gracefully proportioned sculptures, architecture, and paintings. In the Hellenistic period, the populace appreciated these various objects of art for their beauty alone. The culture of Rome excelled in engineering and building, skills intended to organize efficiently a vast empire and provide an aesthetic environment for private and public use. The Romans built temples, roads, bathing complexes, civic buildings, palaces, and aqueducts. One of the greatest of their artistic and engineering accomplishments was the massive-domed temple of all the gods called the Pantheon, which is today one of the most perfectly preserved of all buildings from the classical period.

- The **Medieval** period also produced large numbers of artwork masterpieces. The Romanesque style of art and architecture was preeminent from about 800 to 1200 CE. By then many local styles, including the decorative arts of the Byzantine Empire, the Near East, and the German and Celtic tribes, were contributing to European culture. Common features of Romanesque churches are round arches, vaulted ceilings, and heavy walls that are ornately decorated—primarily with symbolic figures of Christianity. Realism had become less important than the message. The Gothic architecture flourished during this period with the creation of magnificent ribbed vaulting and pointed roofs. The cathedrals in this style are some of the purest expressions of an age. They combine a continued search for engineering and structural improvement with stylistic features that convey a relentless verticality, a reach toward heaven, and the unbridled adoration of God. Soaring and roomy, the construction of the Gothic cathedrals employed such elements as flying buttresses (structure to reinforce a wall) and pointed arches and vaults; a number of sculptures and stained-glass windows that were, for the worshippers, visual encyclopedias of Christian teachings and stories.

- **Renaissance** (14th to 16th century) artists developed new forms and revived classical styles and values, with the belief in the importance of the human experience on Earth and realism. Great sculptors approached true human characterization and realism as they revived elements of Greek architecture. Like the painters of the period, Renaissance architects took a scientific, ordered approach and emphasized perspective and the calculated composition of figures in space. Art became more emotional and dramatic, and because of this the use of color and movement increased, compositions were more vigorous, and references to classical iconography and the pleasures of an idyllic golden age increased. Typical examples of this emotional, dramatic art are Michelangelo's magnificent Sistine Chapel frescoes and his powerful sculptures of David and Moses, Leonardo da Vinci's *Mona Lisa*, Raphael's *School of Athens* fresco, and the increasingly dramatic and colorful works of the Venetian and northern Italian masters Titian, Correggio, Giorgione, and Bellini.

- **Baroque** style emerged in the 17th century in Europe. The baroque style used exaggerated motion, and elaborate and detailed artwork. The movement produced drama, tension, exuberance, and grandeur in sculpture, painting, literature, and music.

- **Rococo art** characterizes the art of the early eighteenth century. Artists of the Rococo era turned the agitated drama of the baroque style into light, pastel-toned, swirling compositions that seem placed in an idyllic land of a golden age.

- **Nineteenth-century art** was characterized by three elements—romanticism and idealism, realism, and impressionism. In the first half of the nineteenth century, landscape painting in England reached a zenith with the works of John Constable and Joseph Mallord William Turner. Turner's awe-inspiring landscapes form a bridge between the spirit of romanticism and the expressionistic brushwork and realism of the Barbizon School in France, whose chief painters were Charles Daubigny and Jean-Baptiste-Camille Corot. Beginning with Barbizon, the French painters of the nineteenth century concentrated increasingly on the reporter-like depiction of everyday life and the natural environment in a free, painterly (gesture and brushwork) style.

- **Realism** rejected traditional means of composing a picture, academic methods of figure modeling and color relations, and accurate and exact rendering of people and objects in favor of an art that emphasized quickly observed and sketched moments from life, the relation of shapes and forms and colors, the effects of light, and the act of painting itself. The realist pioneers were Gustave Courbet (*The Stone Breakers, A Burial at Ormans*), Jean-Francois Millet (*The Sower, The Angelus*), and Honoré Daumier (*The Third-Class Carriage*).

- **Impressionism** began with Edouard Manet in France in the 1860s. French artists continually blurred the boundaries of realism and abstraction. They used light and color to capture the impression of images as opposed to the real "real image." The landscapes and everyday-life paintings of impressionist artists like Claude Monet, Camille Pissarro, Auguste Renoir, Alfred Sisley, and Edgar Degas gave way to the more experimental arrangements of form and color of the great postimpressionists: Paul Gauguin, Vincent van Gogh, Georges Seurat, and Henri Toulouse-Lautrec. Auguste Rodin produced powerful sculptures with the freedom of impressionist style.

- **Twentieth-century art** provided new avenues for artistic expressions including:

- **Surrealism** is one of the new trends in painting that emerged in the 20th century. Inspired by the psychoanalytic writings of Sigmund Freud and Carl Jung, artists made the subconscious and the metaphysical important elements in their work. The influence of psychology is especially evident in the work of the surrealist artist Salvador Dali. Salvador Dali created non-realistic paintings as revealed in dreams, free of conscious controls of reason and conventions.

- **Cubism** and abstract paintings of Pablo Picasso also emerged during the twentieth century. This new type of art represents the most direct call for the total destruction of realistic depiction. Artists challenged common realistic conventions to create new representations of reality or imagination. Cubism is the most important and influential movement of the European painting and sculpture in the early 20th century.

- **Muralists** and social realists between WWI and WWII created art that was physically interesting and whose subjects were accessible to the average person. John Sloan, George Bellows, Edward Hopper, Thomas Hart Benton, Grant Wood, and John Stuart Curry were among those who celebrated the American scene in paintings, frequently in murals for public buildings, and through widely available fine prints. The great Mexican muralists, who usually concentrated on political themes—Diego Rivera, José Clemente Orozco, and David Siqueiros—brought their work to the public both in Mexico and in the United States.

- **Photorealism** also emerged as a new form of art where paintings resemble photos, lifelike; often portraits, still life, and landscapes.

- **Graffiti** is a new and controversial type of art form that emerged in inner cities in America. The controversial nature of this new form of art is caused in the way that the expression is conducted. Traditionally, spray-painting and using brushes, the artists create the work on the surface of private and public buildings with or without the approval of the owners. For some people, graffiti is a nuisance while for others, it becomes a liberating response to the pressure of modern-day living.

- For a comprehensive analysis of the history of art visit *http://witcombe.sbc.edu/ARTHLinks.html*.

Integration of the Arts in the Content Areas

Arts can be easily integrated with content areas. In reading, children begin drawing to represent the main idea of a story. Later in writing, they begin adding words to the drawings. Artworks are also ideal to guide children to notice details about a painting. Through observation and description, children can practice vocabulary words, and communication skills in general. Scientific principles like light, color, and texture can be easily introduced through artwork. The study of insects like the butterfly can be used to guide children to identify colors and shapes. Art concepts of space, proportion and balance can also be introduced through mathematics instruction. For example, a Native American or Mexican quilt can be easily incorporated to teach color, balance, and culture. Nature is the best representation of arts; and so, teachers should take advantage of this gift to make content area education more meaningful and enjoyable for children.

Evaluating Works of Art

To judge the quality of a work in visual art, students should be given basic criteria for assessment. The main principle of the criteria can be derived through questions similar to the ones presented below:

- What is the purpose of the author? Does the work achieve its purpose?
- Has the artist spoken with a unique voice, regardless of style, or could this artwork just as easily be the work of someone else?
- Is the style appropriate to the expressed purpose of the work?
- Is the work memorable and distinctive?
- Was it created to meet social or cultural needs?
- Has the artist used all the technical elements available to the particular discipline with accomplished skill?

Often after answering such questions, a student might be able to determine the specific timeframe of the painting and the type of style.

When addressing these questions, students should be able to describe a work of art using terms such as line, color, value, shape, balance, texture, repetition, rhythm, and shape. They should be able to discuss some of the major periods in the history of the visual arts. It is important that students be able to confront a work and judge its aesthetic merits, regardless of their ability to recognize it from memory.

References

Texas Education Agency. 2006. Texas Knowledge and Skills.
 http://www.tea.state.tx.us/teks/
Wallace, L. 2006. Utah Education Network (UEN).
 http://www.uen.org/
Witcombe, C. L. 1995. Art History. Sweet Briar College, VA.
 http://witcombe.sbc.edu/ARTHLinks.html

Competency 025 (Music)

The teacher understands concepts, processes, and skills involved in the creation, appreciation, and evaluation of music and uses this knowledge to plan and implement effective learning experiences in music.

The main goal of music education is to introduce students to the concepts and skills involved in experiencing music, and the aesthetic and personal dimensions of music. It is also expected that teachers will guide children in music understanding and discrimination, music's role in society and the context in which it is created. Children are expected to study music structure, increase listening awareness, and develop sensitivity to its expressive qualities.

Curriculum Requirements

To accomplish these goals the state of Texas has organized the music curriculum around four basic strands—perception, creative expression, historical and cultural heritage, and critical evaluation. Children in elementary education and beyond are required to demonstrate a level of mastery in each of the basic music strands. Table 5-2 presents an overview of the music curriculum in grades K–4.

Music and the Content Areas

Music does not exist in a vacuum. The historical or cultural context of a piece of music, and the development of various instruments, is vital for understanding

Table 5-2. Music Education Strands for K–4 (TEA, 2006)

Grades	Perceptions	Creative Expressions	Historical/Cultural	Critical Evaluation
K–2	Identify sounds of voice and instruments from various musical families. Identify instruments visually; Use music terminology to explain sounds and performance.	Sing songs from diverse cultures, and play simple rhythm instruments. Read simple expressions of music notation.	Relate music to historical periods. Sing songs from diverse cultures. Identify relationships between music and other subjects.	Classify sounds as high and low in pitch. Show appropriate behavior during live performance.
3–4	Use music terminology to explain sounds and performance. Categorize a variety of musical sounds from the various types of instruments such as woodwind, brass, string, percussion, keyboard, and electronic instruments.	Play a classroom instrument independently or in a group. Read and write simple musical notations. Identify musical symbols and terms referring to dynamics and tempo.	Identify music from diverse cultures and from various historical periods. Identify aurally excerpts of music from diverse genres, styles and periods.	Distinguish between beat/rhythm, high/low, loud/soft, fast/slow. Define basic criteria for evaluating musical performance.

musical expressions. Students should know and be able to discuss the context of music by making connections among social studies, reading or language arts, and the fine arts. For example, when students are reading stories about the American Revolution, they should be aware that it occurred during the period known as the classical period in music history. Listening to a piece of music by Franz Joseph Haydn or Wolfgang Amadeus Mozart, and talk about how they reacted to the Old World. You also might want to compare the classical works to a colonial American tune by William Billings as an effective way to help students understand the historical, cultural, and societal contexts of music.

Similarly, the music of the Beatles, the assassination of John F. Kennedy, the Hippie movement, and the war in Vietnam all took place within the same approximate time frame. The teacher can ask students to find contrasts and similarities among these artistic and social events and look for ways that the historical context affected music and ways that music affected and reflected history.

These examples from American history are easy for most students to grasp. However, the objective seeks to have teachers and students consider the role of music in history and culture beyond the American experience. By having students listen to music from Mexico, the Caribbean islands, China, Japan, Germany, Australia, or Africa when they are studying these cultural groups, the students' learning experience is enriched and becomes more memorable for them. It is even more valuable for students to view performances of the music and dance of these cultures. Seeing the costumes and the movement are an important part of understanding the culture.

Terminology for Music Education

One of the key elements in music education is to introduce children to the vocabulary and concepts they need to describe and analyze music. Some of the key music concepts for children in K–4 follow:

- The **tone** is the musical sound of the voice; it may describe the quality of the sound. For instance, one might say that someone sings with a "nasal tone," a "thin tone," or a "full tone." A synonym for tone is **timbre**.
- **Tempo** stands for the word "time" and it describes the speed or pace of a song or music. The tempo is described as the number of beats per second (BPS).

- **Pitch** describes the vocal or instrumental production of sounds. Pitch can be described as high or low. It is often confused with volume. Volume can be loud and soft, while pitch is described as high or low. Vocal pitch can be classified, from the lowest to the highest, as bass, baritone, tenor, alto, mezzo soprano, or soprano. For example, Placido Domingo and Luciano Pavarotti, who sing with a deep and strong voice, are tenors.
- **Meter** is a musical term used to describe the rhythm of a composition based on the repetitive patterns or pulses of strong and weak beats. Children can easily be taught to count the beats of song by tapping the foot or clapping.

Elements of Music

There are several elements use to make music—rhythm, melody, form, texture, timbre, and dynamics. Descriptions of the elements follow.

- **Rhythm** is the contrast among the various lengths of musical tones. For instance, in "The Star-Spangled Banner," the rhythm is short, short, medium, medium, medium, long. To indicate the lengths of the tones, musical notation uses various types of notes and rests. The sheet music uses simultaneous combinations of musical tones to indicate **harmony**. Harmony is the performance of two or more different pitches produced simultaneously to accompany a melody.
- **Melody**, on the other hand, is the succession of the notes. Melody is the horizontal linear succession of sounds and silences ordered by time. Sometimes the teacher may refer to the melody as the tune.
- **Form** is the structure of the song, or the way that it is put together. Sometimes there is a refrain that is repeated, or sometimes there is a chorus that is used after each verse.
- **Texture** is the context in which simultaneous sounds occur. The sounds can be chords (harmony) or even counterpoint (concurrent melodies of equal importance).
- **Timbre or tone** refers to the quality of the musical sound.
- **Dynamics** refers to the volume or the loudness of the sound or the note. The two basic dynamic indications are *p* (for *piano*, meaning softly or quietly) and *f* (for *forte*, meaning loudly or strong).

Musical elements work together to express ideas, emotions, settings, time, and place using sound.

Music in the Classroom

Music is the arrangement of sounds for voice and musical instruments and, like dance, requires training and repetitive practice. Making music is part of our daily activities. Mothers sing to their babies. Children beat sticks together, make drums, and sing during their play. Adults whistle or sing along with tunes on the radio. Sound and music naturally draw people together. Music is an important part of culture, religious practice, and personal experience for all people. Some people become professional musicians, whereas others whistle, sing, or play for their own enjoyment and nothing more.

It is important that students have the opportunity to experience as many ways to make music as possible. It is through the acquisition of basic skills in singing and playing instruments that people grow in their ability to express themselves through music. As students develop skills, they are also exposed to basic musical concepts such as melody, harmony, rhythm, pitch, and timbre (tone). With experience, students come to make decisions about what is acceptable or not acceptable within a given cultural or historical context and thereby develop their own aesthetic awareness. Music making is a natural part of the human experience.

Vocal Performance

Children's **vocal ranges** vary from one child to the next. The voice ranges of girls and boys remain about the same until the boys' voices begin to change, which is usually sometime during junior high. The voice of the average child is similar to the voice of an adult in terms of range but not quality. The teacher should not encourage children to imitate the heavier and fuller quality of the mature adult voice. Children can sing high, but as with an adult voice, tension results when the pitch is too high. When selecting vocal literature (music for singing), the teacher must consider the age-appropriate range of the students and their vocal abilities.

The materials used for a quality music program in any grade should reflect various musical periods and styles, cultural and ethnic diversity, and a gender balance. The goal of a quality music program is to make students aware that music is both a part of and a reflection of many cultures and many ethnic groups. The teacher should provide and encourage students to sing, play, and listen to music of many cultural and ethnic groups. The teacher should include diverse styles (basic musical languages) and genres (categories). Dividing music into categories can be difficult. Styles are constantly emerging. Many songs can be categorized by multiple genres. Nevertheless, the main groupings are classical, gospel, jazz, blues, rhythm and blues, rock, country, electronic, electronic dance, melodic music, hip hop, rap, punk, reggae, and contemporary African music.

Instruments in Music Education

There is a difference between the study of simple instruments and the study of orchestral instruments. In Texas, children do not usually begin the study of orchestral instruments prior to middle school, and then, a music teacher—not the classroom teacher—gives instruction in orchestral instruments. The instruments that the classroom teacher normally uses in K–4 include the **rhythmic instruments** (e.g., triangle, tambourine, blocks, and sticks); **melodic instruments** (e.g., melody bells and simple flutes); and **harmonic instruments** (e.g., chording instruments, like the autoharp).

Rhythmic Instruments

After the students have a chance to move along with music and after singing games and action songs, they may be ready to try rhythmic instruments. The students will need opportunities to experiment with triangles, tambourines, sticks, and blocks, among others, in order to experience the sounds they make. Students might try striking the tambourine with the hand to get one sound and with the knee to get another, for instance. After this experimentation, the teacher and class will be ready to try something new.

Another approach to music instruction is having students listen to a piece of music and then decide on the instruments they want to play and playing the musical selection again with student accompaniment. This more creative approach is appropriate for young children who cannot read music or even for music readers who want to produce their own performance techniques.

Melodic Instruments

Melodic bells are instruments that the child strikes with a mallet. The child may use the bells before they learn an instrument like the flute. In Texas, teachers can introduce these melodic instruments with the music instruction in upper elementary, but the actual teaching of these musical instruments is generally postponed until middle school.

Harmonic Instruments

The rectangular wooden base of an autoharp has wire strings stretched across it. The child can press the wooden bars and strums the wires to produce chords. Students can experiment with harmony using the autoharp. They will find that sometimes a variety of chords "sound right" but that at other times only one chord works.

Reading and Interpreting Simple Music Notation

Music notation is a way of writing music. Teaching students to use, read, and interpret music notation will heighten their enjoyment of music. Students can begin with simple music notation. For example, students might try listening to a simple melody and making dashes on the board or on their papers to indicate the length the notes. As children sing the nursery rhyme "Three Blind Mice," for instance, they would mark dashes of similar length for the words/notes *three* and *blind*.

With **traditional music notation**, the students use the lines and spaces on the musical staff. Students will observe that there are four spaces and five lines on the musical staff. They may also notice that the appearance of the notes indicates the length, and the placement of the notes on the staff indicates the various tones.

Nontraditional music notation is something that many students in the upper grades may have noticed in their books. In the South, for example, many of the hymnals use a nontraditional type of music notation called shape notes. Instead of the elliptical note head in the traditional notation, the heads of the notes are in various shapes to show the position of the notes on the major scale. Another nontraditional music notation is Braille notation. Braille music uses the Braille reading system so that visually impaired children can learn to read music.

The National Anthem

The "Star-Spangled Banner" is the national anthem of the United States. Francis Scott Key wrote the poem after a British attack during the War of 1812. Eventually, music was added to the poem, and in 1931, it officially became the American national anthem. A fragment of the anthem follows:

Oh, say, can you see, by the dawn's early light,
What so proudly we hailed at the twilight's last gleaming?
Whose broad stripes and bright stars, thro' the perilous fight'
O'er the ramparts we watched, were so gallantly streaming.
And the rockets red glare, the bombs bursting in air,
Gave proof through the night that our flag was still there.
Oh, say, does that star-spangled banner yet wave
O'er the land of the free and the home of the brave?

The Second National Anthem

In 1938 and on the verge of WWII, Irving Berlin wrote one of the most memorable peace songs—"God Bless America" (Library of the Congress, 2006). This song became an instant hit and became a patriotic touchstone for Americans during WWII. Today, this composition is one of the most beloved songs in the nation. The song has been performed and recorded by many artists, but it has been Ray Charles' version that best represents the emotions and the fervor of our "second national anthem." A fragment of the song follows.

While the storm clouds gather far across the sea,
Let us swear allegiance to a land that's free,
Let us all be grateful for a land so fair,
As we raise our voices in a solemn prayer.

God Bless America,
Land that I love.
Stand beside her, and guide her
Thru the night with a light from above.
From the mountains, to the prairies,

To the oceans, white with foam
God bless America, My home sweet home.

Texas Patriotic Songs

In 1929 the Texas Legislature adopted "Texas, Our Texas" as the state song. The authors of the song were William J. Marsh and Gladys Yoakum Wright. A fragment of the song follows (Texas State Library, 2006):

Texas, our Texas! All hail the mighty State!
Texas, our Texas! So wonderful so great!
Boldest and grandest, Withstanding ev'ry test;
O Empire wide and glorious, You stand supremely blest.

[Refrain] God bless you Texas! And keep you brave and strong,
That you may grow in power and worth, Thro'out the ages long.

Texas, O Texas! Your freeborn single star,
Sends out its radiance to nations near and far.
Emblem of freedom! It sets our hearts aglow,
With thoughts of San Jacinto and glorious Alamo.

Another song linked to the state history is "The Yellow Rose of Texas," which was first published in 1853 by an author with the initials "J.K." (Folk Music, 2006). The tune was popular among the Confederate soldiers during the American Civil War. A fragment of the song follows:

There's a yellow rose of Texas
That I am going to see,
No other fellow knows her,
No other, only me.
She cried so when I left her,
It like to break my heart,
And if I ever find her
We never more will part.

Popular Music of Texas and the United States

The American Southwest, and specifically Texas, has played an important role in the development of music. The state has pioneered multiple musical developments including tejano music, mariachi, country music, and the blues.

Tejano music is one the forms of folk and popular music developed by Mexicans and Mexican-Americans in the Southwest. Tejano music represents a blend of traditional Mexican music like Corridos with influence from German and Czech music. The Polka is a European type of dancing music brought by the Czechs to Texas, and it is an important component of Tejano music. The accordion is a featured instrument in Tejano music. This instrument was invented in Europe and brought to Texas by both German and Czech immigrants. More recently, Tejano music has been influenced by rock, the Blues and Cumbia—folk music from Colombia. The combination of all these influences helped to created this new type of music called Tejano. In recent years, this music has been introduced to mainstream America by well known artists like Selena Quintanilla and Emilio Navaira, and groups like the Kumbia Kings and La Mafia.

Mariachi is a type of musical group, that is originally from Mexico. The kind of group can be as small as six to seven people or as large as fifteen. Traditionally, a mariachi group has at least two violins, two trumpets, and different kinds of string instruments, including a guitarrón—a large six-string acoustic bass guitar. Mariachi music was made popular in the world by Gaspar Vargas and the Mariachi Vargas de Tecalitlán. This pioneer band was formed in 1897 and today, the fifth generation of the Mariachi Vargas is still performing worldwide.

Country music is a combination of popular musical forms developed in the Southern United States. Its origin can be traced to various sources like folk music, Celtic music, blues, and gospel music, not to mention the old cowboy songs from the days of the cattle drives. Similar to the blues, and the Mexican Corridos, country music tells stories about family and personal struggles. Country music is now part of the mainstream music scene. Some of the best known country artists are Willie Nelson, Johnny Cash, Hank Williams, Dolly Parton, and George Strait.

The Blues is a vocal and instrumental form of music that evolved in the United States in predominantly African American communities. The style, emotions, and spirituality represented in the music represents the experience and the suffering of African slaves and the cultural tradition of West Africa. The blues has been a major influence on later American and Western popular music. It has influenced jazz, rock and roll, hip-hop, and country music. Some of the artists who represent this genre are John Lee Hooker, Muddy Waters, and B.B. King.

Evaluating Musical Performance

People respond to music naturally. They do not need prompting or help to respond to it. However, to share their thoughts and feelings about music, students must learn how to put their responses into musical terminology. Some people call music a language, but it does not function as a spoken language. It does not provide specific information, instructions, or reactions. Rather, music sparks thoughts, feelings, and emotions.

To put their experiences into words, musicians and artists have developed vocabularies and approaches to discussing music and art. This does not mean there is only one way to respond to or talk about music or art. However, it is easier for students to understand music and musicians, art and artists, if they can use the kind of vocabulary and approaches that musicians or artists use to discuss their work.

People cannot express themselves or effectively communicate if they do not understand the structures and rules that underlie the "language" that they are trying to use. Although music does not provide the kind of specific communication that spoken language does, it has its own structures. When students are able to think about and discuss music, they gain a deeper understanding of the music and can better express their responses to that music.

The aesthetic experience is what draws people to music. The experience is one that most people have had, but one that some people cannot easily describe. In fact, words seem clumsy when it comes to something that can be so profound and wonderful. The type of music, the period, or the performer does not necessarily limit the aesthetic experience. It is possible to have an aesthetic experience when listening to a child sing or while listening to a professional orchestra performing a symphony by Beethoven. The important thing is to share that aesthetic experience. It is part of what makes music and art special.

There are many ways to encourage exploration of and growth through aesthetic responsiveness. A common experience is a crucial starting point. After students listen attentively to several pieces of music, the teacher might ask them to describe how each piece made them feel. It is often best to write their responses down before starting a discussion. Then, the teacher might ask them to explain why each piece of music made them feel the way they described.

Young students will likely provide simple, straightforward emotional responses to music (e.g., "It made me feel happy!"). Older students should explore why the music affected the feelings that it did and use both musical concepts (e.g., "It made me feel happy because it was in a major key") and nonmusical associations (e.g., "It made me feel happy because it sounded like a circus, and I like to go to the circus"). Through this kind of sharing, along with teacher insights and readings about how other people have responded to music, students come to a deeper understanding of their personal responses to music, other art forms, and possibly the world. In addition, teachers should provide students with practical ways to express their responses or reactions to what they experience in life outside the musical or artistic genres.

In addition to having aesthetic experiences, recognizing their value, and being able to discuss or share those experiences, teachers and students must attempt to foster an appreciation for the arts and their ability to create meaning. The arts provide an opportunity to explore and express ideas and emotions through a unique view of different life experiences. It is through the experience of music, or any art form, that people begin to transcend their mundane day-to-day experiences and reach beyond to a richer life experience.

References

Library of the Congress. 2006. American Treasures of the Library of the Congress *http://www.loc.gov/exhibits/treasures/trm019. html*

Folk Music. 2006. Folk Music of England, Scotland, Ireland, Wales and America. *http://www.contemplator.com/bibliog.html*

Texas Education Agency. 2006). Texas Knowledge and Skills. *http://www.tea.state.tx.us/teks/*

Texas State Library and Archives Commission Website. 2006. *http://www.tsl.state.tx.us/ref/abouttx/statesong.html*

Competency 026 (Health)

The teacher uses knowledge of the concepts and purposes of health education to plan and implement effective and engaging health instruction for all children.

The Texas Essential Knowledge and Skills curriculum provides developmentally appropriate content and strategies for teaching health education to children in grades K–12. Some of the key components of the TEKS require children to develop an understanding of their body, proper nutrition practices, safety procedures, and to use reliable information to make personal health decisions. Some of the topics introduced in grades K-4 are:

1. Identify and consume healthy food choices
2. Strategies to avoid health and safety risks
3. Strategies for protection against sexual predators
4. Role of the media and the internet in influencing health decisions
5. Assertive behaviors to deal with demands to engage in risky behaviors
6. Gang prevention programs
7. Drugs and alcohol preventions programs
8. Knowledge of the human body
9. Safety procedures in school and the community

Additional information about these and other important health considerations for teachers follow.

Nutrition and Its Role in Promoting Health

Along with exercise, a healthy diet is vital to good health and longevity. The elements of good nutrition, the role of vitamins, elimination of risk factors, and strategies to control weight are all part of a healthy lifestyle.

In the spring of 2005, the U.S. Department of Agriculture (USDA) changed the food pyramid to guide Americans in how to eat healthily. As shown in Figure 5-1, the food pyramid has six rainbow-colored divisions. The climbing figure reminds us all to be active.

The food groups indicated on the pyramid (left to right) are as follows:

1. Grains
2. Vegetables
3. Fruits
4. Fats and oils
5. Milk and dairy products
6. Meat, beans, fish, and nuts

Complex carbohydrates, which include vegetables, fruits, high-fiber, whole grain breads, and cereals, should comprise at least one-half of the diet. These foods provide fiber, which helps digestion, reduces constipation, and reduces the risk of colon cancer. Complex carbohydrates also provide water, which is vital to the entire body.

Proteins should make up about one-fifth of the diet. Proteins are used to build and repair the body. Protein sources include fish, beans, peas, lentils, peanuts, and other pod plants. Red meat also contains protein, but because it is high in saturated fat, one should eat it less often. **Saturated fat** is present also in cocoa butter, palm oil, and coconut oil. There is a link between high-fat diets and many types of cancer. Diets high in saturated fats cause the body to produce too much **low-density**

Figure 5-1. USDA Food Pyramid
Source: U.S. Department of Agriculture, *Steps to a Healthier You*, www.mypyramid.gov.

lipoprotein (LDL), which is one type of **cholesterol**. The other type of cholesterol is **high-density lipoprotein (HDL)**. Some cholesterol is essential to brain functions and to the production of certain hormones, but too much LDL cholesterol encourages the buildup of plaque in the arteries. LDL cholesterol can be controlled through proper diet, and HDL cholesterol levels can be raised by exercise. **Triglycerides** are other types of fat in the blood that are important to monitor; triglycerides seem to be inversely proportional to HDLs.

Unsaturated vegetable fats are preferable to saturated fats. Unsaturated fats appear to offset the rise in blood pressure that accompanies too much saturated fat and may lower cholesterol and help with weight loss. Unsaturated fats are present in vegetable products and in olive oil. Although whole milk products contain saturated fat, the calcium they contain is vital to health. For this reason, some weight-loss diets recommend dairy products in the form of skim milk and low-fat cheese.

Vitamins are essential to good health; however, a person must be careful not to take too much of certain vitamins. The fat-soluble vitamins, A, D, E, and K, are stored in the body, and excessive amounts will cause some dangerous side effects. All other vitamins are water-soluble and are generally excreted through the urinary system and the skin when taken in excess. **Minerals** are essential to good health. Some of the minerals needed for appropriate body function are: sodium, potassium, zinc, iron, calcium, phosphorus, and magnesium. For a more detailed list of nutritional supplements (i.e. vitamins and minerals) please see the website of the National Institute of Health for their recommendations at *http://dietary-supplements.info.nih.gov/Health_Information/Dietary_Reference_Intakes.aspx*.

Health and Wellness

One of the primary reasons for the teaching of physical education is to instill a willingness to exercise and to encourage students to make good decisions about their health. To that end, it is important to understand the benefits of participating in a lifelong program of exercise and physical fitness.

The benefits of a consistent program of diet and exercise are many and varied. Improvements in cardiac output, maximum oxygen intake, mood stabilization,

and enhancing the blood's ability to carry oxygen are just a few of these benefits. Another aspect of physical education concerns awareness and avoidance of the risks that are present in our everyday lives. Some risk factors include being overweight, smoking, using drugs, having unprotected sex, and excessive unmanaged stress. Education is the key to minimizing the presence of these risk factors. Unfortunately, because of the presence of peer pressure and the lack of parental control, education is sometimes not enough.

Weight Control Strategies

Statistics show that Americans get fatter every year. Even though countless books and magazine articles are available on the subject of weight control, often the only place a student gets reliable information about diet is in the classroom. The unfortunate reality is that people who are overweight on average, do not live as long as those who are not. Being overweight has been isolated as a risk factor in various types of cancer, heart disease, gall bladder problems, and kidney disease. Chronic diseases such as diabetes and high blood pressure are also aggravated by, or caused by, being overweight.

Conversely, being underweight presents a great many problems. Our society often places too much emphasis on losing weight and being thin. Women are especially prone to measuring their self-worth by the numbers they read on the bathroom scale. Young girls are especially susceptible to these messages and eating disorders can result. Anorexia nervosa and bulimia are becoming more common at younger ages. According to the National Institute of Health:

> Eating disorders are not due to a failure of will or behavior; rather, they are real, treatable medical illnesses in which certain maladaptive patterns of eating take on a life of their own. The main types of eating disorders are anorexia nervosa and bulimia nervosa. A third type, binge-eating disorder, has been suggested but has not yet been approved as a formal psychiatric diagnosis. Eating disorders frequently develop during adolescence or early adulthood, but some reports indicate their onset can occur during childhood or later in adulthood.

Ideal weight and a good body fat ratio should be the goals when trying to lose weight. A correlation may exist between body fat and high cholesterol. Exercise is the key to a good body fat ratio. Exercise helps keep the ratio low, improves cholesterol levels, and prevents heart disease.

In order to lose weight, calories burned must exceed calories consumed. No matter what kind of diet is tried, that principle applies. There is no easy way to maintain a healthy weight. Again, the key is exercise. If calorie intake is restricted too much, the body goes into starvation mode and operates by burning fewer calories. Just a 250-calorie drop a day combined with a 250-calorie burn will result in a loss of one pound a week. Crash diets, which bring about rapid weight loss, are not only unhealthy but also ineffective. Slower weight loss is more lasting. **Aerobic exercise** is the key to successful weight loss. Exercise speeds up metabolism and causes the body to burn calories. Timing of exercise will improve the benefits. Exercise before meals speeds up metabolism and helps suppress appetite. Losing and maintaining weight is not easy. Through education, people will be better able to realize that maintaining a healthy weight is crucial to a healthy life and should be a constant consideration.

Students as young as kindergarteners and first graders can learn how to recognize advertisements that might lead them to unhealthy behavior (e.g., for candy or sugar-laden cereal). By third or fourth grade, children should be able to demonstrate that they are able to make health-related decisions regarding advertisements in various media. Teachers can encourage students to (1) avoid alcohol, tobacco, stimulants, and narcotics; (2) get plenty of sleep and exercise; (3) eat a well-balanced diet; (4) receive the proper immunizations; and (5) avoid sharing toothbrushes, combs, hats, beverages, and food with others.

In addition, any study of the physical environment—in science, social studies, or other subjects—should relate the contents to health whenever possible. Examples include the effects of pollution on health; occupational-related disease (e.g., "black lung" disease); the health care options available to people in different parts of the world and in different economic circumstances; differentiation between communicable and non-communicable diseases; and the importance of washing their hands frequently. Older children should be able to explain the transmission and prevention of communicable diseases, and all children should learn which diseases cannot be transmitted through casual contact.

Stress Management

Stress is the product of any change, either negative or positive. Environmental factors such as noise, air pollution, and crowding; physiological factors such as sickness and physical injuries; and, finally, psychological factors such as self-deprecating thoughts and negative self-image cause stress. In addition to the normal stressors that everyone experiences, some students may be living in dysfunctional families, some may be dealing with substance abuse and addictions, and some may be experiencing sexual abuse. Students have numerous sources of stress in their lives.

Because life is a stressful process, it is important that students and teachers learn acceptable ways to cope with stress. The first step in coping with stress is to recognize the role that stress plays in our lives. A teacher might lead a class through a brainstorming activity to help the students become aware of the various sources of stress affecting them. Next, the teacher could identify positive ways of coping with stress, including positive self-talk, physical exercise, proper nutrition, adequate sleep, balanced activities, time management techniques, good study habits, and relaxation exercises.

Students facing stress often experience a wide range of emotions. They may be sad, depressed, frustrated, or afraid. Effective teachers realize that students' emotions play a significant role in students' classroom performance and achievement. Thus, they should seek to create a classroom environment supportive of students' emotional needs. They should have appropriate empathy and compassion for the emotional conflicts facing students, as well as a realistic awareness that students need to attain crucial academic and social skills that will give them some control over their environment as they become increasingly independent individuals and, eventually, productive citizens.

First Aid

First aid is the immediate, temporary care of an injured or ill person. Occasionally, during physical education classes or during the school hours, injuries and illnesses occur. Therefore, a basic knowledge of first aid is important for physical education teachers and other instructors. However, a teacher should not attempt first aid if the procedures are unclear. A course in first aid is important for the classroom teacher and they are readily available from the local American Red Cross.

The following are some common injuries and a brief description of their emergency treatments:

- A **fracture** is a break in a bone. Fractures can be simple, multiple (many breaks in the bone) or **compound** (a break in the bone and the skin). Appropriate first aid for fractures: Immobilize, use ice to control swelling, and seek medical aid. In the case of a compound fracture, it is important to stop the bleeding.
- **Traumatic shock** is the severe compression of circulation caused by injury or illness. Symptoms include cool sweaty skin and a rapid weak pulse. Appropriate first aid for shock: Minimize heat loss, and elevate the legs without disturbing the rest of the body. Seek medical help.
- A **sprain** is an injury to a joint caused by the joint being moved too far or away from its range of motion. Both ligaments and tendons can be injured in a sprain. **Ligaments** join bone to bone, and **tendons** join muscle to bone. Appropriate first aid for sprains: Rest, ice, compression, and elevation (RICE).
- A **strain** is a muscle injury caused by overwork. Appropriate first aid for a strain: Use ice to lessen the swelling. Applying some heat after icing can be beneficial although opinion on the value of heat varies.
- **Dislocation** is a joint injury in which bone becomes out of place at the joints. As a result, ligaments can be severely stretched and torn. Appropriate first aid for a dislocation: Immobilize and seek medical help. Some people advocate "popping" the dislocation back into place, but this can be risky for both the injured person and for the person giving the first aid (liability). Therefore, allow the medical professionals to put the joint back in place.
- The symptoms of **heat exhaustion** include cold and sweaty skin, nausea, dizziness, and paleness. Heat exhaustion is not as severe as heat stroke. Appropriate first aid for heat exhaustion: increase water intake, replace salt, and get out of the heat.
- The symptoms of **heat stroke** include high fever, dry skin, and possible unconsciousness. Appropriate first aid for heat stroke: attempt to cool off gradually, get into the shade, and seek medical attention immediately.
- The symptoms of **heart attack** include shortness of breath, pain in the left arm, pain in the chest, nausea, and sweating. Appropriate first aid for a heart attack: elevate the head and chest, give cardiopulmonary resuscitation if indicated, and seek medical assistance.
- The cause of **seizures** is often epilepsy. Appropriate first aid for seizures: Clear the area around the victim to avoid injury during the seizure. Do not place anything in the victim's mouth; seek medical help after the seizure if necessary.
- **Resuscitation** is a first-aid technique that provides artificial circulation and respiration. Remember the ABCs: A is for "airway," B is for "breathing," and C is for "circulation." Check the airway to make sure it is open, and check breathing and circulation.

Child Abuse and Neglect

Child abuse is a common problem in the United States. According to the American Academy of Pediatrics, more than 2.5 million cases of child abuse and neglect are reported annually in the nation (2006). Half of these cases involve neglect while the other half involves physical and sexual abuse. Despite all the media attention given to child abuse and neglect, many teachers still believe that it cannot happen to one of their students. They may think, "This is a nice neighborhood," or "Most of these students have both a mother and a father living at home." However, abuse and neglect may happen to children, possibly even to one of your students.

Abused children typically show signs of **over stimulation**—being "wired," unruly, and/or belligerent. By contrast, the behaviors of neglected children point to **under stimulation**—all they want is to be left alone, and typically they are unsociable, sedate, and withdrawn. The child learns this behavior at home during periods of neglect. The neglect may change the child's behaviors from almost flat (registering no emotion) to anger. Although poor attention, tears, violence, and languid behavior may be indicators of either abuse or neglect, neglected children usually have feelings of hopelessness and cannot adequately control their thoughts. Students either become obsessed by the neglect or refuse to acknowledge that the neglect is really happening.

Visible Signs of Physical Abuse

One of the most obvious visible signs of child abuse is red swelling or bruising caused by being hit. The appearance of marks on a child may be proof of child abuse, and the teacher must report the evidence. Visible signs are also one way teachers can separate real abuse cases from unfounded ones. While marks from the hand, fist, or belt are usually recognizable, other marks in geometric shapes—from eating utensils, paddles, coat hangers, or extension cords—can signify child abuse.

Reporting Suspicions of Abuse

Teachers in Texas are required by law to report any suspicion of child abuse or neglect to the Department of Human Services. Thus, they must be vigilant for possible symptoms or indications of child abuse. Failure to file a report of suspicion of child abuse or neglect has consequences, and it can result in legal action against the teacher. After the report, the teacher should realize that the child—already needing support—may feel that the educator has exposed the child's private life. While accepting the child's feeling of betrayal, the teacher can explain that the report was necessary and assure the child of protection against reprisals for telling about the abuse. Sometimes the child benefits from just knowing that others do care about his or her well-being.

Body Systems

The body has a system of interrelated subsystems working together to keep the system functioning properly. **Cells** are the building blocks of the human body. **Tissues** are groups of similar cells working to perform a specific job. Different kinds of tissues may work together for a larger purpose; a group of tissues working together is called an **organ**. A group of organs working together in a special activity is an **organ system**. There are several organ systems in humans.

Musculoskeletal System

The human skeleton consists of more than 200 bones held together by connective tissues called **ligaments**. Contractions of the **skeletal muscles**, to which the bones are attached by **tendons**, affect movements. The nervous system controls muscular contractions.

Nervous System

The nervous system has two divisions: the **somatic**, which allows voluntary control over skeletal muscle, and the **autonomic**, or involuntary, which controls cardiac and glandular functions. Nerve impulses carried by cranial or spinal chord nerves that connect the brain to skeletal muscles cause **voluntary movement**. **Involuntary movement**, or reflex movement, occurs in direct response to outside stimulus. Various nerve terminals, called **receptors,** constantly send impulses to the central nervous system. Each type of receptor routes nerve impulses to specialized areas of the brain for processing.

Circulatory System

The **heart** pumps blood in the circulatory system. The blood passes through the right chambers of the heart and through the lungs, where it acquires oxygen, and back into the left chambers of the heart. Next, the heart pumps the blood into the main artery, the **aorta**, which branches into increasingly smaller arteries. Beyond that, blood passes through tiny, thin-walled structures called **capillaries**. In the capillaries, the blood gives up oxygen and nutrients to tissues and absorbs metabolic waste products containing carbon dioxide. Finally, blood completes the circuit by passing through small **veins**, joining to form increasingly larger vessels until it reaches the largest veins, which return it to the right side of the heart.

Immune System

The body defends itself against foreign proteins and infectious microorganisms by means of a complex immune system. The immune system is composed of a dual system that depends on recognizing a portion of the surface pattern of the invader and the generation of **lymphocytes** and **antibody** molecules to destroy invading molecules.

Respiratory System

Respiration results from the expansion and contraction of the **lungs**. In the lungs, oxygen enters tiny capillaries, where it combines with hemoglobin in the red blood cells and is carried to the body's tissues. At the same time, carbon dioxide passes through capillaries into the air contained within the lungs. Inhaling draws air that is higher in oxygen and lower in carbon dioxide into the lungs; exhaling forces air that is high in carbon dioxide and low in oxygen from the lungs.

Digestive and Excretory Systems

Food provides the energy required for sustenance of the human body. After the fragmenting of food by chewing and mixing with **saliva**, digestion begins. Chewed food passes down the esophagus into the **stomach**, where gastric and intestinal juices continue the digestion process. Thereafter, the mixture of food and secretions makes its way down the **alimentary canal** using the rhythmic contraction of the smooth muscle of the **gastrointestinal tract**.

Motor Skills Development

Physical changes play a significant role in the development of children as they gradually gain control of the movements and functions of their bodies. As they develop physically, children refine their motor skills, enabling them to engage in increasingly complex lessons and activities. For teachers to be able to identify patterns of physical development, they must create educational activities that are developmentally appropriate for their students' physical abilities.

Children between the ages of 3 and 4 have mastered standing and walking. At this stage, children are developing **gross motor skills**, including the ability to hop on one foot and balance, climb stairs without support, kick a ball, throw overhand, catch a ball that has bounced, move forward and backward, and ride a tricycle. Children between the ages of 3 and 4 are also developing fine motor skills, such as using scissors, drawing single shapes, and copying shapes like capital letters.

By age 4 or 5, when most children enter school, they are developing the gross motor ability to do somersaults, swing, climb, and skip. These skills require increasing coordination. In addition, children at this age can begin to dress themselves using zippers, buttons, and possibly tying shoes. They can eat independently using utensils. Children at this age are increasingly capable of copying shapes, including letters and numbers. They can cut and paste and draw a person with a head, body, arms, and legs. These **fine motor skills** develop quickly in children of this age.

By age 6, children can bounce a ball, skate, ride a bike, skip with both feet, and dress themselves independently. As the student develops year by year, the physical

skills, both fine and gross motor, become increasingly complex and involve more muscles and more coordination. By age 9, children can complete a model kit, learn to sew, and cook simple recipes. By age 10, children can catch fly balls and participate in all elements of a softball game.

Recognizing the basic milestones that most children will achieve by a certain age will assist teachers in making decisions about academic lessons and tasks. In addition, teachers may be able to identify children who may not be reaching their developmental milestones with the rest of the class. In short, the physical ability of students to engage in simple to complex activities in school gradually increases as they develop. Teachers must adjust and adapt classroom and playground activities to be developmentally appropriate for the specific skill levels of students. To this end, it is important for teachers to be able to identify the physical development patterns of their students.

Human Growth and Development

A teacher does not have to be an expert in anatomy and physiology to see the physical changes that accompany students' growth and maturity. The preschool child has trouble grasping pencils and crayons in a manner that facilitates handwriting; however, even most 2-year-olds can grasp crayons sufficiently to make marks on papers and thus enjoy the creative excitement of art.

Physiological changes play a significant role in the development of children as they increase their control of bodily movements and functions and refine their motor skills. Their ability to engage in simple to complex classroom and playground activities increases as they develop. Teachers must adjust and adapt classroom and playground activities to be developmentally appropriate for students' various skill levels. Girls, on average, reach maturational milestones before boys. Physical changes may cause embarrassment to both females and males when they draw unwelcome attention. These changes almost always create some discomfort as adolescents find the body they were familiar and comfortable with to be quite different, sometimes seemingly overnight. To facilitate this transition, teachers need to make children aware that these changes are part of their natural development.

Social and Emotional Health

Many major factors relate to and are necessary to build both social and emotional health. It is critically important for teaches to develop a basic understanding of the principles of human development and its multiple dimensions—physical, mental, emotional, and social. Additionally, teachers must appreciate a dynamic and interactive view of human development.

This approach to understanding human development is one that recognizes that human beings do not develop in a vacuum. People exist in an environment that, friendly or unfriendly, supportive or non-supportive, evokes and provokes reactions from individuals. Moreover, human development is not a one-way street with the environment doing all the driving. People also act in certain ways to shape and form their environment.

A constant interaction or interplay occurs between people and their environments. Thus, effective teachers must be sensitive to and knowledgeable of both personal characteristics of students (internal factors) and characteristics of their environment. Internal factors, beyond the general characteristics that humans share as they grow and mature, also include students' personality characteristics, their self-concept and sense of self-esteem, their self-discipline and self-control, their ability to cope with stress, and their general outlook on life.

Self-Concept   Empowerment has many components, one of which is **self-concept**, or self-esteem. A good definition of self-concept is what we think and believe to be true about ourselves, not what we think about others and not what they think about us.

Related to self-concept is self-efficacy. Simply stated, **self-efficacy** is the confidence you have in your ability to cope with life's challenges. Self-efficacy refers to your sense of control over life or over your responses to life. Experts say that ideas about self-efficacy get established by the time children reach age 4. Because of this early establishment of either a feeling of control or no control, classroom teachers may find that even primary grade students believe that they have no control over their lives, that it makes no difference what they do or how they act. Therefore, it is all the more important that teachers attempt to help all students achieve coping skills and a sense of self-efficacy. Self-concept appears to be a combination of self-efficacy and self-respect as seen against a background of self-knowledge.

Mental and Emotional Disorders in Children

Mental and emotional disorders present various emotional and physical signs. **Depression** can manifest itself in an overall lack of interest in activities, constant crying, or talk of suicide. **Anxiety** or obsessive thoughts are another indication of a possible mental or emotional disorder. Physical signs include a disruption in eating or sleeping patterns, headaches, nausea and stomach pain, or diarrhea. The teacher needs to consider these signs as a cause for serious concerns and treatment.

Psychotic disorders, such as schizophrenia, are serious emotional disorders. These disorders are rare in young children and difficult to diagnose. One of the warning signs for psychotic disorders is that the student experiences a complete break from the reality of his or her surroundings. Schizophrenics may have difficulty expressing themselves, resulting in unusual speech patterns or even muteness. Schizophrenics, who are more likely to be boys than girls, may also exhibit facial expressions that are either markedly absent of emotion or overly active.

Infantile autism is a serious emotional disorder that appears in early childhood. Characteristics include withdrawn behavior and delayed or absent language and communication skills. Symptoms of autism can appear in children between four and eighteen months of age. Autistic children will usually distance themselves from others and may be unable to experience empathy. In addition, they often cannot distinguish or appreciate humor. Autistic children may have a preoccupation with particular objects or may perform particular activities repeatedly. While autistic children can range in all levels of intelligence, some children may have particular skills in focused areas, such as music or math. Diagnosis might inaccurately determine mental retardation, hearing/auditory impairment, or brain damage. Treatment for autistic children may involve therapy, drugs, or residential living. However, only five percent of autistic children ever become socially well-adjusted adults. Many of these high-functioning autistics are placed in the regular classroom, some with personal aides to facilitate their success.

Factors That Contribute to Substance Use and Abuse

Drug and alcohol problems can affect anyone, regardless of age, sex, race, marital status, place of residence, income level, or lifestyle. However, there are certain identifiable risk factors for substance abuse. **Risk factors** are characteristics that occur statistically more often for those who develop alcohol and drug problems, as either adolescents or adults, than for those who do not develop substance abuse problems. These factors include individual, familial, social, and cultural characteristics.

Individual Characteristics

Some of the personal characteristics that have been linked to substance abuse are: aggressiveness, emotional problems, inability to cope with stress, and low self-esteem. Feelings of failure and a fragile ego can also contribute to this problem. The presence of physical disabilities, physical or mental health problems, or learning disabilities can add to the student's vulnerability to substance abuse. In many ways, students who are at risk for academic problems are also susceptible to substance abuse problems.

Family Characteristics

Associated with substance abuse among youth are several family characteristics. First, and perhaps most important, is the alcohol or other drug dependency of a parent or both parents. This characteristic might relate to another significant factor: parental abuse and neglect of children. Antisocial and/or mentally ill parents are factors that put children at risk for drug and/or alcohol abuse. In addition, high levels of family stress such as large, overcrowded family conditions; family unemployment or underemployment; and parents who have little education or who are socially isolated are also risk factors. Single parents without family or other support; family instability; a high level of marital and family conflict or violence; and parental absenteeism due to separation, divorce, or death can also increase children's vulnerability to substance abuse. Finally, other important factors to consider are the lack of family rituals, inadequate parenting, little child-to-parent interaction, and frequent family moves. These factors describe children without affiliation or a sense of identity with their families or community. Any of these family factors could lead to a substance abuse problem in a student.

Social and Cultural Characteristics

Living in an economically depressed area with high unemployment, inadequate housing, a high crime rate, and a prevalence of illegal drug use are social characteristics that can put an individual at risk for substance abuse. Cultural risk factors include minority status involving racial discrimination, differing generational levels of assimilation, low levels of education, and low achievement expectations from society at large.

All the recognized risk factors are only indicators of the potential for substance abuse. They are not necessarily predictive of an individual's proclivity to drug or alcohol abuse. Some children who are exposed to very adverse conditions grow up to be healthy, productive, and well-functioning adults. Yet, knowing the risk factors, teachers are better able to identify children vulnerable to substance abuse and develop prevention education strategies. If teachers recognize these risk factors in some of their students, there are certain things that teachers can do to increase the chances that the youngster or adolescent will resist the lures of illegal and dangerous alcohol and drug abuse.

Identify Signs and Symptoms of Substance Use and Abuse

Sometimes it can be difficult to tell if someone is using illegal drugs or alcohol. Usually, people who abuse drugs or alcohol (including young people) go to great lengths to keep their behavior a secret. They deny and/or try to hide the problem. However, certain warning signs can indicate that someone is using drugs or drinking too much alcohol:

- Lying to teachers and family members
- Avoiding people who are longtime friends or associates
- Having slurred speech
- Complaining of headaches, nausea, or dizziness
- Having difficulty staying awake in class

These examples, in and of themselves, are insufficient to confirm a substance abuse problem, but in combination and when displayed consistently over time, they are strong indicators. Teachers should record their observations and keep written reports of the behavioral changes they witness. Moreover, they should report their suspicions to the appropriate school authorities.

School Violence and Antisocial Behaviors

Some of the elements that contribute to school violence are: (1) overcrowding, (2) poor design and use of school space, (3) lack of disciplinary procedures, (4) student alienation, (5) multicultural insensitivity, (6) rejection of at-risk students by teachers and peers, and (7) anger or resentment at school routines. On the other hand, factors contributing to school safety include (1) a positive school climate and atmosphere, (2) clear and high performance expectations for all students, (3) practices and values that promote inclusion, (4) bonding of the students to the school, (5) high levels of student participation and parent involvement in school activities, and (6) opportunities to acquire academic skills and develop socially. Effective teachers need to be alert to the signs of potentially violent behavior, acknowledging that signs can easily be misinterpreted and misunderstood. Warning signs should be used to get help for children, not to exclude, punish, or isolate them.

Imminent Warning Signs of Violence

Some of the imminent warning signs of school violence are: (1) serious physical fighting with peers or family members; (2) serious destruction of property; (3) rage for seemingly minor reasons; (4) detailed threats of lethal violence; (5) possession and/or use of firearms and weapons; and (6) other self-injurious behaviors or threats of suicide. Teachers have to become vigilant to these signs of violence and notify the appropriate authorities of these behaviors.

Violence prevention strategies at school range from adding social skills training to the curriculum to installing metal detectors at the entrances to buildings. Schools should teach all students procedures in conflict resolution and anger management, and should explain the school, rules, expectations, and disciplinary policies.

Competency 027 (Physical Education)

The teacher uses knowledge of the concepts, principles, skills, and practices of physical education to plan and implement effective and engaging physical education activities for young children.

In 1986, the National Association for Sport and Physical Education appointed a committee to develop a working definition of the characteristics that physically educated people ought to exhibit (NASPE, 2006). As a result of this initiative, the NASPE introduced the following definition.

A physically educated person is someone who:

- has learned skills necessary to perform a variety of physical activities;
- knows the implications of and the benefits from involvement in physical activities;
- participates regularly in physical activity and is physically fit;
- values physical activity and its contribution to a healthful lifestyle.

With this definition in mind, a committee of the same organization developed the National Standards for Physical Education (NASPE, 2006). The national standards for physical education are:

- **Standard 1:** Demonstrates competency in motor skills and movement patterns needed to perform a variety of physical activities.
- **Standard 2:** Demonstrates understanding of movement concepts, principles, strategies, and tactics as they apply to the learning and performance of physical activities.
- **Standard 3:** Participates regularly in physical activity.
- **Standard 4:** Achieves and maintains a health-enhancing level of physical fitness.
- **Standard 5:** Exhibits responsible personal and social behavior that respects self and others in physical activity settings.
- **Standard 6:** Values physical activity for health, enjoyment, challenge, self-expression, and/or social interaction.

The Texas Essential Knowledge and Skills

In conjunction with the national initiative, The Texas Essential Knowledge and Skills (TEKS) requires children to demonstrate knowledge and skills for movement that provide the foundation for enjoyment, continued social development through physical activity, and access to a physically active lifestyle. All children are expected to develop muscular strength and endurance of the arms, shoulders, abdomen, back and legs. They are also expected to become aware of how the muscles, bones, heart, and lungs function in relation to physical activity. Some of the key skills and activities required in the state K–4 curriculum are listed below (TEC, 2006).

Kindergarten

Children should be able to

1. play with other children within boundaries during games and activities;

2. develop muscular strength and endurance of the arms, shoulders, abdomen, back, and legs such as hanging, hopping, and jumping;

3. demonstrate knowledge of a variety of relationships such as under, over, behind, next to, through, right, left, up, down, forward, backward, and in front of;

4. roll sideways (right or left) without hesitating;

5. toss a ball and catch it before it bounces twice.

First Grade

Children should be able to

1. demonstrate proper foot patterns in hopping, jumping, skipping, leaping, galloping, and sliding;

2. demonstrate the ability to work with a partner such as leading and following;

3. clap in time to a simple rhythmic beat; create and imitate movement in response to selected rhythms; jump a long rope; and demonstrate on cue key elements in overhand throw, underhand throw, and catch;

4. create and imitate movement in response to selected rhythms;

5. demonstrate control in balancing and traveling activities.

Second Grade

Children should be able to

1. demonstrate skills of chasing, fleeing, and dodging to avoid or catch others;

2. demonstrate mature form in walking, hopping, and skipping;

3. demonstrate a variety of relationships in dynamic movement situations such as under, over, behind, next to, through, right, left, up, or down;

4. demonstrate simple stunts that exhibit personal agility such as jumping with one and two foot takeoffs and landing with good control;

5. demonstrate on cue key elements of hand dribble, foot dribble, kick and strike such as striking balloon or ball with hand.

Third Grade

Children should be able to

1. demonstrate mature form in jogging, running, and leaping;

2. demonstrate control and appropriate form such as curled position and protection of neck in rolling activities;

3. transfer on and off equipment with good body control such as boxes, benches, stacked mats, horizontal bar, and balance beam;

4. clap echoes in a variety of one measure rhythmical patterns;

5. demonstrate key elements in manipulative skills such as underhand throw, overhand throw, catch and kick.

Fourth Grade

Children should be able to

1. change speed during straight, curved, and zig zag pathways;

2. catch a football pass on the run;

3. jump and land for height and distance absorbing force such as bending knees and swinging arms;

4. perform basic folk dance steps such as schottische (German folk dance), and step-together-step;

5. demonstrate key elements in manipulative skills such as volleying, hand dribble, foot dribble, punt, striking with body part, racquet, or bat.

The activities and skills for children in K–4 are designed to keep children active, to develop the fitness necessary for appropriate physical development, and to maintain a healthy body and mind.

Physical Fitness and Health

The axiom "Use it or lose it" certainly holds true for the human body. Our bodies thrive on **physical activity**, which is any bodily movement produced by skeletal muscles and resulting in energy expenditure. Physical fitness enables a person to meet the physical demands of work and leisure comfortably. A person with a high level of physical fitness can enjoy a better quality of life and minimize the development of life threatening diseases. Unfortunately, Americans tend to be relatively inactive.

Lack of activity can cause many problems, including flabby muscles, a weak heart, poor circulation, shortness of breath, obesity, coronary artery disease, hypertension, type 2 diabetes, osteoporosis, and certain types of cancer. Overall, mortality rates from all causes are lower in physically active people than in sedentary people. In addition, physical activity can help people manage mild-to-moderate depression, control anxiety, and prevent weakening of the skeletal system.

By increasing physical activity, a person may improve heart function and circulation, respiratory function, and overall strength and endurance. All of these lead to improved vigor and vitality. Exercise also lowers the risk of heart disease by strengthening the heart muscle, lowering pulse and blood pressure, and lowering the concentration of fat in both the body and the blood. It can also improve appearance, increase range of motion, and lessen the risk of back problems associated with weak bones and osteoporosis.

Every person should engage in regular physical activity and reduce sedentary activities to promote health, psychological well-being, and a healthy body weight. On most days of the week, children should engage in at least 60 minutes of physical activity.

Proper hydration is important during physical activity. To help prevent dehydration during prolonged physical activity or when it is hot, people should (1) consume fluid regularly during the activity and (2) drink several glasses of water or other fluid after the physical activity is completed (USDA, 2005).

Physical Education Activities for Children

Children in early childhood are not concerned with physical fitness; instead they are interested in having fun. Based on this premise, a physical education program for this age group should reflect this interest. The child who is actively involved in fun physical activities will get the same benefits as children in a highly structured physical fitness program.

Movement Education

During play activities, a child engages in meaningful activities impacting the total body and emphasizing movement education. **Movement education** is the process by which a child is helped to develop competency in movement. It has been defined as learning to move and moving to learn. Movement competency requires the student to manage his or her body. This body management is necessary to develop both basic and specialized activities. Basic movement skills are needed for the child's daily living and play. Specialized skills are required to perform sports and other activities that have very clear techniques. Basic skills must be mastered before the child can develop specialized ones.

The child controls his or her movement during non-locomotor (stationary) activities, in movements across the floor or field, through space, and when suspended on an apparatus. To obtain good body management skills is to acquire, expand, and integrate elements of motor control. This is done through wide experiences in movement, based on a creative and exploratory approach. It is important that children not only manage their body with ease of movement, but also realize that good posture and body mechanics are important parts of their movement patterns. In other words, a child with good motor control is a child who is graceful. This is important not just for playing games and sports, but simply for safety. Children without this skill are more prone to accidents and injury.

Perceptual Motor Competency

Perceptual motor competency is another consideration in body management. Perceptual motor concepts that are relevant to physical education include those that give attention to balance, coordination, lateral movement, directional movement, awareness of space, and knowledge of one's own body. Basic skills can be divided into three categories, locomotor, non-locomotor, and manipulative skills (IDE, 2001). A movement pattern might include skills from each category.

Locomotor Skills Locomotor activities describe the type of movement children have to master in order to travel or move within a given space. These include walking, running, leaping, jumping, hopping, galloping, sliding, and skipping.

Non-Locomotor Skills Non-locomotor activities are used to control the body in relation to the force of gravity. These are done while in a stationary position, i.e., kneeling or standing. Some of these activities are: pushing, pulling, bending, stretching, twisting, turning, swinging, shaking, bouncing, and rising and falling.

Manipulative Skills Manipulative skills are used when a child handles and play with an object. Most manipulative skills involve using the hands and the feet, but other parts of the body may be used as well. Hand-eye and foot-eye coordination are improved with manipulative objects. Throwing, batting, kicking, and catching are important skills to be developed using balls and beanbags. Starting a child at a less challenging level and progressing to a more difficult activity is an effective method for teaching manipulative activities. Most activities begin with individual practice and later move to partner activities. When teaching throwing and catching, the teacher should emphasize skill performance, principles of opposition, weight transfer, eye focus, and follow through. Some attention should be given to targets when throwing because students need to be able to catch and throw to different levels. Reaching is a "point-to-point" arm movement that is very common in our daily activities. In fact, reaching and grasping are typically used together to serve a number of purposes like eating, drinking, dressing, or cooking. The reaching/grasping task requires an "eye-hand" coordination and control of movement timing for a successful attempt.

Children need to develop the appropriate muscular and eye coordination to achieve a variety of daily tasks required to function effectively in their environment. These tasks are developmental in nature but teachers can facilitate the mastery of these by engaging children in enjoyable activities where these basic movements are required. Table 5-3 presents a few examples of movement activities appropriate for grades K–4.

For detailed information on physical education activities for 3–5 year old children visit the Iowa Department of Education (IDE, 2001). Physical fun for little ones. http://www.state.ia.us/educate/ecese/cfcs/physical_fun.

Specialized Skills Specialized skills are related to various sports and other physical education activities such as dance, tumbling, gymnastics, and specific games. To teach a specialized skill, the instructor must present and use explanation, demonstration, and drill. Demonstration can be done by other students, provided the teacher monitors the demonstration and gives cues for proper form. Drills are excellent to teach specific skills but can become tedious unless they are done in a creative manner. Using game simulations to practice skills is an effective method to maintain interest during a practice session.

Teachers must also remember to use feedback when teaching a skill or activity. Positive feedback is much more conducive to skill learning than negative feedback. The typical intimidation tactics of physical education coaches will not work for children at this age. Appropriate feedback means correcting with suggestions to improve. If a student playing kickball continually misses or kicks the ball out of play, he or she is aware that something is not right. The teacher should indicate what the problem is and tell the student how to succeed in kicking the ball to the play area.

Movement education enables the child to make choices of activity and the method they wish to employ. Teachers can structure learning situations so the child can be challenged to develop his or her own means of movement. The child becomes the center of learning and is encouraged to be creative in carrying out the movement experience. In this method of teaching,

Table 5-3. Motor Skills Activities for K–4 Students

Key Movements	Mastery	Activities
Running	4–5 years	Free play, short races and musical chairs
Jumping	5 years	Hopscotch, rope jumping, Jumping Jacks (advanced)
Hopping	4–6 years	Dancing activities and Hopscotch
Skipping	4–6 years	Marching and songs of motion (guide children to conduct specific activities such as skipping, jumping, etc.)
Catching	3–6 years	Playing catch, passing the ball, Frisbee
Striking—ball	6–7 years	Batting practice using underhand throws or using a batting tee
Kicking	4–6 years	Kick ball and soccer
Throwing	5–6 years	Playing catch, throwing to a target, bean bag toss

the child is encouraged to be creative and progress according to his/her abilities. The teacher is not the center of learning, but offers suggestions and stimulates the learning environment. Student-centered learning works especially well when there is a wide disparity of motor abilities. If the teacher sets standards that are too high for the less talented students, they may become discouraged and not try to perform.

Basic movement education attempts to develop the children's awareness not only of what they are doing but how they are doing it. Each child is encouraged to succeed in his or her own way according to his or her own capacity. If children succeed at developing basic skills in elementary school, they will have a much better chance at acquiring the specialized skills required for all sports activities.

Aerobic Exercise

Exploration of movement activities through fun activities constitutes the main focus of the physical education curriculum in the early grades. However, the curriculum can provide for more organized activities like yoga or low impact aerobic exercise. Aerobic exercise involves both muscle contraction and movement of the body. Aerobic exercise requires large amounts of oxygen and when done regularly, will condition the cardiovascular system. Some aerobic exercises are especially suited to developing aerobic

training benefits, with a minimum of skill and time involved. Examples of good aerobic activities are walking, running, swimming, and bicycling. These activities are especially good in the development of fitness because all of them can be done alone and with a minimum of special equipment. In order to be considered true aerobic conditioning, an activity must require a great deal of oxygen, it must be continuous and rhythmic, it must exercise major muscle groups and burn fat as an energy source, and it must last for at least 20 minutes at an individual's target heart rate.

Children can participate in low impact aerobics training but parents and teachers must monitor their performance. Children will probably try to keep up with adults, and initially they may not have the strength or flexibility to maintain the pace. This could lead to undue fatigue, needless muscle soreness or injury.

Adaptive Physical Education

The Americans with Disabilities Act (ADA) requires the placement of students in the least restrictive environment (ADA, 2006). For most "handicapped children" the least restrictive environment is the regular classroom, which includes participation in physical education activities. The challenge in teaching physical education to handicapped children is tailoring activities to fit each child. For example, blind or partially sighted students can participate in dance, and some gymnastic and tumbling activities. These students can also participate in some other activities with modifications. A beeper ball together with verbal cue can be used for T-ball or even for softball. If a beeper is not available, the teacher can put the student in position and assist in aiming and cueing when to hit the ball. For students using assistive devices like walkers or crutches, allow them to hit the ball from a seated position and use the crutch to bat (IDE, 2001). If the child is unable to run, allow a substitute runner. Many games and activities can be modified for the handicapped. Sometimes all it takes is a little ingenuity to change activities so handicapped students can enjoy participating.

Anatomy and Physiology

Effective physical education teachers possess an understanding of the human body and how physical activity can impact it. Knowledge of anatomy and physiology can guide teachers in the selection and implementation of games and physical activities. **Anatomy** describes the structure, position, and size of various organs. Because our bones adapt to fill a specific need, exercise is of great benefit to the skeletal system. Bones that anchor strong muscles thicken to withstand the stress. Weight-bearing bones can develop heavy mineral deposits while supporting the body. Because joints help provide flexibility and ease of movement, it is important to know how each joint moves. Types of joints are ball and socket (shoulder and hip), hinge (knee), pivot (head of the spine), gliding [carpal (wrist) and tarsal (ankle) bones], angular (wrist and ankle joints), partially movable (vertebrae), and immovable (bones of the adult cranium).

Muscles are the active movers in the body. In order to properly teach any physical education activity, the functions and physiology of the muscles must be understood. Because muscles move by shortening or contracting, proper form should be taught so the student can get the most out of an activity. It is also important to know the location of each muscle. This knowledge will help in teaching proper form while doing all physical education activities. Understanding the concept of antagonistic muscles, along with the related information concerning flexors and extensors, is also vital to the physical educator. Imagine trying to teach the proper form of throwing a ball if you do not understand the mechanics involved. Knowledge of anatomy and physiology is also necessary to teach proper techniques used in calisthenics as well as all physical activities. Some physical education class standbys are frequently done improperly or done when the exercise itself can cause harm.

References

ADA. 2006. Americans with Disability Act home page. *http://www.usdoj.gov/crt/ada/adahom1.htm*

American Academy of Pediatrics. 2006. Child abuse and neglect. Excerpted from *Caring for Baby and Young Child: Birth to Age 5*, Bantam 1999.

Iowa Department of Education. 2001. Physical fun for little ones. http://www.state.ia.us/educate/ecese/cfcs/physical_fun.

NASPE. 2006. National Association for Sports and Physical Education website. http://www.aahperd.org/NASPE

National Institute of Mental Health. 2001. *Eating Disorders: Facts About Eating Disorders and the Search for Solutions. http://www.nimh.nih.gov/Publicat/eatingdisorders.cfm*

TAC 2006. Texas Administrative Code. TAC. Title 19, Part II Chapter 115. Texas Essential Knowledge and Skills for Health Education. *http://www.tea.state.tx.us/rules/tac/chapter115/index.html*

U.S. Department of Agriculture. 2005. *Steps to a healthier you. http://www.mypyramid.gov.*

TExES

Texas Examinations of Educator Standards

101 Generalist EC-4

Practice Test

Answer Sheet

1. Ⓐ Ⓑ Ⓒ Ⓓ
2. Ⓐ Ⓑ Ⓒ Ⓓ
3. Ⓐ Ⓑ Ⓒ Ⓓ
4. Ⓐ Ⓑ Ⓒ Ⓓ
5. Ⓐ Ⓑ Ⓒ Ⓓ
6. Ⓐ Ⓑ Ⓒ Ⓓ
7. Ⓐ Ⓑ Ⓒ Ⓓ
8. Ⓐ Ⓑ Ⓒ Ⓓ
9. Ⓐ Ⓑ Ⓒ Ⓓ
10. Ⓐ Ⓑ Ⓒ Ⓓ
11. Ⓐ Ⓑ Ⓒ Ⓓ
12. Ⓐ Ⓑ Ⓒ Ⓓ
13. Ⓐ Ⓑ Ⓒ Ⓓ
14. Ⓐ Ⓑ Ⓒ Ⓓ
15. Ⓐ Ⓑ Ⓒ Ⓓ
16. Ⓐ Ⓑ Ⓒ Ⓓ
17. Ⓐ Ⓑ Ⓒ Ⓓ
18. Ⓐ Ⓑ Ⓒ Ⓓ
19. Ⓐ Ⓑ Ⓒ Ⓓ
20. Ⓐ Ⓑ Ⓒ Ⓓ
21. Ⓐ Ⓑ Ⓒ Ⓓ
22. Ⓐ Ⓑ Ⓒ Ⓓ
23. Ⓐ Ⓑ Ⓒ Ⓓ
24. Ⓐ Ⓑ Ⓒ Ⓓ
25. Ⓐ Ⓑ Ⓒ Ⓓ
26. Ⓐ Ⓑ Ⓒ Ⓓ

27. Ⓐ Ⓑ Ⓒ Ⓓ
28. Ⓐ Ⓑ Ⓒ Ⓓ
29. Ⓐ Ⓑ Ⓒ Ⓓ
30. Ⓐ Ⓑ Ⓒ Ⓓ
31. Ⓐ Ⓑ Ⓒ Ⓓ
32. Ⓐ Ⓑ Ⓒ Ⓓ
33. Ⓐ Ⓑ Ⓒ Ⓓ
34. Ⓐ Ⓑ Ⓒ Ⓓ
35. Ⓐ Ⓑ Ⓒ Ⓓ
36. Ⓐ Ⓑ Ⓒ Ⓓ
37. Ⓐ Ⓑ Ⓒ Ⓓ
38. Ⓐ Ⓑ Ⓒ Ⓓ
39. Ⓐ Ⓑ Ⓒ Ⓓ
40. Ⓐ Ⓑ Ⓒ Ⓓ
41. Ⓐ Ⓑ Ⓒ Ⓓ
42. Ⓐ Ⓑ Ⓒ Ⓓ
43. Ⓐ Ⓑ Ⓒ Ⓓ
44. Ⓐ Ⓑ Ⓒ Ⓓ
45. Ⓐ Ⓑ Ⓒ Ⓓ
46. Ⓐ Ⓑ Ⓒ Ⓓ
47. Ⓐ Ⓑ Ⓒ Ⓓ
48. Ⓐ Ⓑ Ⓒ Ⓓ
49. Ⓐ Ⓑ Ⓒ Ⓓ
50. Ⓐ Ⓑ Ⓒ Ⓓ
51. Ⓐ Ⓑ Ⓒ Ⓓ
52. Ⓐ Ⓑ Ⓒ Ⓓ

53. Ⓐ Ⓑ Ⓒ Ⓓ
54. Ⓐ Ⓑ Ⓒ Ⓓ
55. Ⓐ Ⓑ Ⓒ Ⓓ
56. Ⓐ Ⓑ Ⓒ Ⓓ
57. Ⓐ Ⓑ Ⓒ Ⓓ
58. Ⓐ Ⓑ Ⓒ Ⓓ
59. Ⓐ Ⓑ Ⓒ Ⓓ
60. Ⓐ Ⓑ Ⓒ Ⓓ
61. Ⓐ Ⓑ Ⓒ Ⓓ
62. Ⓐ Ⓑ Ⓒ Ⓓ
63. Ⓐ Ⓑ Ⓒ Ⓓ
64. Ⓐ Ⓑ Ⓒ Ⓓ
65. Ⓐ Ⓑ Ⓒ Ⓓ
66. Ⓐ Ⓑ Ⓒ Ⓓ
67. Ⓐ Ⓑ Ⓒ Ⓓ
68. Ⓐ Ⓑ Ⓒ Ⓓ
69. Ⓐ Ⓑ Ⓒ Ⓓ
70. Ⓐ Ⓑ Ⓒ Ⓓ
71. Ⓐ Ⓑ Ⓒ Ⓓ
72. Ⓐ Ⓑ Ⓒ Ⓓ
73. Ⓐ Ⓑ Ⓒ Ⓓ
74. Ⓐ Ⓑ Ⓒ Ⓓ
75. Ⓐ Ⓑ Ⓒ Ⓓ
76. Ⓐ Ⓑ Ⓒ Ⓓ
77. Ⓐ Ⓑ Ⓒ Ⓓ

78. Ⓐ Ⓑ Ⓒ Ⓓ
79. Ⓐ Ⓑ Ⓒ Ⓓ
80. Ⓐ Ⓑ Ⓒ Ⓓ
81. Ⓐ Ⓑ Ⓒ Ⓓ
82. Ⓐ Ⓑ Ⓒ Ⓓ
83. Ⓐ Ⓑ Ⓒ Ⓓ
84. Ⓐ Ⓑ Ⓒ Ⓓ
85. Ⓐ Ⓑ Ⓒ Ⓓ
86. Ⓐ Ⓑ Ⓒ Ⓓ
87. Ⓐ Ⓑ Ⓒ Ⓓ
88. Ⓐ Ⓑ Ⓒ Ⓓ
89. Ⓐ Ⓑ Ⓒ Ⓓ
90. Ⓐ Ⓑ Ⓒ Ⓓ
91. Ⓐ Ⓑ Ⓒ Ⓓ
92. Ⓐ Ⓑ Ⓒ Ⓓ
93. Ⓐ Ⓑ Ⓒ Ⓓ
94. Ⓐ Ⓑ Ⓒ Ⓓ
95. Ⓐ Ⓑ Ⓒ Ⓓ
96. Ⓐ Ⓑ Ⓒ Ⓓ
97. Ⓐ Ⓑ Ⓒ Ⓓ
98. Ⓐ Ⓑ Ⓒ Ⓓ
99. Ⓐ Ⓑ Ⓒ Ⓓ
100. Ⓐ Ⓑ Ⓒ Ⓓ
101. Ⓐ Ⓑ Ⓒ Ⓓ
102. Ⓐ Ⓑ Ⓒ Ⓓ

Practice Test for Generalist EC–4 Certification

Questions 1–102

> **Instructions:** Select the best answer.

1. Identify the statement that best describes the relationship between the eight social studies strands and the TEKS in the implementation of the Texas curriculum.

   (A) There is no connection between the TEKS and the social studies strands.
   (B) The social studies strands have been used as a foundation for the development of the state curriculum.
   (C) The strands apply to programs at the university level and the TEKS applies to K–12 curricula.
   (D) The strands apply to programs at the high school level, while the TEKS applies to all grade levels.

2. The state curriculum officially introduces children to Texas history in

   (A) prekindergarten.
   (B) first grade.
   (C) third grade.
   (D) fourth grade.

3. Children in prekindergarten and kindergarten might have problems understanding how the Earth is represented in globes and flat representations because children at this age

   (A) might not be developmentally reading to understand symbolic representations.
   (B) might pay more attention to the colors and features of globes and maps than the concepts being taught.
   (C) might not be interested in maps and globes.
   (D) might have problems recognizing the Earth's features presented on the 12-inch globe representation.

4. To apply the concept of time zones, students need to have a clear understanding of

   (A) the International Date Line.
   (B) the Earth's yearly revolution.
   (C) the concept of the meridians of longitude.
   (D) the concept of the parallels of latitude.

5. The Sumerians, Akkadians, Babylonians, and Assyrians were some of the civilizations that flourished in Mesopotamia—the land between the rivers. What rivers are being alluded to in this statement?

   (A) Nile and Amazon
   (B) Tigris and Euphrates
   (C) Nile and Indus
   (D) Volga and Danube

6. Identify the modern-day country that encompasses most of the territory of ancient Mesopotamia.

   (A) Iran
   (B) Pakistan
   (C) Kuwait
   (D) Iraq

7. Identify two key historical concepts or characters of the Middle Ages.

   (A) the Greek and the Roman Empires
   (B) the feudal system and the Crusades
   (C) Stonehenge and the rise of Islam
   (D) the Renaissance and Alexander the Great

8. The most advanced pre-Columbian civilizations of Mesoamerica were the

   (A) Aztecs and Incas.
   (B) Maya and Aztecs.
   (C) Toltecs and Pueblos.
   (D) Olmecs and Iroquois.

9. Identify the statement that best describes the country of Iraq.

   (A) It is a linguistically and ethnically homogeneous Muslim nation.
   (B) It is a Muslim nation with multiple ethnic groups within its borders.
   (C) It is located in Southeast Asia.
   (D) It is a province of Pakistan.

10. If in the United States we are enjoying a warm winter, what season are the people of Brazil having?

    (A) spring
    (B) summer
    (C) winter
    (D) fall

11. The imperial forces of Japan attacked Pearl Harbor on Sunday, December 7, 1941. Once the attack began, the officer in charge called President Roosevelt and notified him of the attack. During the communication, the president was able to hear the noise of the bombs exploding and the struggle of the battle. Recently, a reporter from the *Dallas Morning News* was researching the details of the attack and found a transcription of the official diary of Emperor Hirohito, where he indicated the following: "The Imperial forces of Japan destroyed the American fleet in Hawaii Monday, December 8, 1941." If the attack occurred on December 7, why did the official document from the Japanese government indicate that the attack happened on December 8? Select the statement that best explains this discrepancy.

    (A) The Americans knew that the attack was going to happen and assumed that it had happened the day before.
    (B) The U.S. government had spies in Japan and they knew when the attack was going to take place.
    (C) There is a one-day difference between the two regions.
    (D) Emperor Hirohito learned about the attack the day after and he assumed that it happened on that day.

12. Indian tribes from the Central and Great Plains of Texas are better known than their counterparts from the Coastal Plains because

    (A) they had a more advanced civilization.
    (B) they were sedentary and built better ceremonial sites and permanent structures.
    (C) they domesticated the horse, which made them better hunters and warriors.
    (D) they had an abundance of food sources and were stronger.

13. Probably as a response to the war in the Middle East, OPEC cut the production of oil. As a result of this action, the cost of gasoline increased to almost $3.00 per gallon in 2005. What is the economic principle or statement that is best represented by this situation?

    (A) During war, the prices of fossil fuels increase.
    (B) The American economy is dependent on foreign oil.
    (C) The law of supply and demand determines the prices of goods and services.
    (D) OPEC was boycotting the United States.

14. The Fifteenth Amendment of the U.S. Constitution was ratified in 1870 to grant

    (A) black women and men the right to vote.

(B) citizenship for blacks.
(C) freedom of slaves.
(D) black men the right to vote.

15. The U.S. Constitution was designed so that no single branch of the government—executive, judicial, or legislative—could exert full control over the other two. This unique feature of the Constitution is known as

    (A) judicial review.
    (B) the pocket veto.
    (C) checks and balances.
    (D) habeas corpus.

Use the information in this scenario to answer questions 16 and 17:

> **Scenario:** Mr. Jamie Mackey has seven ELLs in his class who are having difficulties pronouncing English words containing the letters *sh* and *ch*. To support these students, he organizes small-group instruction to address their specific needs. He introduces pronunciation and vocabulary concepts through a chart. The chart is color-coded to guide students in the pronunciation of phonemes; i.e., he uses blue for the /sh/, green for /ch/, brown for /k/. Every week, he adds new words to the chart until he is satisfied that students have mastered the grapheme-phoneme correspondence. The chart for this week is shown below.

16. Based on the information provided in the chart, what is the primary reason for the confusion that ELLs experience with these two phonemes?

    (A) They cannot distinguish the difference between the two phonemes.

(B) They cannot pronounce either of the two phonemes.
(C) They might not be interested in learning these differences.
(D) The grapheme-phoneme correspondence is inconsistent.

17. What might be the advantages of using the chart above to teach pronunciation?

    (A) The chart provides examples of the grapho-phonemic consistency of English.
    (B) The students become aware of the words that follow grapheme-phoneme correspondence and those that do not.
    (C) The chart can be used to teach the intonation pattern of the language.
    (D) Children get exposed to vocabulary words and develop graphophonemic awareness.

18. Identify the number of syllables and the number of phonemes present in the word *thought*.

    (A) two syllables and three phonemes
    (B) one syllable and three phonemes
    (C) three syllables and six phonemes
    (D) two syllables and three phonemes

19. Marcus can separate a word into its individual phonemes and put it back together to re-create the original word. However, he has problems separating words into syllables and identifying the syllable with the primary stress. Based on this scenario, Marcus needs additional support with

    (A) phonological awareness.
    (B) phonemic awareness.
    (C) syllabication.
    (D) word stress.

1. *sh*—/sh/	2. *ch*—/ch/	3. *ch*—/k/	4. *ch*—/sh/	5. *s*—/sh/	6. *t*—/sh/
shower	church	Christmas	chef	sure	caution
short	chart	chemistry	Chevron	sugar	contribution
shell	choice	chrome	Chevrolet	mission	communication

20. Mr. Rovira guides five-year-old children in the recitation of the following utterance—"**R**ound the **r**ugged **r**ock the **r**agged **r**ascal **r**an." Children have fun with the activity and try to say it without errors. What literary technique is he using?

    (A) alliteration
    (B) tongue twister
    (C) nursery rhyme
    (D) memorization drills

21. Ms. Thomas introduces new vocabulary words within the context of a sentence and through the use of visuals. Once children understand the concept linked to the word, she repeats individual words, pausing after each syllable. Once children can separate the word into syllables, she guides them to separate syllables into individual phonemes. What skills is Ms. Thomas introducing with the latter activity?

    (A) the intonation pattern of the language
    (B) phonological awareness
    (C) vocabulary development
    (D) pronunciation drills

22. When teaching the grapheme-phoneme correspondence of English, teachers must

    (A) make the activity interesting to all students.
    (B) monitor the children so they do not pronounce the letters with a foreign accent.
    (C) create an atmosphere of cooperation among students from diverse ethnic and linguistic backgrounds.
    (D) control the inconsistency of the grapheme-phoneme correspondence of English by presenting consistent sounds first.

23. Ms. Jefferson has guided first-grade students to read polysyllabic words until they can read them fluently. Later, students are asked to separate the words into syllables, and finally she guides students to identify the main stress in each word. What skill is Ms. Jefferson emphasizing?

    (A) alphabetic awareness
    (B) reading fluency
    (C) phonological awareness

    (D) syllabication

24. Ms. Jefferson also uses monosyllabic words to present the concept of onset and rimes. Identify the pair of words that best represent this concept.

    (A) *want-ed—walk-ed*
    (B) *very—berry*
    (C) *think-ing—eat-ing*
    (D) *s-ank—b-ank*

25. The use of phonics instruction in conjunction with components from the whole language approach are typical for programs emphasizing a

    (A) skills-based approach.
    (B) balanced-reading approach.
    (C) meaning-based approach.
    (D) humanistic approach.

26. John Goodman used the term *miscues* in reading to describe the type of

    (A) variation that occurs when children attempt to put words in writing.
    (B) variation that occurs when children try to decode and guess the meaning of printed words.
    (C) errors that occur when children try to communicate orally in their native language.
    (D) discrepancy that occurs between the schemata of the child and the one intended by the author.

27. Identify the statement that best describes the advantages of using the language experience approach to teach reading to language minority students.

    (A) It provides the schema or experiential background to facilitate the comprehension of the story.
    (B) It uses the vocabulary and the experience common to both language minority and mainstream students.
    (C) It minimizes the possibility of errors due to idiomatic expressions from both L1 and L2.
    (D) It facilitates reading by ensuring a positive match between L1 and L2.

28. Identify the main benefit of the shared book experience.

    (A) Stories are shared in a warm, supportive environment.
    (B) The whole class can read with the teacher.
    (C) Children like big books.
    (D) It contains attractive pictures and big letters.

29. Identify the statement that best describes sight words.

    (A) Sight words are prevalent in environmental print.
    (B) Sight words occur frequently in print.
    (C) Children decode sight words using semantic and structural clues.
    (D) Children have difficulty spelling sight words.

30. Knowledge of the two words used to create compound words can help students in the interpretation of the compound word. However, there are examples of compound words in which the meaning of the two components does not contribute to, and often interfere with, the interpretation of the new word. Identify the set of compound words that fall into this category.

    (A) *doghouse*, *autograph*, and *boathouse*
    (B) *greenhouse*, *White House*, and *mouthwash*
    (C) *butterfly*, *nightmare*, and *brainstorm*
    (D) *hotdog*, *birdhouse*, and *underground*

31. When teaching English to ELLs of Spanish background, Ms. Rico introduced a list of Greek and Latin prefixes common to Spanish and English. She explained the spelling patterns and the meaning of each of the prefixes. She presented examples of words that contain the prefixes, and led students to decode these based on the meaning of the prefixes. What decoding strategy is Ms. Rico using?

    (A) contextual
    (B) structural
    (C) pictorial
    (D) syntactic

32. Ms. Fuentes frequently leads students in choral reading to promote reading fluency. She also takes declarative statements from the story and asks students to change them to questions or exclamations. Students have fun generating these changes. What is the main purpose of the latter activity?

    (A) To emphasize listening and speaking skills
    (B) To teach the intonation pattern of the language
    (C) To teach singing and music skills
    (D) To make the class more enjoyable

33. By second grade, students are generally guided to discontinue the practice of pointing to the words being read. What is the rationale for this change of strategy?

    (A) Students get tired of pointing to the words while reading.
    (B) Students find this practice annoying and typical of younger children.
    (C) This practice can interfere with the development of reading fluency.
    (D) This practice is archaic and does not seem to help in the reading process.

34. Vocabulary development is a key predictor of success in reading. Identify a strategy that parents can use with preschool children to promote vocabulary development in a fun and relaxed environment.

    (A) Use flash cards and concrete objects to introduce vocabulary words.
    (B) Play a game where the parent and the child teach each other a new word every day.
    (C) Play games where children have to name antonyms and synonyms.
    (D) Ask children to memorize a list of vocabulary words every day.

35. The main purpose for teaching sight words is to promote instant recognition of characters and words. Instant recognition of words can improve students'

    (A) reading fluency.
    (B) decoding skills.
    (C) reading comprehension.
    (D) writing skills.

36. The main purpose of family literacy programs is

    (A) to teach ESL to Spanish-speaking parents and to provide training in cross-cultural communication.
    (B) to keep children busy while parents attend literacy classes.
    (C) to empower parents to help and be involved in the education of their children.
    (D) to empower child and adult English language learners by providing meaningful education.

37. Identify the factor(s) that most likely can affect the development of early literacy among preschool children.

    (A) Parents read frequently to their children and have books available at home.
    (B) Parents teach children to use the dictionary and guide them to select the best definition based on the context of the words.
    (C) Parents have available reference materials and electronic translation programs to promote early bilingualism among children.
    (D) Parents take their children to the library and bookstores to obtain books.

38. Mike is a four-year-old monolingual, Spanish-speaking child. His parents read Spanish books to him every day. As a result of their effort, Mike has mastered directionality in reading and basic decoding skills. He can also decode words by linking two syllables. Based on his literacy growth, what might be the next logical step for the parents to promote his growth?

    (A) Stop reading to him to encourage self-sufficiency.
    (B) Continue reading to him and introduce comprehension strategies.
    (C) Continue challenging the child by introducing books for advanced first graders.
    (D) Stop teaching Spanish reading and introduce English only.

39. The main purpose of an intergenerational literacy initiative is to

    (A) improve the literacy development of adults and the community.
    (B) use children as a reason to involve parents in school activities.
    (C) promote literacy among children using the support of parents and other family members.
    (D) improve reading skills beginning in preschool and continue improving throughout life.

40. Identify the steps that best describe the writing process.

    (A) Develop an outline of the intended writing project, complete an initial draft, and edit for content.
    (B) Complete an initial draft, revise for the accuracy of content, and publish.
    (C) Brainstorm for ideas, develop an outline, complete an initial draft, edit, and publish.
    (D) Write an initial draft, share it with peers, review for grammaticality, and publish.

41. In project-oriented activities, students are guided to produce knowledge instead of reproduce knowledge. Identify the strategy that best represents this difference.

    (A) Students are presented with a problem, they are asked to discuss it, and they find possible solutions.
    (B) Students recite the pledge of allegiance and later they discuss the meaning of the words.
    (C) Students are presented with a problem and given three possible solutions to the problem.
    (D) Students are given a list of solutions and a list of problems; they are supposed to match the two.

42. Identify the strategies to lead the child from the stage of learning to read to the stage of reading to learn.

    (A) Expose children to different kinds of literature and vocabulary words specific to content areas.
    (B) Introduce children to different kinds of text and how to scan to locate and retrieve information.
    (C) Allow students to read without interruption for at least 20 minutes a day.
    (D) Introduce the concepts of connotation and denotation in words and phrases.

43. Vocabulary development is a key predictor of success in reading in the content areas for all students, but especially for children new to the English language. Identify the best strategy to introduce vocabulary development for ELLs from diverse cultural and linguistic backgrounds.

    (A) Teach content vocabulary through direct, concrete experience as opposed to definitions.
    (B) Identify key vocabulary words in the content area and provide children with a translation of each word.
    (C) Teach content vocabulary in a comparative fashion, contrasting the meaning of vocabulary words in the various languages represented in class.
    (D) Deemphasize the importance of lexicon, introduce the words in context, and guide children to derive the meaning using context clues.

44. Mary, a well-educated teacher, visited one of her favorite English professors in college. After having lunch with him, she said good-bye to the professor and he replied with the following statement: "Good-bye and drive careful." Mary looked at him in shock and smiled. Why was Mary in shock?

    (A) The professor looks old and unhappy.
    (B) The professor exhibited faulty agreement in his speech.
    (C) The speech of the professor was unintelligible.
    (D) The professor used a colloquial expression.

45. The writing portion of the fourth-grade TAKS test has two components—a multiple-choice portion and a writing sample. The writing sample of the test is evaluated using a

    (A) multiple-choice format.
    (B) rubric with discrete language components.
    (C) four-point rubric.
    (D) six-point rubric.

46. A second-grade student began writing a composition about his friend in the following way: (1) George is my friend. (2) Mary is my best friend.

(3) Rachel are my friends too. What type of support does this child need to write a more cohesive and standard writing sample?

    (A) spelling and agreement instruction
    (B) use of active and passive voice
    (C) agreement and sentence connectors
    (D) use of appropriate capitalization and punctuation

47. Identify the most appropriate strategy(ies) to meet the needs of children at the emerging stage of writing development.

    (A) Identify errors in the writing sample and guide children to self-correct.
    (B) Provide a prompt and guide children to write a composition based on it.
    (C) Read stories and ask children to retell the story while you write it down.
    (D) Allow the child to read for at least 30 minutes every day.

48. The main purpose of an interactive/dialogue journal is to allow

    (A) children opportunities to practice speaking and writing skills.
    (B) children opportunities to communicate freely in a written form.
    (C) students opportunities to receive corrective feedback from peers.
    (D) students opportunities to practice listening, speaking, reading, and writing.

49. Convergent research on linear versus curvilinear rhetorical patterns shows that Spanish-speaking English language learners and young children in general have a tendency to follow a curvilinear approach in writing. What strategies can teachers use to support these students?

    (A) Teach pronunciation and application of grammar structures.
    (B) Guide children to develop an outline for the story, and provide them with guiding questions to keep them focused on the topic and the audience.
    (C) Provide a speaking checklist to help students stick to the topic.

(D) Provide examples of stories written in a linear fashion and ask students to modify them by adding their own information.

50. A rubric to rate English composition in kindergarten and first grade should not place heavy emphasis in the mastery of spelling because

(A) the use of phonemic and invented spelling is part of specific stages of writing development in children.

(B) the use of standard spelling is not important in the development of compositions.

(C) spelling addresses visual memory and should not be given great value.

(D) the development of standard spelling requires students to use structural and phonics rules effectively.

51. English writing samples from Spanish-dominant ELLs may contain which of the following key features?

(A) The stories are simple in content and written in a linear fashion.

(B) The stories might have complex sentence patterns and sophisticated words from Spanish.

(C) The stories might be perceived as disjointed and lacking logical sequencing.

(D) They might switch from Spanish to English within the same sentence.

52. In assessment, minimal pairs are used to teach and assess   *ex. pin & bin - difference in one sound*

(A) morphology.

(B) phonology.

(C) syntax.

(D) lexicon.

53. If a child is reading an average of 90 percent of the words correctly, he or she is reading at the

(A) independent level.

(B) frustration level.

(C) comprehension level.

(D) instructional level.

54. In compliance with the NCLB legislation, Texas adopted an instrument to assess the English achievement of ELLs—the Texas Observation Protocol (TOP). The TOP assesses the listening, speaking, reading, and writing components of English. In addition to the writing samples required, this instrument uses _____ to assess the linguistic performance of children in English.

(A) a rating scale containing three options (agree, disagree, uncertain)

(B) a multiple-choice test with four choices (A, B, C, and D)

(C) a series of open-ended questions to guide the teacher in the collection of data

(D) a checklist identifying specific literacy components

55. Running records, teacher observations, and speaking checklists are examples of

(A) teacher-developed assessment instruments.

(B) informal literacy assessment.

(C) formal literacy assessment.

(D) objective literacy instruments.

56. In Ms. Waler's class, students were asked to interview family members to identify strategies they will use to solve a given mathematical problem. What might be the main benefit of this activity?

(A) It will provide a multicultural view for problem solving and will validate home cultures.

(B) It will validate the students' native language and achievements.

(C) It will free the teacher to address other administrative issues.

(D) It will establish the community as a guiding force in the development of the school curricula.

57. The main advantage of using hands-on activities in mathematics is to

(A) enhance students' ability to think abstractly.

(B) make the lesson more enjoyable.

(C) lead students to active learning and guide them to construct their own knowledge.

(D) promote equity, equality, and freedom for the diverse ethnic groups in the nation.

58. One of the reasons that might explain the low performance of English language learners in mathematics word problems is the lack of

    (A) mathematical intelligence needed to do well in these kinds of tests.
    (B) vocabulary development to understand technical terms and concepts in mathematics.
    (C) a conceptual framework needed to do well in problems that require high-order thinking skills.
    (D) interest and the ability to deal with abstractions and number concepts.

59. Children having problems deciding on the value of a dime versus ten pennies might be experiencing problems with

    (A) centration.
    (B) conservation.
    (C) ordering or seriation.
    (D) classification.

60. Perform the indicated operation: $(-36) - 11$.

    (A) 47
    (B) 25
    (C) −47
    (D) −25

61. Simplify: $6 \times 2 + 3/3$.

    (A) 18
    (B) 5
    (C) 10
    (D) 13

62. Simplify to a single term in scientific notation: $(2 \times 10^3) \times (6 \times 10^4)$.

    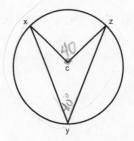

    (A) 12×10^7
    (B) 1.2×10^{12}
    (C) 1.2×10^8
    (D) 12×10^{12}

63. Identify the mathematic properties involved in the following problem: $(6 + 2) + 5 = 6 + (2 + 5)$.

    (A) Distributive property
    (B) Associative property of addition
    (C) Property of zero
    (D) Associative property of multiplication

64. How many lines of symmetry do all nonsquare rectangles have?

    (A) 0
    (B) 2
    (C) 4
    (D) 8

Use the figure below to answer the question that follows. Assume that point C is the center of the circle. Angles xyz and xcz intercept minor arc xz. The measure of angle xyz is 40°.

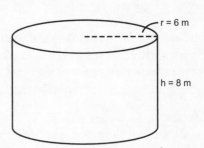

65. What is the measure of major arc xyz?

    (A) 140°
    (B) 280°
    (C) 160°
    (D) 320°

66. What is the approximate volume of the following cylinder?

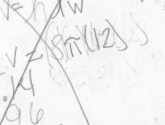

    (A) 904 cm³
    (B) 301 cm³
    (C) 151 cm³
    (D) 452 cm³

67. Mrs. Cameron plans to buy carpeting for her living room floor. The room is a rectangle measuring 14 feet by 20 feet. She wants no carpet seams on her floor, even if that means that some carpeting will go to waste. The carpeting she wants comes in 16-foot-wide rolls. What is the minimum amount of carpeting that will have to be wasted if Mrs. Cameron insists upon her no-seams requirement?

(A) 40 square feet
(B) 60 square feet
(C) 80 square feet
(D) 100 square feet

68. One of the key methodological considerations that teachers have to account for when developing thematic instruction for children in prekindergarten through grade 2 is

(A) the integration of all concepts.
(B) the development of age-appropriate instruction for children.
(C) the development of interesting and challenging activities for all learners.
(D) the integration of problem-solving strategies.

69. Based on TEKS, the earliest that teachers can introduce mathematics reasoning to children is

(A) first grade.
(B) kindergarten.
(C) third grade.
(D) second grade.

70. In the early grades, mathematic and spatial reasoning are introduced in learning centers through the use of manipulatives. What is the main advantage of using learning centers to introduce mathematic and spatial reasoning?

(A) Children explore and learn reasoning skills indirectly using concrete objects in informal settings.
(B) Children can play and enjoy the benefits of manipulatives.
(C) Children are taught mathematics concepts deductively using manipulatives and other concrete objects in an informal format.

(D) Children are exposed to the state curriculum in a highly structured learning environment.

71. The main value of using real-life situations to teach problem-solving skills involving mathematics is that the children in grades K–4 can see

(A) the connection between the school curriculum and mathematics.
(B) the value of mathematics in solving daily situations.
(C) that mathematics is an important part of the Texas curriculum.
(D) that the use of learning centers has a specific value in life.

72. The Texas TEKS requires a teacher to address the following four strands in art education:

(A) history, perception, performance, and creativity.
(B) creativity, emotion, Native American art, and European impressionists.
(C) perception, creative expressions, historical and cultural heritage, and critical evaluation.
(D) critical evaluation, visual arts and perception, color combinations, and body and finger painting.

73. Diego Rivera, José Clemente Orozco, and David Siqueiros are some of the best representatives of

(A) photorealism.
(B) muralists.
(C) surrealism.
(D) impressionism.

74. Identify the painter who best represents the cubism art movement.

(A) Salvador Dali
(B) Goya
(C) Michelangelo
(D) Pablo Picasso

75. The concept of value as an element of art describes the use of

(A) space to create perspective.
(B) line to highlight parts of a work.

(C) light to represent the mood of the artist.

(D) space to place objects on different planes.

76. Pitch is the relative _____ of a musical sound.

   (A) duration or length
   (B) loudness or softness
   (C) high and low
   (D) rhythm

77. Select the letter that contains the correct sequence of Kodaly rhythm syllables for this song line—"Happy Birthday to you!"

   (A) Ta Ta Ta Ta Ta ta-a
   (B) Ti Ti Ta Ta Ti Ti ta
   (C) Ti ti ta ti ti ta ta
   (D) Ti Ti Ta Ta Ta ta-a

78. The state song of Texas is

   (A) "The Yellow Rose of Texas."
   (B) "Texas, Our Texas."
   (C) "God Bless America."
   (D) "The Alamo."

79. Identify a modern popular music genre with a strong German, Mexican, and Czech influence.

   (A) mariachi
   (B) country
   (C) tejano
   (D) salsa

80. By ages four and five, children are generally able to perform somersaults, climb, and skip. They also begin dressing themselves using buttons and zippers. These kinds of activities represent an example of

   (A) gross motor skills.
   (B) required curriculum components in school.
   (C) fine motor skills.
   (D) a transition point from early childhood to adulthood.

81. The dance exercises most appropriate for children in grades 1–2 are

   (A) walk and/or skip.
   (B) run and/or skip.

   (C) skip and slide.
   (D) skip and step-hop.

82. The *E* in the acronym RICE, a treatment process for sprains, represents

   (A) exercise.
   (B) elevation.
   (C) evaluation.
   (D) expose.

83. Based on the Individuals with Disabilities Education Act (IDEA), children with crutches or any other types of assistive devices should

   (A) not be allowed to participate in physical education activities.
   (B) be allowed to participate like any other student.
   (C) be provided with appropriate modification for participation in physical education activities.
   (D) be provided with a special physical education class designed for them.

84. To complete an effective aerobic workout, exercise should be performed at an individual's target heart rate for a minimum of

   (A) 15 minutes.
   (B) 20 minutes.
   (C) 30 minutes.
   (D) 45 minutes.

85. Which of the following is a locomotor skill?

   (A) bending
   (B) catching
   (C) throwing
   (D) hopping

86. What percentage of a daily diet should be composed of carbohydrates?

   (A) 20%
   (B) 25%
   (C) 40%
   (D) 50%

87. The most appropriate and safe exercises for kindergarten and first-grade students are

    (A) jogging and walking.
    (B) games that require physical activity.
    (C) games that require endurance.
    (D) contact sports.

Use the information in this scenario to answer questions 88–90:

Scenario: Mr. Vargas organized a lesson to introduce fourth-grade students to the concept of marine habitats. As a focus, he presented two 25-gallon aquariums. Aquarium A has a variety of plants, 10 snails, and 25 unique varieties of small fishes. Aquarium B also contains a variety of plants, three snails, and five small fish of the same variety. He organized the students in groups of five. Once the groups were formed, students were asked to discuss the appropriateness of the combinations of plants and the number of animals. The ultimate goal is to predict the success of the habitats, including successful breeding, among the animals.

88. The main science objective of Mr. Vargas's lesson is to

    (A) guide students to communicate with peers.
    (B) promote scientific inquiry and problem-solving skills using scientific data.
    (C) work in cooperative groups.
    (D) keep students engaged and interested in the scientific concepts presented in class.

89. After a lengthy discussion, students agreed that Aquarium B had a better chance to establish and maintain a successful habitat. What information led students to make this decision?

    (A) The size of the aquarium
    (B) The ratio of plants and animals
    (C) The number of plants
    (D) The number of fish

90. Students also agreed that aquarium B had a better chance of successful breeding among the fish. What information did students use to arrive at this conclusion?

    (A) The ratio of plants and fish
    (B) The number of fish in each tank
    (C) The size of the tanks
    (D) The types of fishes in each tank

91. To make the science curriculum cognitively accessible to English language learners in grades K–2, teachers use thematic units and incorporate

    (A) techniques from various foreign language methods.
    (B) scientific exploration and hands-on activities.
    (C) a variety of instructional strategies and sophisticated scientific tools.
    (D) the use of chemicals and human specimens used by scientists.

92. George placed a metal spoon on an open flame and the spoon became so hot that it burned his hands. What scientific principle represents this type of energy transfer?

    (A) Radiation
    (B) Conduction —thermal energy
    (C) Convection —heating liquids
    (D) Kinetic energy

93. Vinegar is composed of two substances—acetic acid (a colorless liquid) and water. This combination of substances is an example of a

    (A) compound.
    (B) mixture.
    (C) chemical.
    (D) substance.

94. Traditionally, matter has been classified into three states:

    (A) rock, soil, and minerals.
    (B) ice, snow, and water.
    (C) liquid, gas, and solid.
    (D) nickel, lava, and magma.

95. The United States is probably the only industrialized country in the world that uses the English system of measurement in daily life, except for science and engineering. What is the rationale for using the metric system in scientific research and engineering?

(A) The metric system is widely used in the world.
(B) The English system is an archaic and outdated system used mostly in business.
(C) The metric system is more precise than the English system.
(D) The English system allows for the easy computation of measurements.

96. Living things are classified into five groups: monera, protista, fungi, plants, and animals. Some of these groups are unicellular, while the others are made up of multiple cells; however, there is only one group that has prokaryotic cells. What kingdom contains prokaryotic cells?

(A) Monera
(B) Protista
(C) Fungi
(D) Plants

Use the information in this scenario to answer questions 97 and 98:

Scenario: Corals are invertebrates that generally live in a symbiotic relationship with algae. Some of them build reefs, others do not. Most of them filter water to obtain nutrients for survival.

97. Based on this description, corals belong to which of the following kingdoms?

(A) Monera
(B) Animal
(C) Plant
(D) Fungi

98. The term *symbiotic* in this case means that corals

(A) are parasites attached to algae.
(B) share the same environment with algae.
(C) exchange services with other organisms.
(D) are living organisms.

99. The key function of the food chain in the ecosystem is to

(A) control the number of animals.
(B) preserve the types of plants in the habitat.
(C) maintain a balance among organisms.
(D) maintain a balance between fungi and dead matter.

100. Germaine, a fourth-grade student, notices that the shape of South America is similar to the shape of Africa. To demonstrate this, he cut off the South American map, placed it next to the map of Africa, and found an almost perfect match. He was amazed by his discovery and asked the teacher if Africa was once part of South America. What type of theory or scientific principle can the teacher introduce to make Germaine's discovery a teachable moment?

(A) theory of evolution of the species
(B) theory of intelligent design
(C) theory of transcontinental migration
(D) theory of plate tectonics

101. The main function of Earth's atmosphere is to

(A) protect and preserve life.
(B) prevent the contamination of Earth.
(C) create a vacuum between Earth's crust and its mantle.
(D) recycle water and gases.

102. Earthquakes are caused by

(A) thermal activity in the core.
(B) the movement of continental plates.
(C) the melting of rocks and minerals.
(D) the movement or rotation of Earth.

TExES

Texas Examinations of Educator Standards

101 Generalist EC-4

Answers: Practice Test

Practice Test Answers, Sorted by Competency

Question	Competency	Answer	Did you answer correctly?
16	001	D	✓
17	001	B	✓
18	001	B	✓
19	002	A	✗
20	002	A	✓
21	002	B	✓
22	003	D	✓
23	003	C	✓
24	003	D	✓
25	004	B	✓
26	004	B	✗
27	004	A	✗
28	004	A	✓
29	005	B	✓
30	005	C	✓
31	005	B	✓
32	006	B	✓
33	006	C	✓
34	006	A	✗
35	006	A	✗
36	007	C	✗
37	007	A	✓
38	007	B	✓
39	007	C	✓
40	008	C	✓
41	008	A	✓
42	008	B	✓
43	008	A	✓

Question	Competency	Answer	Did you answer correctly?
44	009	D	✓
45	009	C	✗
46	009	C	✓
47	009	C	✓
48	010	B	✗
49	010	B	✓
50	010	A	✓
51	010	C	✓
52	011	B	✓
53	011	D	✗
54	011	D	✓
55	011	B	✗
56	012	A	✗
57	012	C	✓
58	012	B	✓
59	012	B	✓
60	013	C	✓
61	013	D	✓
62	013	C	✓
63	013	B	✓
64	014	B	✓
65	014	B	✓
66	014	A	✗
67	014	A	✓
68	015	B	✓
69	015	B	✗
70	015	A	✓
71	015	B	✓

Question	Competency	Answer	Did you answer correctly?
2	016	D	✓
3	016	A	✓
4	016	C	✓
5	017	B	✓
6	017	D	✓
7	017	B	✓
8	017	B	✓
9	018	B	✓
10	018	B	✓
11	018	C	✓
12	018	C	✓
13	019	C	✓
14	019	D	✗
15	019	C	✓
1	020	B	✓
88	020	B	✓
89	020	B	✓
90	020	D	✓
91	020	B	✓
92	021	B	✓
93	021	B	✓
94	021	C	✓
95	021	C	✗
96	022	A	✓

Question	Competency	Answer	Did you answer correctly?
97	022	B	✓
98	022	C	✓
99	022	C	✓
100	023	D	✓
101	023	A	✓
102	023	B	✓
72	024	C	✓
73	024	B	✗
74	024	D	✓
75	024	C	✗
76	025	C	✓
77	025	D	✓
78	025	B	✓
79	025	C	✓
80	026	C	✗
81	026	A	✗
82	026	B	✓
86	026	D	✗
83	027	C	✓
84	027	B	✗
85	027	D	✓
87	027	B	✗

Answer Key

1. (B)	27. (A)	53. (D)	78. (B)
2. (D)	28. (A)	54. (D)	79. (C)
3. (A)	29. (B)	55. (B)	80. (C)
4. (C)	30. (C)	56. (A)	81. (A)
5. (B)	31. (B)	57. (C)	82. (B)
6. (D)	32. (B)	58. (B)	83. (C)
7. (B)	33. (C)	59. (B)	84. (B)
8. (B)	34. (A)	60. (C)	85. (D)
9. (B)	35. (A)	61. (D)	86. (D)
10. (B)	36. (C)	62. (C)	87. (B)
11. (C)	37. (A)	63. (B)	88. (B)
12. (C)	38. (B)	64. (B)	89. (B)
13. (C)	39. (C)	65. (B)	90. (D)
14. (D)	40. (C)	66. (A)	91. (B)
15. (C)	41. (A)	67. (A)	92. (B)
16. (D)	42. (B)	68. (B)	93. (B)
17. (B)	43. (A)	69. (B)	94. (C)
18. (B)	44. (D)	70. (A)	95. (C)
19. (A)	45. (C)	71. (B)	96. (A)
20. (A)	46. (C)	72. (C)	97. (B)
21. (B)	47. (C)	73. (B)	98. (C)
22. (D)	48. (B)	74. (D)	99. (C)
23. (C)	49. (B)	75. (C)	100. (D)
24. (D)	50. (A)	76. (C)	101. (A)
25. (B)	51. (C)	77. (D)	102. (B)
26. (B)	52. (B)		

General Education Practice Test
Detailed Explanations of Answers

1. (B)

The social studies strands are systematically integrated throughout the social studies state curriculum in grades K–12. Choice A is incorrect based on the previous explanation. C and D are incorrect because the social studies strands are used in public education as well as in higher education. **Competency 020**

2. (D)

TEKS introduces social studies from the known to the unknown. Students begin studying themselves and from there go to the school, community, and finally to the state. The focus on TEKS for fourth grade is the history of Texas. Choice A is incorrect because TEKS is available only in K–12. For prekindergarten, teachers use instructional guidelines. B is incorrect because the focus of first grade is the school and the community. C is incorrect because in grade 3, the focus is the individual and how each affects the community. **Competency 016**

3. (A)

Choice A is correct because maps use symbolic representation, and children at that age rely mostly on concrete experiences for learning. The abstraction typical of maps' legends and other symbolic representations might not be developmentally appropriate for this age group. B is a plausible statement but not the best answer. Children initially will be inclined to use the globe as toys and pay attention to colors, but eventually they will

understand its function through classroom instruction. C is incorrect because it presents an opinion not supported in the scenario. D is probably a true statement: Children will have problems conceptualizing how the Earth can be represented in a small 12-inch globe, but this choice is not the best answer because it addresses only one component of the question—globe representation. **Competency 016**

4. (C)

The Earth is divided into 24 zones based on the meridians of longitude, which are determined using the rotation of the Earth and its exposure to sunlight. This rotation creates day and night, and consequently the concept of time. Choice A is incorrect because the International Date Line is only one of 24 meridians of the Earth. Choice B is incorrect because the term *revolution* describes the movement of the Earth around the sun, which affects the seasons but not necessarily the time zones. Choice D is incorrect because the parallels of latitude do not affect the time zones. **Competency 016**

5. (B)

The convergence of the Tigris and the Euphrates created a fertile region where some of the greatest civilizations of the world emerged. This part of the world has been called the Fertile Crescent and it is part of the area called the Cradle of Civilizations. Choice A is incorrect because the Nile gave birth to the Egyptian civilization, and the Amazon River is located in

South America, far away from Mesopotamia. Choice C is incorrect because the Indus River is located in modern-day India. Choice D is incorrect because the Volga and Danube rivers are located in Europe. **Competency 017**

6. (D)

The country of Iraq is located in the region known as Mesopotamia. A is incorrect because the country of Iran is located east of the Tigris River. Choice B is incorrect because Pakistan is located further southeast of the rivers. Choice C is also incorrect because the Kingdom of Kuwait is located southwest of the area and south of Iraq. **Competency 017**

7. (B)

The feudal system characterized life in the Middle Ages. The attacks of the barbaric tribes forced people to live under the protection of a lord, usually within the walls of a castle. Muslim Turks took Jerusalem in 1095, and a year later, Christians began the Crusades to rescue the Holy Land. Choice A is incorrect because both the Greek and Roman empires are part of the Ancient World. Choice C is incorrect because one of the events is part of the Ancient World—Stonehenge. Choice D is incorrect because Alexander the Great ruled the Ancient World. **Competency 017**

8. (B)

The Maya and the Aztecs occupied the area of Central America and Southern Mexico called Mesoamerica. Both groups were accomplished builders, astronomers, and mathematicians. Choice A is incorrect because the Inca civilization was not a Mesoamerican group. They developed an advanced civilization in South America, in present-day Peru and Ecuador. Choice C is incorrect because only the Toltecs were from Mesoamerica; the Pueblo Indians were from present-day New Mexico in North America. Choice D is incorrect because only the Olmecs were a Mesoamerican group. The Iroquois civilizations developed in North America. **Competency 017**

9. (B)

Iraq is a Muslim nation with multiple ethnic groups within its borders. The largest groups are the Shi'a Muslims, Sunni Muslims, and the Kurds. A is incorrect. The multiple groups living in Iraq speak Arabic, Kurdish, Turkish, Assyrian, and other languages. Choice C is incorrect because Iraq is located in the Middle Eastern part of Asia. Choice D is incorrect because Pakistan is a Muslim country from the region but there is no political association between the two nations. **Competency 018**

10. (B)

Brazil is located in the Southern Hemisphere, and the United States is located in the Northern Hemisphere; thus, if the United States is in winter, then in Brazil it is summer. Choices A, C, and D are incorrect based on the previous explanation. **Competency 018**

11. (C)

There is a difference of one day from Honolulu to Tokyo. Honolulu is located west of the International Date Line (IDL), while Japan is east of the line. That is, if we travel from Honolulu toward the east on December 7 and pass the IDL to get to Tokyo, we would get there on December 8. The attack was recorded on December 7, 1941, in Honolulu, but the equivalent date for Japan was December 8, 1941. A, B, and D are incorrect because they do not explain the real reason for the date confusion. Additionally, the scenario does not provide information to support the position that Emperor Hirohito was confused about the dates. **Competency 018**

12. (C)

The Apache and the Comanche domesticated the horse and became skillful hunters and warriors. These skills allowed them to fight the whites for many years for control of the Central and Great Plains of Texas. Choice A is incorrect because the tribes from the plains were nomads and did not develop an advanced civilization. B is incorrect because both the Comanche and the Apache were nomads and did not leave permanent constructions.

D is incorrect because the tribes from the area had to hunt for survival and they had to move continuously to find adequate food supplies. **Competency 018**

13. (C)

Reducing the production of oil while keeping the same demand for the product creates an imbalance between supply and demand. This imbalance results in a price increase. A is incorrect. War generally increases the demand and prices in general, not only the price of fossil fuels. B is incorrect because the statement does not explain the economic principle required in the question. It just presents a true statement—the American economy depends on foreign oil. D presents an opinion that fails to address the true question. **Competency 019**

14. (D)

The Fifteenth Amendment granted black males the right to vote. A is incorrect because the voting right was given to black males only, not women of any race. B is incorrect because the Fourteenth Amendment granted citizenship to former slaves. C is incorrect because the Thirteenth Amendment granted freedom to slaves. **Competency 019**

15. (C)

The U.S. Constitution set up a system so that each branch has the power to control or regulate the power of the other two. Choice A is incorrect because judicial review addresses only the power of the judicial branch to review legislation enacted by Congress and signed by the president. If the legislation is unconstitutional, it can be invalidated. B is incorrect because it addresses the power of the president to veto or refuse to sign legislation approved by Congress. D is incorrect because habeas corpus is one of the civil rights that guarantees people the right to a quick trial by jury. **Competency 019**

16. (D)

A visual analysis of columns 4, 5, and 6 shows that the phoneme /sh/ can be represented by at least four

different graphemes—*ch, s, ss,* and *t*—in words like *chef, sure, mission,* and *caution.* The grapheme *ch* is also inconsistent. Column 3 shows that the grapheme *ch* represents the sound /k/. This inconsistency affects the ability of ELLs to separate the two phonemes. A, B, and C are incorrect because the scenario does not provide evidence to suggest that ELLs cannot establish a difference or pronounce the two phonemes, or that they might not be interested in learning the difference between the two. **Competency 001**

17. (B)

The chart provides examples of words that follow grapheme-phoneme correspondence. It also provides examples of words that use different graphemes to represent the sounds. This chart provides students with tangible information to help them deal with graphophonemic inconsistencies. A is incorrect because this particular chart places more emphasis on graphophonemic inconsistencies than on consistencies. C is incorrect because the chart presents words in isolation; thus, it cannot present information about the intonation pattern used in sentences or larger units. D is a plausible answer, but it does not capture the true intent of the activity. The chart is designed to deal with specific, inconsistent sounds only. **Competency 001**

18. (B)

The word *thought* is a long word, even though it is monosyllabic. It has three phonemes. The word contains two consonant diagraphs, *th* and *ght*, and a vowel digraph, *ou,* representing one sound each for a total of three sounds. A, C, and D are incorrect based on the previous explanation. **Competency 001**

19. (A)

The child is having problems with word stress and syllabication, and both terms are part of phonological awareness. B is incorrect because the child is not having problems with phonemic awareness. He has mastered the ability to separate phonemes and blend them back to re-create the word. C and D are incorrect because none of them individually explains the needs of the child. The reality is that the child needs support in both components; thus, C or D individually cannot be the correct answer. **Competency 002**

20. (A)

Alliteration is a technique to emphasize the connection between the consonant and the sound that it represents. In this particular case, the tongue twister is used to emphasize the sound of the /r/. B is incorrect because the technique goes beyond the use of a tongue twister. Tongue twisters are examples of alliteration and they emphasize pronunciation and fluency. C is incorrect because the utterance does not represent an example of traditional nursery rhymes. Nursery rhymes are short poems, stories, or songs written to entertain children. The most famous nursery rhyme is the Mother Goose collection from England. **Competency 002**

21. (B)

The answer calls for syllabication and phoneme segmentation. Both concepts are part of phonological awareness. Choice A is incorrect because sentence analysis was not the primary concern in the scenario. The intonation pattern describes the rhythm and pitch used in phrases and sentences. C is incorrect because in the latter activity, the issue is the phonological analysis of words. Vocabulary development was emphasized in the first part of the scenario only. D is incorrect because the scenario does not address pronunciation at all. **Competency 002**

22. (D)

Teachers have to present the consistent sounds of English first to develop self-confidence among children. Once children master those initial grapheme-phoneme correspondences, they can attempt more challenging components. Choice A is incorrect because it deals with a generic well-accepted practice, but it does not address the question. B is incorrect because the alphabetic principle does not specifically deal with the issue of the development of foreign accents. C is incorrect because it failed to address the question. It is always important to

create an atmosphere of collaboration among students, but this statement does not address the linguistic nature of the questions. **Competency 003**

23. (C)

Syllabication and word stress are part of the concept called phonological awareness. Choice A is incorrect because the activity goes beyond establishing the connection between letters and sounds typical of the alphabetic principle. B is incorrect because the development of fluency goes beyond the analysis of individual words. The development of phonological awareness is a prerequisite for the development of fluency. D is incorrect because the concept of syllabication is only one of two elements presented in the scenario—syllabication and word stress. **Competency 003**

24. (D)

Onsets represent the first phoneme of a syllable or a monosyllabic word like the word presented in choice Choice D. Rimes follow the onset, and are linked to the concept of word families. The rime *ank* can be used to create multiple words, like *blank, tank, rank,* and *flank*. Choices A and C are generally used to represent verb tenses and cannot be considered the typical rime or word family. Choice B is incorrect because the two words do not represent onset and rimes. Instead, the example of *very–berry* represents a minimal pair—two words that differ in only one phoneme. **Competency 003**

25. (B)

A balanced-reading approach uses best practices from both phonics and whole language. It also places emphasis on the use of authentic literature and the literature-based approach to construct meaning. Choice A is incorrect because the skills-based approach emphasizes mostly phonics instruction. C is incorrect because the meaning-based approach emphasizes mostly the whole language approach. D is incorrect because there is no connection between humanistic psychology and the question. **Competency 004**

26. (B)

Miscue analysis describes the variation that students produce in their attempts to read or decode words. Goodman suggested that only those miscues affecting meaning should be taken into account. A is incorrect because *miscues* is a term to describe reading not necessarily writing attempts. C is incorrect because Goodman does not identify miscues as errors, plus the concept does not apply to attempts to communicate orally, such as conversation. D is incorrect because there is no connection between miscues and the schema theory. **Competency 004**

27. (A)

The main reason for the creation of the language experience approach (LEA) was to eliminate the discrepancy between the background knowledge that the child brings to the reading process and the experiential background required to understand the story, i.e., the schema of the author. B is incorrect because it eliminates the need to discuss the schema of the story by exposing children to a common experience and guiding them to dictate a story using the experience. C is incorrect because students will use their own vocabulary in the story; if they use idioms, these are probably known to children in the group. D is incorrect because the main purpose of LEA is not to contrast L1 and L2. **Competency 004**

28. (A)

The overall purpose of the shared book experience is to guide children to be successful in reading and to develop an interest in learning to read. The story is read to the students in a very supportive environment using visuals to enhance comprehension. The main goal is to make reading an enjoyable activity and to motivate children to read on their own. B is incorrect because reading with the whole class is a by-product of the shared book experience, but it is not the main goal. C and D are true statements. Traditionally, books used in shared reading use big letters and attractive pictures, and children like big books, but these features are not the main reason for conducting shared reading. **Competency 004**

29. (B)

Sight words occur frequently in writing, and often the best way to teach them is by instant recognition. Choice A is not correct because environmental print does not necessarily contain sight words. Street signs and store names can have very unique names that cannot be taught as sight words. C is incorrect because sight words are taught to be recognized instantly, without analyzing their structural or semantic representation. D is incorrect because most sight words are short and easy to spell. Because they occur so frequently in reading, spelling is facilitated. **Competency 005**

30. (C)

The words *butterfly, nightmare,* and *brainstorm* may get students confused because they do not provide a reliable point of view to comprehend their meaning. A, B, and D are incorrect because they contain information to help children in the comprehension process. Words like *doghouse, underground,* and *mouthwash* provide clear indications of the intended meaning. **Competency 005**

31. (B)

The analysis of the structure of the words for decoding and comprehension is definitely part of structural analysis. Choice A is incorrect because context goes beyond individual words. C is incorrect because pictorial clues describe any kind of visual information, like pictures and charts. D is incorrect because syntactic clues use whole sentences and determine meaning based on the position of words within sentences. **Competency 005**

32. (B)

When children change declarative sentences to questions or exclamations, they have to change the intonation pattern of the language. Choice A is incorrect because sentence transformations are not designed necessarily to teach listening skills. C is incorrect because there is no connection between the linguistic transformation requested and teaching singing and music. Conducting sentence transformation can be an enjoyable activity; however, making the class more enjoyable is just a derivative of the process. D is definitely incorrect. **Competency 006**

33. (C)

Pointing to the words as they are read is designed to establish the connection between speech and print. However, after the skill has been mastered, it is discontinued so students can engage in fluent reading. A and B are incorrect because they offer nonsubstantial reasons for the strategy change. D is incorrect because the practice of pointing to the words as they are being read is not archaic; it is indeed an effective practice for beginning readers. **Competency 006**

34. (A)

The use of flash cards with pictures representing concepts and concrete objects can definitely be effective in teaching vocabulary to preschool children. B is incorrect because parents can teach a word every day to the child, but the child might not be able to participate effectively because preschoolers generally do not have the vocabulary development to teach parents new words. C is also incorrect because preschoolers might not have the necessary vocabulary development to participate in a game dealing with antonyms and synonyms. D is incorrect because the practice of memorizing vocabulary is quite boring and ineffective for children of all ages. **Competency 006**

35. (A)

When children don't have to struggle to decode words, reading fluency is facilitated. B is incorrect because, by definition, no decoding is necessary when the reader recognizes the word instantly. C is incorrect because comprehension goes beyond the instant recognition of words. Readers have to analyze the schema of the writing and evaluate other elements to achieve reading comprehension. Instant recognition of words can improve spelling skills; however, it does not necessarily improve the writing process. **Competency 006**

36. (C)

A family literacy program involves family members, and its main goals are to emphasize the value of literacy and to support children's efforts in becoming literate. Choice A is incorrect because the goals of literacy go beyond teaching English to ELLs to provide cross-cultural communication. B is incorrect because the program is primarily aimed at promoting literacy among children. Teaching literacy to parents can also be part of the program, but it is a secondary goal. D presents a strong distracter because in a certain way, a family literacy program can empower children and adults; however, the option is too generic. **Competency 007**

37. (A)

Reading to children and having books available for them provide children with reading readiness skills and can promote interest in reading. B is incorrect because the use of dictionary skills might not be developmentally appropriate or interesting enough for preschool children. C is incorrect because the children might not be ready for electronic translation programs, and translation is not the best strategy for promoting literacy development. D is incorrect because getting books for children without additional support will not develop early literacy among children. **Competency 007**

38. (B)

Reading to children in any language can promote interest in reading and decoding skills. Promoting reading comprehension is the next logical step. Choice A is incorrect because reading to children should not be interrupted, especially during the preschool years. Actually, reading to children can be beneficial even for advanced readers. C is incorrect because the scenario does not provide evidence to suggest that the child is ready for more challenging first-grade books. D is incorrect because reading skills acquired in the first language can transfer to the second language. Additionally, students should be exposed to reading in the dominant language first. **Competency 007**

39. (C)

Intergenerational literacy programs are designed to involve parents and family members in the education of their children. Choice A is incorrect because the literacy development of adults and the community is neither the only nor the primary purpose of an intergenerational literacy program. Children are the most important component in this process. Involving parents is an important component of the program, but it is not the purpose of the program; thus, B is incorrect. Traditionally, intergenerational literacy initiatives are designed for the early grades, and successful programs can affect the child for life; however, the program traditionally does not go beyond the elementary grades; thus, D is incorrect. **Competency 007**

40. (C)

Brainstorming for ideas and developing an outline of the writing project are paramount for process writing. A, B, and D are incorrect because they do not contain brainstorming as the initial component of the process. **Competency 008**

41. (A)

When students are presented with a problem and they are asked to discuss it and provide solutions based on the information, they are creating or producing knowledge. B is incorrect because children are just reciting and analyzing the meaning of the words in the pledge of allegiance. C and D are incorrect because in both choices (and in choice B) students are selecting choices given to them, not creating new ones. **Competency 008**

42. (B)

The main purpose of reading to learn is to obtain content information efficiently and effectively. One way to accomplish this task is to make students aware of the format used in the content areas and to guide them to retrieve the information by reading for the main idea or scanning for information. Choice A is incorrect because it addresses only one component of the process—vocabulary development. C is incorrect because it does not address the issue of the complexity of expository writing. D is incorrect because it addresses only the issue of vocabulary development—connotation and denotation. **Competency 008**

43. (A)

The best way to teach vocabulary to ELLs is to present the word together with a visual or concrete representation—a word concept. The introduction of word concepts can avoid any possible cultural conflict with similar concepts in the students' cultures. B is incorrect because translation can teach the word but fail to teach the concept that the word represents. C is incorrect because it would be very difficult to teach every single word in a contrasting fashion. Plus, most ESL classes contain speakers of various languages, which makes this activity impractical. D is incorrect because with ELLs, we cannot deemphasize the role of vocabulary development. Using context alone to obtain meaning will not work for children new to the English language. **Competency 008**

44. (D)

The professor used a colloquial expression commonly used in Texas. In the expression *drive careful*, the adjective *careful* was used to modify the verb. In Standard English, adjectives cannot modify verbs; the expression requires an adverb to create the standard version—*drive carefully*. A and C are incorrect because the scenario does not provide evidence to substantiate the information. B is incorrect because the statement does not show faulty agreement in number. **Competency 009**

45. (C)

The writing sample of the TAKS test is evaluated holistically using a four-point rubric, where a score of 3 or 4 is required to show mastery. The actual score is a combination of the multiple-choice score and the score of the writing sample. A is incorrect because only one part of the test is evaluated with a multiple-choice format. B is incorrect because the writing sample is evaluated holistically as opposed to being evaluated with a rubric containing specific (discrete) language features.

D is incorrect based on previous explanations. **Competency 009**

46. (C)

The three sentences can be combined with appropriate connectors to avoid repetitions. In this particular case, the conjunctions can be used to create compound sentences. Sentence 3 shows faulty agreement, which suggests that the child can also benefit from this kind of instructional support. A and B are incorrect because the writing sample does not show problems with spelling or the use of active and passive voice. D is incorrect because the writing sample does not show problems with capitalization and punctuation. **Competency 009**

47. (C)

Reading a story and asking a child to retell it promote interest in writing. When the teacher writes down the dictated story, the child can see the connection of oral and written work. A and B are incorrect because the children at the emerging stage don't have sufficient command of written language to correct their own writing or write a composition based on prompts. D is incorrect because reading for 30 minutes a day without any kind of explicit or implicit writing support might not be effective for children at the emerging stage for writing. **Competency 009**

48. (B)

The use of interactive journals allows children opportunities to communicate in meaningful and real-life situations. A and D are incorrect because listening and speaking abilities are not emphasized in interactive journals. C is incorrect because corrective feedback is not encouraged in communication activities. Teachers can provide indirect corrective feedback through modeling. **Competency 010**

49. (B)

During the prewriting stage, students should be guided to develop an outline that reflects the order of the ideas in the composition. They also can benefit from guiding questions to keep them focused on the topic and the intended audience. Choice A is incorrect because learning about grammar structures and pronunciation will not necessarily affect the organization and coherence of the composition. C is incorrect because it addresses speaking ability as opposed to the writing process. D is a strong distracter but not the best answer. Modeling effective writing is always a good strategy, but examples only might not provide the necessary guidance to make permanent changes in the students' writing style. B is a better choice because it provides a strategy that, once learned, can be used in multiple future situations. **Competency 010**

50. (A)

Children go through predictable stages of spelling development. During the initial stages, children invent words and use phonics skills as a foundation for spelling, which often results in nonstandard spelling. B and C are incorrect because spelling might not be the most important element in writing, but it is definitely important for effective writing. D is incorrect because it does not address the question. It just indicates that spelling requires phonics and structural rules, but it does not say why a rubric should not place heavy emphasis on spelling. **Competency 010**

51. (C)

The English writing samples of ELLs from a Spanish background often follow a curvilinear progression and might include multiple stories embedded within the narrative. This deviation from the linear progression expected in English writing creates the impression that the story is disjointed and lacks coherence. Based on the previous explanation, Choice A is incorrect—children might not produce compositions following a linear progression. The composition of children might contain complex sentences and an occasional use of Anglicized words or even Spanish words, but these features do not represent the main characteristics of English compositions from Latino children. Based on this explanation, B and D are incorrect. **Competency 010**

52. (B)

In minimal pairs, students are required to identify whether two sets of words are different or the same based on the phoneme sequence contained in each word. For example, the words *vine* and *fine* are different because they differ in at least one phoneme, i.e., the /v/ and /f/. Choice A is incorrect because morphology is not taken into account when comparing the two words. C is incorrect because there is no connection between minimal pairs and syntax. D is incorrect because lexicon deals with vocabulary development, and minimal pairs attempt to test whether children can understand how phonemes change the meaning of the words. **Competency 011**

53. (D)

When children miss about 10 percent of the words in a passage, comprehension problems will occur. Children at the instructional level need continuous support and guidance from the teachers. Choice A is incorrect because students at the independent level of reading are able to understand 95 percent of the words. C is incorrect because the term *comprehension level* is not a technical descriptor for reading levels. B is incorrect because students at the frustration level can read less than 89 percent of the words correctly. With this low level of word recognition, they will have severe comprehension problems. **Competency 011**

54. (D)

The TOP contains a checklist of specific skills for teachers to document when these behaviors occur during observation. A and B are incorrect because the TOP does not contain rating scales or multiple-choice questions. C is incorrect because the TOP is a checklist identifying the specific linguistic features for observation. **Competency 011**

55. (B)

All three instruments, running records, teacher observations, and the checklist, are examples of infor-

mal assessment. Choice A is incorrect because at least one of the instruments, running records, is not a teacher-developed instrument. C is incorrect based on the information previously stated. D is incorrect because all three instruments require some level of subjectivity. **Competency 011**

56. (A)

People across the world solve mathematics problems using a variety of strategies and processes. When community members are allowed to share their problem-solving strategies, children get a broader view of mathematics concepts. B makes sense and the activity can validate students' native language and achievement, but these elements do not constitute the real purpose for inviting community members to share problem-solving skills. C is incorrect because freeing teachers from administrative tasks is not the real purpose of the activity. D is incorrect because an isolated activity with parents is not generally enough to make the community the guiding force in the development of school curriculum. **Competency 012**

57. (C)

Hands-on activities can make the curriculum more relevant and guide children to construct their own knowledge. Hands-on activities can probably lead children to think abstractly (see choice A), but the activity is not designed exclusively to accomplish this goal. Hands-on activities can make the class more interesting and enjoyable (see choice B), but they are not the reasons for the activities. D is incorrect because there is no evidence to suggest that hands-on activities can promote equity, equality, or freedom among students. **Competency 012**

58. (B)

Vocabulary development and the technical mathematics terms used in word problems can affect students' ability to comprehend and solve word problems. A and C are incorrect because there is no evidence to suggest that ELLs lack mathematics intelligence or the conceptual framework to do well in mathematics. D is incorrect because there is no evidence to suggest that ELLs might lack interest or the ability to do well in mathematics. **Competency 012**

59. (B)

Children in prekindergarten and kindergarten might have problems understanding the concept of conservation. They might pay attention to the quantity (10 cents) as opposed to the implied value of the currency. Choice A is incorrect because the issue of centration was not relevant in the question; centration refers to the tendency to focus on one characteristic while ignoring the others. C is incorrect because ordering and seriation did not play a role in the confusion of the child; seriation requires students to match two or more objects with two or more components in a sequence. D is incorrect because classification involves the simultaneous use of two or more variables to classify or categorize objects, and children were not required to classify objects in the scenario. **Competency 012**

60. (C)

When subtraction involves any negative numbers, a good rule to use is, "Don't subtract the second number. Instead, add its opposite." Using that rule, the original expression, $(-36) - 11$ becomes $(-36) + (-11)$. To be "in debt" by 36, then to be further "in debt" by 11, puts one "in debt" by 47, shown as -47. **Competency 013**

61. (D)

When presented with a simplification problem involving several different operations, the universally accepted order of operations must be used. In this case, working from left to right, the multiplication (6×2) and the division ($3 \div 3$) must be completed first, giving $12 + 1$, or 13. **Competency 013**

62. (C)

The correct answer is 1.2×10^8. Because multiplication is commutative (factors can be multiplied in any order), multiply the 2 and the 6 (giving 12) and 10^3 and 10^4 (giving 10^7). Note: To multiply exponential expressions with like bases, add the exponents. This gives 12×10^7. That expression is not in scientific notation (the first number must be between 0 and 10), so change the 12 to 1.2, and 10^7 into 10^8 to "compensate." **Competency 013**

63. (B)

The associative property of addition states that the order of the addends do not affect the results. Choice A is incorrect because the distributive property addresses the combination of addition and multiplication and the question addresses only addition. C is incorrect because the property of the zero is not used in the question. D is incorrect because the question does not address multiplication. **Competency 013**

64. (B)

If you can fold a two-dimensional figure so that one side exactly matches or folds onto the other side, the fold line is a line of symmetry. The figure below is a nonsquare rectangle with its two lines of symmetry shown.

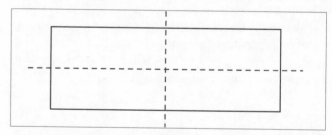

You might think that lines drawn from opposite corners are lines of symmetry, but they're not. The two halves would be the same size and shape, but wouldn't fold onto each other. Note that the question asked about nonsquare rectangles. Squares (which *are* rectangles) have *four* lines of symmetry. Based on the information provided, A, C, and D are incorrect. **Competency 014**

65. (B)

Angle *xyz* is an inscribed angle (its vertex is on the circle). Angle *xcz* is a central angle (its vertex is at the circle's center). When two such angles intercept (or "cut off") the same arc of the circle, a specific size relationship exists between the two angles. The measure of the central angle will always be double the measure of the inscribed angle. In this case, that means that the measure of angle *xcz* must be 80°. Thus, minor arc *xz* also measures 80°. Every circle (considered as an arc) measures 360°. That means that major arc *xyz* measures 280° (360 – 80). The explanation shows that A, C, and D are incorrect. **Competency 014**

66. (A)

The formula for finding the volume of a cylinder is: $V = \pi r^2 h$. This means that the volume is equal to pi (about 3.14) times the measure of the radius squared times the height of the cylinder. In this case, that's $3.14 \times 6^2 \times 8$, or $3.14 \times 36 \times 8$, or about 904. Note that the final answer is given in cubic centimeters. Based on this explanation, B, C, and D are incorrect. **Competency 014**

67. (A)

The only way carpet from a 16-foot-wide roll will cover Ms. Cameron's floor without seams is if she buys 20 feet of it. She can then trim the 16-foot width to 14 feet so that it fits her floor. Buying 20 feet of a 16-foot-wide roll means that she will have to buy 320 square feet. Her living room has an area of only 280 square feet (14 feet × 20 feet), so she'll be wasting 40 square feet (320 – 280), but no more. Based on this analysis, choices B, C, and D are incorrect. **Competency 014**

68. (B)

Children in grades prekindergarten to grade 2 have unique developmental characteristics, like limited vocabularies and attention spans, that require appropriate planning to insure that children benefit from instruction. A, C, and D are important considerations when planning instruction, but none of them are as important as planning instruction based on the developmental characteristics of children. **Competency 015**

69. (B)

TEKS requires children in kindergarten to explore and work with basic mathematic reasoning. In first grade and up, the level and sophistication of logical thinking increases in complexity. Based on prior statements, A, C, and D are incorrect. **Competency 015**

70. (A)

Learning centers allow children opportunities to explore mathematics reasoning in a play and low-anxiety format. B is incorrect because it addresses only one component of the benefit—the use of manipulatives. C is incorrect because, traditionally, learning centers are not used to teach deductively—direct teaching. Instead, students learn inductively through the use of manipulatives and the input from teachers. D is incorrect because learning centers do not use a highly structured format. On the contrary, learning centers are designed to be a low-anxiety environment where children can explore on their own. **Competency 015**

71. (B)

Children can see that knowledge of mathematics has a functional value in their lives. A and C are incorrect because most children cannot conceptualize that the activities that they do in mathematics are part of a school or state curriculum. D is incorrect because children in K–4 generally cannot make extrapolations between activities in the learning centers and their intrinsic value in life. **Competency 015**

72. (C)

Children are expected to be exposed to various forms of art, to study features of each, and to communicate using sensory-appropriate art terminology. They are also expected to produce artwork, and evaluate their own and the artworks from various groups. Based on the previous explanations, A, B, and D are incorrect. **Competency 024**

73. (B)

Diego Rivera, José Orozco, and David Siqueiros are the best representatives of the muralist movement in Mexico and perhaps in the world. Choice A is incorrect because photorealists do not use murals to present their work. Instead, canvases are generally used to create the artwork. C and D are incorrect because surrealism and impressionism do not use the social realism typical of the work of the Mexican muralists. **Competency 024**

74. (D)

Pablo Picasso is the best representative of cubism. Choice A is incorrect because Salvador Dali is linked to a different movement called surrealism. Both surrealism and cubism are art movements of the twentieth century. C is incorrect because Michelangelo is a painter of the Renaissance period and he used realism in his art. **Competency 024**

75. (C)

The values of light and darkness are used to create the three-dimensional quality of figures and to represent the mood of the artist. A, B, and D describe elements of art but the results of each are different than that produced by light and darkness. However, each of the choices provided correctly describes how these elements contribute to the creation of art. **Competency 024**

76. (C)

Pitch describes how high or low sounds are produced. Choice A is incorrect because it describes characteristics of rhythm. Based on this explanation, D (rhythm) is also incorrect. B is incorrect because it describes features of dynamics (volume)—loud and soft. **Competency 025**

77. (D)

The question addresses basic understanding of the standard Kodaly rhythm syllables. The three basic syllables included are *ta*, which would be notated as a quarter note on a staff; *Ti*, which would be notated as an eighth note on a staff; and *Ta-a*, which would be notated as a half note on the staff. If a person sings the common tune "Happy Birthday" to him- or herself, it should be apparent that the definite answer is D. B is a good answer and would be the rhythm for the final statement if two notes were sung on the word *to*, which is often done. Choice A begins with the wrong note. C begins with the correct note but ends with the wrong note. **Competency 025**

78. (B)

In 1929, the Texas State Legislature adopted "Texas, Our Texas" as the state song. Choice A is incorrect. "The Yellow Rose of Texas" is a well-known song in the state. It is a patriotic song popularized by Texan soldiers during the American Civil War. C is incorrect because the song "God Bless America" is a patriotic song for the whole nation. D is incorrect because the Alamo is a patriotic symbol but not the title of a specific song. **Competency 025**

79. (C)

Tejano music has strong influences from the music and instruments of Mexican, German, and Czech immigrants. Choice A is incorrect because mariachi music is originally from Mexico with no specific influence from German or Czech groups. B is incorrect because there is no clear connection between the music from Mexico and country music. D is incorrect because salsa music does not have specific connections with Mexican, German, or Czech groups. Instead, salsa music has been influenced by Spanish, Indian, and African music. **Competency 025**

80. (C)

Performing somersaults, climbing, skipping, and dressing themselves require children to master fine motor skills. Based on this explanation, A is incorrect. B is a plausible answer but it is too generic in nature; thus it is not the best answer. D is incorrect because children will have to go through various years of development to arrive at the adult stage of development. **Competency 026**

81. (A)

The simplest steps used are "walk and/or skip" and are therefore appropriate for grades 1 and 2. The steps "run and/or skip" (see choice B) and "skip and slide" (see choice C) are more difficult and therefore are suggested for grades 2 and 3. Even more difficult is the "step-hop" (see choice D), and it is incorporated in dances appropriate for grades 3–6. **Competency 026**

82. (B)

Elevation is a key component to the RICE treatment process for sprains. The other components are rest, ice, and compression. Choice A is incorrect because one should not return to exercise until significant healing has been achieved, though bearing a tolerable amount of weight on the sprain has been shown to help quicken the healing process. C is incorrect because *evaluation* is not a technical term used in the treatment of sprains. D is incorrect because the sprain should be bandaged properly to prevent exposure and thus prevent re-injury. **Competency 026**

83. (C)

The ADA required school districts to place special education children in the least restrictive educational environment; thus, an orthopedic handicapped student would be placed in mainstream classrooms. Students are required to receive physical education using appropriate accommodations to allow their successful participation. Choice A is incorrect because only in extreme cases are special education children excluded from participating in the school curriculum. B is partially correct, but it fails to mention the need to make accommodations for successful participation in physical education activities. D is incorrect because it adopts an extreme position not applicable to limited mobility. **Competency 027**

84. (B)

Cardiovascular exercise for a minimum of 20 minutes per session, as part of an exercise program, will lead to effective physical results with a proper nutritional diet. (A) and (C) are obviously incorrect based on the previous statement. Forty-five minutes (D) is an effective time period when performing lower-paced activities like a weight-lifting exercise session. **Competency 027**

85. (D)

Locomotor activities describe the types of movement that children use to move from one place to the other. In this case, hopping is the only choice that accomplishes this goal. Choice A is incorrect because bending is not a locomotor activity. B and C are also incorrect because they are manipulative skills. **Competency 027**

86. (D)

Complex carbohydrates should comprise at least half of the calories consumed for the healthy diet of an active person. Carbohydrates are the primary and most efficient source of energy for the body. Proteins should make up about 20 percent (see choice A) of the caloric intake of an active person. Based on the previous explanations, B and C are incorrect. **Competency 026**

87. (B)

Games involving physical activity are the best way to exercise children in kindergarten. Choice A is incorrect because, traditionally, jogging might be inappropriate for children at this early age. C and D are incorrect because contact sports and sports that require endurance are not developmentally appropriate for kindergarten students. **Competency 027**

88. (B)

Using high-interest activities like observing an aquarium can motivate scientific inquiry and problem-solving skills. Choices A and C are incorrect because both describe nonscientific objectives. Choice D presents a generic statement that fails to address the main scientific objective. **Competency 020**

89. (B)

A healthy aquatic system should have sufficient space and conditions to support life. Aquarium A has a large number of animals for a small 25-gallon aquarium. Overpopulation can pollute the environment and affect the balance of the ecosystem. The size of the aquarium (see choice A), the number of plants (see choice C), and the number of fish (see choice D) contribute to the success of the habitat, but individually, they cannot justify the students' decision. **Competency 020**

90. (D)

Fish of the same kind have a better chance of reproducing themselves. Aquarium B contains fish of the same kind, while aquarium A has different varieties. A, B, and C present elements that can affect the overall habitat, but they do not provide key information about the chances of successful breeding. **Competency 020**

91. (B)

The state curriculum requires students to engage in scientific exploration in grades K–12. Hands-on experimentation promotes active learning and is beneficial to all students, but it is especially important and developmentally appropriate for children in grades K–2. Choice A is incorrect because the incorporation of foreign language methods is a very broad statement, and it does not say specifically which method will be used or how it will be implemented. C is also incorrect because the statement is vague and does not describe the types of sophisticated tools. Traditionally, in K–2, the tools used are very simple and concrete. D is incorrect because the state curriculum does not require the use of chemicals and human specimens in the early grades. **Competency 020**

92. (B)

Conduction is a form of heat transfer. The metal of the spoon serves as a conductor of the heat emanating from the open flame. Choice A is too generic because radiation describes different kinds of energy produced naturally by the sun and artificially by microwaves and cellular phones. C is incorrect because it does not describe the type of transfer of energy presented in the scenario. However, convection is also a form of heat

transfer carried through movement of matter. For example, the heating of water in a pan creates movement of the liquid from the bottom to the top, forcing cold water down to the bottom of the pan, where it is heated. **Competency 021**

93. (B)

A mixture is a physical combination of two or more substances that retain their own chemical properties; i.e., the mixture can be separated into the original substances—acetic acid and water. Choice A is incorrect because in a compound, the substances are chemically combined, and in the case of vinegar the substances are only mixed physically. C and D are incorrect because they lack the specificity required of the answer. **Competency 021**

94. (C)

Matter can change from liquid to solid to gas in a cyclical fashion. A is incorrect because all three represent examples of solid matter. B is incorrect because it presents only examples of the states and fails to address the stages represented. D is incorrect because it presents just examples of solid and liquid matter. **Competency 021**

95. (C)

The metric system is a very precise system that allows for the measurement of very small amounts of matter. For example, the metric system uses measurements divided into thousands (millimeters or milligrams), while the English system uses larger units of measurement, like inches and ounces. A and D contain perhaps true statements and opinions but they fail to address the question. D is incorrect; the English system does not have a simple way to compute measures. On the other hand, the metric system is based on 10 and the computations are a lot easier. **Competency 021**

96. (A)

The monera kingdom is composed of unicellular organisms and primitive cells called prokaryotic. B, C, and

D are incorrect because all three have more sophisticated cellular systems called eukaryotic. **Competency 022**

97. (B)

Corals are invertebrates that fall under the animal kingdom. These small organisms can reproduce themselves sexually or asexually. Choice A is incorrect because unlike corals, the kingdom monera is made up of unicellular organisms with very rudimentary cellular organization. C and D are incorrect because corals are described in the question as invertebrates, a classification used exclusively for members of the animal kingdom. **Competency 022**

98. (C)

Corals live in a symbiotic relationship with algae because both exchange nutrients or other kinds of services in order for both to survive. Choice A is incorrect because corals are not parasites living off algae. Instead, parasites and corals provide support services to each other for their mutual survival. B and D might be true statements, but they do not define the term *symbiosis*. **Competency 022**

99. (C)

An ecosystem needs to have a balance among organisms to ensure the ability of the system to support life. A, B, and D are incorrect because they merely represent examples of how the system maintains a balance. **Competency 022**

100. (D)

The teacher can discuss the theory of continental drift, which gave rise to the current theory of plate tectonics. According to this theory, the crust of the Earth is broken down into several floating tectonic plates, which move and change locations. Choice A is incorrect because it describes how organisms evolve throughout history. It also alludes to the work of Charles Darwin. B is incorrect because it refers to the religious belief that the universe was created by a supreme being. C describes the process by which organisms living on one continent manage to migrate to other continents or to other regions within a continent. **Competency 023**

101. (A)

The main function of the atmosphere is to serve as a buffer between space and the Earth's crust. This buffer provides the ideal conditions to protect and preserve life on Earth. B and D present two functions that can be linked to the atmosphere, recycling water and gases; however, they fail to highlight the real function of the atmosphere. C is completely incorrect; the atmosphere is above the crust, not beneath it. **Competency 023**

102. (B)

The movement of the plates causes intense seismological activity near the faults, resulting in earthquakes. A and C have some merit because thermal activity can have some implications, but these choices do not provide specific answers to the question. D is totally incorrect; there is no known connection between the rotation of the Earth and earthquakes. **Competency 023**

Index

A

Activation energy, 120
Acute angle, 64
Adaptation for survival, 126–127
Adaptive physical education, 157–158
Addends, 58
Addition, 57
    with algebraic expressions, 61
    associative property of, 58
    commutative property, 58
Aerobic exercise, 147, 157
Aerobic respiration, 123
Age of Discovery, 88
Age of Reason, 93
Alamo, 101
Alcohol abuse, 152–153
Algebra
    algebraic expressions, 61
    multiplication of binomials, 61
    operations with algebraic expressions, 60–61
Algorithm, 57
Alimentary canal, 151
Alliteration, 11
Alphabetic principle, 13–15
    defined, 13
    grapheme-phoneme correspondence in English, 13–14
    stages of learning, 14–15
    teaching grapheme-phoneme correspondence, 15
    writing systems, 13
Alphabetic writing, 13
Amazon River, 106
Amendments, 110
American government, 109–111
American history
    American Revolution, 93–95
    ancient civilizations of Americas, 90–91
    Article of Confederation, 95
    Battle of Gettysburg, 96
    Civil War, 96
    Cold War, 99
    colonization, 92–93
    Continental Congress, 94–95
    economic development, 97
    Enlightenment–Age of Reason, 93
    indentured servant system, 93
    Ku Klux Klan, 97
    Manifest Destiny, 95–96
    Monroe Doctrine, 95
    Reconstruction Era, 96–97
    slavery in U.S., 96
    Spanish American War of 1898, 97
    U.S. Constitution, 95
American Revolution, 93–95
Americas, ancient civilizations of, 90–91
Analysis, critical thinking skills, 34
Anasazi, 91
Anatomy, 158
Ancient period, art style in, 136
Ancient World, 87
Anecdotal records, informal reading inventories, 45–46
Angles, 64
    measurement of, 65–66
    vertical, 66
Animals, 123
    cells, 123
    life cycle of, 126
    reproduction, 127
Antibody, 149
Anxiety, 151
Aorta, 149
Aphasia, 9
Appalachian Highlands, 105
Application, critical thinking skills, 34
Arabic number, 57
Arabs, mathematics and, 74
Archimedes, 74
Area, 65
    for polygons, 66
Art. *See* Music; Visual arts
Article of Confederation, 95
Articulation problems, 9
Associative property, 58
Atlantic–Gulf Coastal Plains, 105

Atoms, 118
Audience, writing process, 42–43
Authentic literature-based texts, 18
Authentic multicultural literature, 19
Automaticity, 25
Autonomic nervous system, 149
Aztecs, 75, 91

B

Babbling, 5
Babylonians, mathematics and, 73
Balance, principle of art, 136
Balanced reading program, 13, 18
Banking, 112
Bar graphs, 68, 80
Baroque style, 137
Bell-shaped curve, 47
Bill of Rights, 110
Binomials, multiplication, 61
Biography, 20
Bloom, Benjamin, 34
Blue moon, 132
Blues, 143–144
Body systems, 124, 149–150
Bolshevik Revolution in Russia, 97
Boston dialect, 6
Bottom-up approach to reading, 17–18
Burns, Susan, 13

C

Capillaries, 149
Carbohydrates, 145
Cells, 122–124, 149
Celsius, 59
Centration, 53
Chang Jiang, 106
Charts
    for social studies information, 81–83
    types of, 82–83
Checklists, informal reading inventories, 45
Checks and balances, system of, 110
Chemical energy, 120
Chemical properties, 118
Chemical sedimentary rock, 128
Child abuse and neglect, 148–149
Children's literature, 19–21
Cholesterol, 146
Chomsky, Noam, 4
Choral reading, 25
Circle, area formula for, 66

Circulatory system, 124, 149
Citizenship, 111
Civil War, 96
Classical period, art style in, 136
Clastic sedimentary rock, 128
Clay, Mary, 26
Climate zones, 131
Cloze test, 30
Cluttering, 8–9
Cognates, 84
Cold War, 99
Colonization of America, 92–93
Color
    element of art, 135
    physical property of matter, 118
Colorado River, 107
Communication disorders, 8–9
Commutative property, 58
Competency
    001 oral language, 3
    002 phonological and phonemic awareness, 10
    003 alphabetic principle, 13–15
    004 literacy development, 15–21
    005 word analysis and decoding, 22
    006 reading fluency, 25
    007 reading comprehension, 26
    008 research and comprehension skills in content
        areas, 31
    009 writing conventions, 35
    010 development of written communication, 40
    011 assessment of developing literacy, 44
    012 mathematics instruction, 51
    013 number concepts, patterns, and algebra, 56
    014 geometry, measurement, probability and statistics,
        63
    015 mathematical process, 70
    016 social science instruction, 77
    017 history, 87
    018 geography and culture, 104
    019 government, citizenship and economics, 109
    020 science instruction, 115
    021 physical science, 117
    022 life science, 122
    023 earth and space science, 127
    024 visual arts, 133
    025 music, 139
    026 health, 145
    027 physical education, 153
Competition, in ecosystem, 125
Composite numbers, 57
Compositions, for literacy assessment, 48–49
Compound fracture, 148

Compounds, 118
Compound words, 24
Conduction, 121
Conductivity, 118
Confederacy Period, 102
Connecticut, 92
Connotation, 4
Conservation, object, 53
Consolidated Alphabetic Stage, 15
Constitution, U.S., 95
    amendments, 110
Consumers, in ecosystem, 125
Content words, 5
Context clues, 22
Continental Congress, 94–95
Continental Divide, 105
Continental drift, 129
Contrast, principle of art, 136
Convection, 121
Convergent question, 30
Cooperative learning, 86
Coordinates, 104
Core, earth, 129
Coronado, Francisco Vázquez de, 99–100
Country music, 143
Crescent moon, 131
Criterion-referenced tests, for literacy assessment, 47
Critical thinking skills, strategies for developing, 34
Crust, earth, 128
Cube, 65
Cubism, 138
Cultural diffusion, 109
Cultural geography, 104
Culture, communication style and, 7
Curvilinear approach, 7
Customary units of measurement, 69–70
Cylinder, 67

D

Data retrieval charts, 81
D-Day, 98
Decimal places, 59
Decoding, 22–23
Decomposers, in ecosystem, 125
Deductive reasoning, 68
Deflation, 112–113
Deforestation, 107
Delaware, 92–93
Denotation, 4
Density, 118
Dependent clause, 38–39

Deposition, 107
Depression, 151
Derivational morphemes, 23
Description, 42
De Vaca, Cabeza, 99
Dialogue journal, 44
Diameter, 64
Digestive system, 124, 150
Digraphs, 15, 36, 38
Discovery, Age of, 88
Dislocation, 148
Distributive property, 59
Divergent question, 30
Diverse learners, literacy assessment, 49–50
Division, 58
    exponential expressions, 61
    with negative and positive numbers, 63
Dolch, Edward W., 22
Dolch words, 22
Dramatic play, to promote oral communication, 9
DRTA, 33
Drug abuse, 152–153
Dynamics, 140

E

Early readers, 16
Earth
    atmosphere, 129–130
    layers of, 128–129
    movements of, 131
Earth and space science, 127–132
    earth's atmosphere, 129–130
    erosion, 130
    geologic activity, 130
    geology, 127–129
    space science, 131–132
    structure and composition of earth, 127–129
    weathering, 130
Earthquakes, 130
Eating disorder, 146
Ebonics, 6
Ecology, 125
Economic interdependence, 112
Economic principles, 111–113
    federal income tax system, 113
    free enterprise, 112
    globalization, 112
    goods and services, 112
    inflation and deflation, 112–113
    money and banking, 112
    supply and demand, 112
Egyptians, mathematics and, 73

Electrical properties, 118
Electricity, 120
Electrons, 118
Elements, 118
Emergent readers, 16
Emotional disorders, 151
Emphasis, principle of art, 135–136
Energy, 120–121
    conservation of, 120–121
    principles of, 120
English Language Arts and Reading, 3–50
    alphabetic principle, 13–15
    assessment of developing literacy, 44–50
    development of written communication, 40–44
    oral language, 3–10
    phonological and phonemic awareness, 10–13
    reading comprehension, 26–31
    reading fluency, 25–26
    research and comprehension skills in content areas, 31–35
    social studies integration strategies, 85–87
    word analysis and decoding, 22
    writing conventions, 35–40
English language learners (ELL)
    choral reading, 25
    communication style and culture, 7
    connotation, 4
    cooperative learning, 86
    essay tests, 48
    fluency disorders, 9
    graphic organizers, 32, 85
    language interference, 7
    linguistic accommodation testing for, 34–35
    Literacy assessment, 49
    mathematics instruction and, 55–56
    pairing students, 25
    pragmatics, 4
    pre-reading activities, 27
    reading comprehension in content areas, 33–34
    scaffolding, 84–85
    scientific vocabulary, 116
    Sheltered English, 85–86
    social studies instruction and, 84–86
    speaking Checklist, 7–8
    SQ4R, 85
    thematic instruction, 80
Enlightenment, 93
Equilateral triangle, 66
Erosion, 130
Essay tests, for literacy assessment, 48
Estimating, 60
Euclid, 74

Eukaryotic cells, 122–123
Evaluation, critical thinking skills, 34
Even numbers, 57
Excretory system, 124, 150
Executive branch, 109
Exfoliation, 130
Exponential notation, 57
Expository writing, 42
Expressive aphasia, 9

F

Factors, 58
Fahrenheit, 59
Fantasy, 19–20
Fat, dietary, 145–146
Faults, geologic, 130
Federal government, 110–111
Federal income tax system, 113
Federal Reserve System, 112
Fine motor skills, 150
First aid, 147–148
First quarter moon, 131
Flowchart, 82–83, 85
Fluency disorders, 8–9
Force, 120–121
Form, 140
Formal assessments, of literacy, 46–48
Formative evaluation, 46
Fossil fuels, 120
Fractions, 57, 61–62
Fracture, 148
Free enterprise, 112
Freeze-thaw, 130
Frustration reading level, 45
Full Alphabetic Stage, 15
Full moon, 132
Function words, 5
Fungi, 123

G

Galaxies, 131
Gastrointestinal tract, 151
Genki English, 17–18
Genre, 19
Geography
    cultural, 104
    deforestation, 107
    deposition, 107
    largest rivers of world, 106

latitude, 105
locating places and regions on map, 104–105
longitude and time zones, 104
map skills by grade, 107–109
mountains of world, 107
physical, 104
regions of U.S., 105
Texas regions and economic activity, 105–106
Geologic activity, 130
Geology, 127–129
Geometry
angle measure, 65–66
angles, 64
diameter, 64
finding area, 65
finding perimeter, 64–65
formulas for polygons, 66–67
lines of symmetry, 64
polygons, 64
principles and properties of, 63–64
radius, 64
reasoning skills, 67–68
rivers in United States, 106–107
triangle properties, 66
Georgia, 93
Gettysburg, Battle of, 96
Gibbous moon, 132
Global aphasia, 9
Globalization, 112
Globes, using, 79
Goliad, 101
Goodman, Kenneth, 18
Goods, 112
Graffiti, 138
Granite, 128
Graphemes, 3
Graphic organizers, 32, 85
Graphs, 60
bar, 68, 80–81
line, 69
pictorial, 68
pie charts, 69, 81
for social studies information, 80–81
Graves, Donald, 41
Gravity, 129
Great Depression, 97–98
Great Plains, 105
Greeks, mathematics and, 73–74
Griffin, Peg, 13
Gross motor skills, 150
Group Investigation, 86
Guided oral repeated reading, 25

H

Half moon, 131
Hand-puppet show, to promote oral communication, 10
Hardness, 118
Harmonic instruments, 141, 142
Harmony, 140
Harmony, principle of art, 136
Health, 145–153
body systems, 149–150
child abuse and neglect, 148–149
first aid, 147–148
human growth and development, 150
mental and emotional disorders, 151
motor skills development, 150
nutrition, 145–146
school violence, 153
social and emotional health, 151
stress management, 147
substance use and abuse, 152–153
weight control strategies, 146–147
Heart, 149
Heart attack, 148
Heat, 120
temperature and, 121
transfer of, 121
Heat exhaustion, 148
Heat stroke, 148
Hemoglobin, 124
Hexagons, 64
High-density lipoprotein (HDL), 146
Hindus, mathematics and, 74
Hiroshima, 98
Historical fiction, 20
History instruction, 87–104
Age of Discovery, 88
American government, 109–111
American history, 92–97
ancient civilizations of Americas, 90–91
Ancient World, 87
Bolshevik Revolution in Russia, 97
citizenship, 111
D-Day, 98
economic principles, 111–113
Enlightenment—Age of Reason, 93
Great Depression, 97–98
Hiroshima and Nagasaki, 98
Holocaust and creation of Israel, 98
Industrial Revolution and Modern Technology, 89–90
Marshall Plan, 98
Middle Ages, 87–88
Modern World, 89

Revolution and Industry, 88–89
Spanish American War of 1898, 97
of Texas, 99–103
Truman Doctrine, 98–99
war on terrorism, 99
World War I, 97
World War II, 98
Yalta Conference, 98
Hohokam, 91
Holocaust, 98
Holophrastic one-word stage, 5
Homographs, 24
Homonyms, 24, 36
Homophones, 24
Houston, Sam, 101

I

Igneous rocks, 128
Imitation, 4
Immune system, 124, 149
Impressionism, 137
Incas, 91
Indentured servant system, 93
Independent clause, 38–39
Independent reading level, 45
Industrial Revolution and Modern Technology, 89–90
Infantile autism, 151
Inflation, 112–113
Inflectional morphemes, 23–24
Informal assessments, of literacy, 45–46
Instructional reading level, 45
Integers, 57
Intelligibility, 6
Interior Highlands, 105
Interior Plains, 105
Intermontane Plateau, 105
International date line, 104
Intonation patterns, 11
Involuntary movement, 149
Involuntary system, 124
Iroquois, 91
Isosceles, 66
Israel, creation of, 98

J

Jim Crow laws, 97
Journals, 39–40
advantages of, 40
types of, 44

Joyce, David E., 75
Judicial branch, 110
Judicial review process, 110

K

Kernel sentences, 3
Kinetic energy, 120
Kingdoms, 123
Ku Klux Klan, 97

L

Landforms, 128
Language. *See* Oral language
Language acquisition
principles of, 4–5
stages of, 5–6
Language Acquisition Device (LAD), 4
Language experience approach to writing, 39
Language interference, 7
Language play, to promote oral communication, 9–10
Language processing disorders, 9
La Salle, Robert de, 100
Latitude, 79, 105
Laurentian Highlands, 105
Learning log, 44
Learning styles, literacy assessment and, 46
Legislative branch, 110
Lever, 121
Lexicon, 3
Life cycles, 125–126
Life science, 122–127
body systems, 124
cell system, 122–124
ecology, 125
life cycles, 125–126
needs of living organisms, 126–127
Ligaments, 148, 149
Line, 135
Line graphs, 69
Lines of symmetry, 64
Linguistic accommodation testing, 34–35
Lisping, 9
Listening, speaking and, 8
Literacy assessment, 44–50
authentic assessment, 48
classroom tests, 48
criterion-referenced tests, 47
diversity in classroom, 49–50
educator's guide to TEKS-based assessment, 49
English language learners, 49

essay tests, 48
formal assessments, 46–48
informal assessments, 45
informal reading inventories, 45–46
miscue analysis, 46
norm-referenced tests, 47
ongoing assessment, 49
performance-based assessment, 47–48
portfolios, 46
reading levels, 45
rubrics for, 48
running records, 45, 46
scoring compositions, 48–49
Literacy development, 15–21
balanced reading program, 18
bottom-up approach (skills-based), 17–18
children's literature, 19–21
defined, 16
early readers, 16
emergent readers, 16
key principles of competency, 21
newly fluent readers, 16
phonics, 17–18
stages of, 16–17
top-down approach (meaning-based), 18
Whole Language Approach, 18
Literature, for children, 19–21
Literature-based approach, social studies, 80
Local government, 111
Locomotor skills, 156
Longitude, 79, 104–105
Low-density lipoprotein (LDL), 145–146
Lungs, 149
Lymphocytes, 149

M

Machines, 121
Macroeconomics, 111–112
Magnetism, 120
Manifest Destiny, 95–96
Manipulatives for mathematics instruction, 54–55
Manipulative skills, 156
Mantle, 128–129
Maps
locating places and regions on map, 104–105
map skills by grade, 107–109
using, 79
Mariachi, 143
Marshall Plan, 98
Maryland, 92
Mass, 117

Massachusetts, 92
Mathematics instruction, 51–56
addition, 57
algebraic expressions, 60–61
algorithm, 57
associative property, 58
basic computation and place value, 60
cognitive development and mathematics, 53
commutative property, 58
content standards, 52
cube, 65
daily living and mathematics, 71–72
developmental considerations, 53–54, 70–71
distributive property, 59
division, 58
English language learners, 55–56
fractions, 61–62
geometry, 63–67
graphic representations, 68–69
graphs and symbolic representations, 60–61
historical development of mathematics, 73–75
integrating mathematics in content areas, 72–73
manipulatives and, 54–55
multiplication, 58
nomenclature of mathematics, 56
number concepts, 57
order of operations, 59
percent, 62–63
performing operations with negative and positive numbers, 63
principles of mathematics, 51
process standards, 52
property of zero, 58
real-life situations and, 56
reasoning skills, 67–68, 71
rounding numbers, 59
subtraction, 58
Texas Essential Knowledge and Skills (TEKS), 52–53
time, temperature and money, 59–60
units of measurement, 69
volume, 65
Matter, 117–118
Mayans, 74, 75
Mayas, 90
Meaning-based approach to reading, 13, 18
Measurement, units of
customary units, 69–70
metric, 69–70
Medieval period, art style in, 137
Meiosis, 123
Melodic instruments, 141, 142

Melody, 140
Mental disorders, 151
Metamorphic rocks, 128
Meter, 140
Metric units, 69–70, 121
Mexican-American War, 102
Microeconomics, 112
Middle Ages, 87–88
Midpoint, 47
Minerals
  dietary, 146
  geology and, 127–128
Miscue analysis
  defined, 18
  literacy assessment, 46
Mississippi River, 106
Missouri River, 107
Mitosis, 123
Mixtures, 118
Mnemonic devices, 32
Modern fantasy, 19–20
Modern World, 89
Monera, 123
Money, 59–60, 112
Monroe Doctrine, 95
Moon, phases of, 131–132
Morphemes, 3
  derivational, 23
  inflectional, 23–24
Morphology, 3
Motor skills development, 150
Mound Builders, 91
Mountains, 107
Movement, principle of art, 136
Movement education, 155–156
Multicultural literature, 19
Multiplication, 58
  associative property of, 58
  binomials, 61
  commutative property, 58
  exponential expressions, 61
  with negative and positive numbers, 63
Muralist, 138
Musculoskeletal system, 124, 149
Music, 139–144
  in classroom, 141
  content areas and, 139–140
  curriculum requirements, 139
  elements of, 140–141
  evaluating musical performance, 144
  instruments in music education, 141–142
  music notation, 142
  patriotic songs in U.S., 142–143
  popular songs, 143–144
  terminology in music education, 140
  Texas patriotic songs, 143
  vocal performance, 141
Music notation, 142

N

Nagasaki, 98
Narrative, 42
Narrative charts, 81
Natural numbers, 57
Nervous system, 124, 149
Neutrons, 118
New Hampshire, 92
New Jersey, 92
Newly fluent readers, 16–17
New moon, 131
New York, 92
Nile River, 106
Nineteenth century art, 137
No Child Left Behind (NCLB), 49
Nonfiction, 20
Nontraditional music notation, 142
Norm-referenced tests, for literacy assessment, 47
North Carolina, 93
Note taking, 32
Nuclear energy, 120
Number concepts, 57
Numbered Heads Together, 87
Numbering system, 74
Nutrition, 145–146

O

Observations, informal reading inventories, 45
Obsidian, 128
Obtuse angle, 64
Occasion, writing process, 43
Octagons, 64
Odd numbers, 57
Ohio River, 106
Olmecs, 90–91
Oñate, Juán de, 100
Onset, 12
Open words, 5
Oral language, 3–10
  activities to promote oral communication, 9–10
  assessing speaking ability, 6–8
  basic components of language, 3–4
  communication disorders, 8–9
  communication style and culture, 7–8

intelligibility, 6–7
language interference, 7
listening and speaking, 8
principles of language acquisition, 4–5
speaking checklist, 7–8
stages of language acquisition, 5–6
Order of operations, 59
Organ, 149
Organic sedimentary rock, 128
Organizational chart, 82
Organ system, 149
Over stimulation, 148

P

Pacific Mountain System, 105
Pair interview, to promote oral communication, 10
Parallel, 68
Parallelogram, area formula for, 66
Partial alphabetic phase, 15
Patterns, 60
Pedigree chart, 81–82
Pennsylvania, 93
Pentagons, 64
Percent, 62–63
Percentile score, 47
Perceptual motor competency, 156–157
Performance-based assessment, literacy assessment,
    47–48
Perimeter, 64–65
Periodic table, 118
Personal journal, 44
Persuasive writing, 42
Phonation, 8
Phonemes
    defined, 3
    grapheme-phoneme correspondence in English, 13–14
Phonics, 17–18
Phonological and phonemic awareness, 10–13
    balanced reading program, 13
    connection to spelling, 35
    defined, 10–11
    importance for reading, 10–11
    intonation patterns, 11
    rhymes, 11
    special considerations for teaching, 11–12
    strategies for teaching, 12–13
    syllabication, 11
    word stress, 11
Phonology, 3
Photorealism, 138
Photosynthesis, 120, 123–124, 126

Physical activity, 155
Physical education, 153–158
    adaptive physical education, 157–158
    aerobic exercise, 157
    anatomy and physiology, 158
    movement education, 155–156
    perceptual motor competency, 156–157
    physical fitness and health, 155
    standards for, 153
    TEKS for, 154–155
Physical geography, 104
Physical properties, 118
Physical science, 117–122
    force, work and energy, 120–121
    matter, 117–118
    precision and accuracy, 121
    safety management, 122
    scientific tools and uses, 118–119
Physiology, 158
Pictographic writing system, 13
Pictorial graphs, 68
Picture book, 19
Pie charts, 69, 80–81
Pitch, 140
Pivot words, 5
Place value, basic computation and, 60
Planets, 131
Plants, 123
    cells, 123
    life cycle of, 126
    reproduction, 127
Plasmas, 118
Poetry, 20
Polygons, 64
Polyhedron, 67
Portfolios, informal reading inventories, 46
Potential energy, 120
Pragmatics, 4
Predation, in ecosystem, 125
Prefixes, 23
Prehistoric period, art style in, 136
Pre-reading activities, 27
Presentations, to promote oral communication, 10
Prime meridian, 104
Prime numbers, 57
Prior knowledge, 27
    activating, 29–30
    linking to new knowledge, 27
Process writing, 41
Producers, in ecosystem, 125
Prokaryotic cells, 122–123
Property of zero, 58

Proteins, 145
Protista, 123
Protons, 118
Psychotic disorders, 151
Ptolemy, 73–74
Pueblo Indians, 91
Purpose, writing process, 43–44

Q

Quadrilaterals, 64
Question, in SQ4R, 33, 85

R

Radiation, 121
Radius, 64
Rational numbers, 57
Raw scores, 47
Read, in SQ4R, 33, 85
Readers' theater, 26
Reading
    balanced reading program, 13, 18
    becoming more efficient readers, 31
    bottom-up approach (skills-based), 17–18
    children's literature, 19–21
    importance of phonological and phonemic awareness,
        10–11
    literacy assessment, 44–50
    meaning-based approach, 13
    phonics, 17–18
    reading fluency, 25–26
    scanning, 31
    skills-based approach, 13
    skimming, 31
    stages of reading development, 16–17
    top-down approach (meaning-based), 18
    Whole Language Approach, 18
    word analysis and decoding, 22–24
Reading comprehension, 26–31
    activating prior knowledge, 29–30
    assessing, 30–31
    background knowledge, 27
    bias in traditional stories, 28–29
    confirming predictions, 30
    in content areas, 33–34
    determining important ideas, 30
    drawing inferences, 30
    linking prior knowledge to new knowledge, 27
    monitoring, 29–30
    predicting or asking questions, 30
    pre-reading activities, 27
    reading fluency and, 25
    reflecting, 30
    repairing understanding, 30
    setting purpose of reading, 27
    story grammar, 27–28
    synthesizing information, 30
    using parts of book, 30
    visualizing, 30
Reading fluency
    assessing, 26
    choral reading, 25
    comprehension and, 25
    defined, 25
    expectations of, 25
    guided oral repeated reading, 25
    interactive computer programs, 25–26
    key principles of competency, 26
    pairing students, 25
    readers' theater, 26
    silent sustained reading, 26
Reading Proficiency Tests in English (RPTE), 49
Realism, 137
Reason, Age of, 93
Reasoning skills
    geometry, 67–68
    promoting, 71
Receptive aphasia, 9
Receptors, 149
Reciprocal teaching, 33, 85
Recite, in SQ4R, 33, 85
Reconstruction Era, 96–97
Rectangle
    area formula for, 66
    area of, 65
    perimeter of, 64–65
Rectangular solid, 67
Reflect, in SQ4R, 85
Reflective journal, 44
Renaissance period, art style in, 137
Reproduction
    animals, 127
    cell, 123
    plants, 127
Research and comprehension skills in content areas,
    31–35
    becoming more efficient readers, 31
    connecting spelling and phonological and alphabetic
        awareness, 35
    critical thinking skills development, 34
    DRTA, 33
    graphic organizers, 32
    linguistic accommodation testing, 34–35

reading comprehension in content areas, 33–34
reciprocal teaching, 33
representations of information for variety of purposes, 34
SQ4R, 32–33
structure of text, 31
study plans, 32
study skills, 32
summarizing and organization of content, 32
think-aloud, 32
transition from learning to read to reading to learn, 31
Resonance, 8
Respiratory system, 124, 149
Resuscitation, 148
Review, in SQ4R, 33, 85
Revolution, earth, 131
Revolution and Industry, 88–89
Rhode Island, 92
Rhymes, 11
Rhythm
element of music, 140
principle of visual art, 136
Rhythmic instruments, 141
Richter scale, 130
Right angle, 64
Rimes, 12
Rio Grande, 106–107
Risk factors, substance abuse, 152
Rivers
largest in world, 106
in United States, 106–107
Rocks
cycle of formation, 128
types of, 128
Rocky Mountain System, 105
Rococo art, 137
Rotation, earth, 131
Rounding numbers, 59
Rubrics, literacy assessment, 48
Running records, 45, 46

S

Saliva, 151
San Antonio, 100
San Jacinto, Battle of, 101
Saturated fat, 145
Scaffolding, 84–85
Scalene triangle, 66
Scanning, 31
School violence, 153
Science instruction, 115–132
assessing science curriculum, 117
in daily life, 116
data analysis, 116
data gathering, 115–116
developmentally appropriate practices, 117
earth and space science, 127–132
ecology, 125
force, work and energy, 120–121
geologic activity, 130
geology, 127–129
health and safety, 116–117
interpreting and communicating results, 116
life cycles, 125–126
life science, 122–127
matter, 117–118
needs of living organisms, 126–127
NSTA curriculum suggestions, 115
physical science, 117–122
precision and accuracy, 121
safety management, 122
scientific inquiry, 115
scientific tools and uses, 118–119
scientific vocabulary, 116
structure and composition of earth, 127–130
systems of human body, 124
Scientific notation, 57
Scientific tools and uses, 118–119
Scribbling, 36
Sedimentary rock, 128
Seizures, 148
Self-concept, 151
Self-efficacy, 151
Semantic clues, 22
Semantics, 3–4
Semantic web, 85
Sentence structures, 3
Services, 112
Shape, 135
Sheltered English, 85–86
Show and tell, to promote oral communication, 10
Sight words, 22
Silent sustained reading, 26
Simple machine, 121
Skeletal muscles, 149
Skills based approach to reading, 17–18
Skills-based approach to reading, 13
Skimming, 31
Slavery, in U.S., 96
Snow, Catherine, 13
Social science instruction
addressing needs of English language learners, 84–86
cooperative learning, 86

graphic representation of historical information, 80–83
Group Investigation, 86
history, 87–104
integrating other content areas, 80
language arts integration strategies, 85–87
Numbered Heads Together, 87
Sheltered English, 85–86
social studies curricula, 77–79
Student Teams Achievement Divisions (STAD), 86
Think-Pair-Share, 86–87
using maps and globes, 79
using technology information in, 79–80
Solar energy, 120
Solar system, 131
Solutions, 118
Somatic nervous system, 149
South Carolina, 93
Space, element of art, 135
Space science, 131–132
Spanish American War of 1898, 97
Speaking ability
assessing, 6–8
communication style and culture, 7
intelligibility, 6
language interference, 7
speaking checklist, 7–8
Speaking Checklist, 7–8
Special education students, linguistic accommodation testing for, 34–35
Spelling
conventional, 36–37
invented, 36
phonological and phonemic awareness, 35
stages of, 36
transitional, 36
Sprain, 148
SQ4R, 32–33, 85
Square
area of, 65
perimeter of, 65
Stars, 131
State government, 110–111
Stomach, 151
Story grammar, 27–28
Story retelling, 29
Strain, 148
Stress management, 147
Student Teams Achievement Divisions (STAD), 86
Study plans, 32
Study skills, 32
Stuttering, 8–9

Substance use and abuse, 152
Subtraction, 58
with algebraic expressions, 61
Suffixes, 84
Summative evaluation, 46
Supply and demand, theory of, 112
Surrealism, 138
Survey, in SQ4R, 32–33, 85
Syllabication, 11
Syllabic writing, 13
Symmetry, lines of, 64
Syntactic clues, 22
Syntax, 3
Synthesis, critical thinking skills, 34

T

Taxes, 113
Technology, Industrial Revolution and Modern Technology, 89–90
Tectonic plates, 129
Tejano music, 143
Telegraphic stage, 5
Temperature, 59, 121
Tempo, 140
Tendons, 148, 149
Tenochtitlan, 91
Teotihuacan, 91
Terrorism, war on, 99
Texas
interdependence of economy, 113
regions and economic activity, 105–106
Texas, history of, 99–103
Alamo and Goliad, 101
Anglo-American presence in, 101
Battle of San Jacinto, 101
Cabeza de Vaca, 99
Confederacy Period, 102
economic development, 102–103
European colonization, 99–101
before European colonization, 99
First Battle in Gonzales, 101
first missions in Texas, 100
Francisco Vázquez de Coronado, 99–100
French influence in, 100
Juán de Oñate, 100
Mexican-American War, 102
Mexican independence, 101
oil in Texas, 103
Reconstruction Period, 102
Republic Period, 102
Sam Houston, 101

San Antonio, 100
six flags over, 103
state facts and symbols, 103
Texas Declaration of Independence, 101
Texas joins United States, 102
Texas war for independence, 101
time line for, 102
Texas Assessment of Knowledge and Skills, 47
Texas English Language Proficiency Assessment System (TELPAS), 49
Texas Essential Knowledge and Skills (TEKS)
  health, 145
  literacy assessment, 49
  mathematics instruction, 52–53
  physical education, 154–155
  scientific tools and uses, 118–119
  social studies, 77–79
  visual arts, 133–134
Texas Observation Protocols (TOP), 49
Texture, 135, 140
Thematic instruction
  English language learners, 80
  mathematics instruction, 72–73
  social studies, 80
Thermal properties, 118
Think-aloud, 32
Think-Pair-Share, 86–87
Tides, 129–130
Timbre, 140
Time, 59
Time line, 85
Time zones, 104–105
Tissues, 149
Toltecs, 90–91
Tone, 140
Top-down approach to reading, 18
Traditional literature, 19
Traditional music notation, 142
Traumatic shock, 148
Tree diagram, 85
Triangles, 64
  area formula for, 66
  perimeter of, 65
  properties of, 66
  types of, 66
Triglycerides, 146
Truman Doctrine, 98–99
Two-word stage, 5

U

Under stimulation, 148

United States
  American government, 109–111
  American history, 92–97
  Constitution, 95, 110
  regions of, 105
  rivers in, 106–107
Unsaturated vegetable fats, 146

V

Value, element of art, 135
Veins, 149
Venn diagram, 32, 85
Violence, school, 153
Virginia, 92
Visual arts, 133–139
  activities for K-4, 135
  art classroom, 134
  elements of art, 135
  evaluating works of art, 138–139
  fine arts *vs.* visual arts term, 133
  goal of art education, 133
  historical periods of, 136–138
  integration of arts in content areas, 138
  principles of art, 135–136
  TEKS and, 133–134
Vitamins, 146
Vocal ranges, 141
Voice disorders, 8
Volcanoes, 130
Volume, 65, 67, 117
Voluntary movement, 124, 149

W

Water cycle, 129
Weathering, 130
Weight, 117
Weight control strategies, 146–147
Weneger, Alfred, 129
Whole Language Approach, 18
Whole numbers, 57
Wind energy, 120
Word analysis
  compound words, 24
  decoding clues, 22
  derivational morphemes, 23
  Dolch words, 22
  homonyms and homophones, 24
  inflectional morphemes, 23–24
  key principles of competency, 24
  semantic clues, 22

syntactic clues, 22

vocabulary sight words, 22

Word stress, 7, 11

Work, 120–121

World War I, 97

World War II, 98

Write, in SQ4R, 33

Writing, systems of, 13

Writing conventions, 35–40

characteristics of emerging writers, 37

characteristics of newly fluent writers, 37–38

connector used in writing, 38, 39

conventional spelling, 36–37

dependent and independent clause, 38–39

developing readiness for writing, 35–36

dictated materials, 39

early writers, 37

expectations for, 38

interactive journals, 39–40

invented spelling, 36

language experience approach, 39

pseudo letters, 36

random letters, 36

reading to students, 39

routine activities as literacy events, 40

scribbling, 36

spoken and written English connection, 35

stages of spelling, 36

strategies for promoting written communication, 39–40

transitional spelling, 36

Writing process, 40–41

Written communication development, 40–44

integrating technology with language and content, 44

new trends in writing, 41–42

types of writing, 44

writing for a variety of occasions, purposes and audiences, 42–43

writing modes, 42

writing process, 40–41

Y

Yalta Conference, 98

Yangtze River, 106

Z

Zapotecs, 90–91

Zero

concept of, 74

property of, 58